TURNING RETIREMENT FUNDS INTO START-UP DREAMS
FINANCING AND RETIREMENT FUNDING OPTIONS
FOR YOUR START-UP BUSINESS

TURNING RETIREMENT FUNDS INTO START-UP DREAMS FINANCING AND RETIREMENT FUNDING OPTIONS FOR YOUR START-UP BUSINESS

A Private Conversation with a Top Retirement Tax Attorney

Adam Bergman, Esq.

ISBN-13: 9781517732790
ISBN-10: 1517732794
Library of Congress Control Number: 2015916761
CreateSpace Independent Publishing Platform
North Charleston, South Carolina

Contents

Introduction

The popularity of entrepreneurship is one of the most important developments of modern economic life. Entrepreneurs help create new companies, which spurs economic growth, creates jobs, and introduces new technologies, products, and services that improve our living standards and quality of life. From Steve Jobs to Bill Gates, Mark Zuckerburg to Sam Walton—indeed, all the way back to Benjamin Franklin—entrepreneurship is what has made America great and helped her become the most powerful country in the world.

There are financial pitfalls to every new business, however, that can and should be avoided. When Mark Zuckerburg launched Facebook, for example, he was forced to give up a percentage of the company to Eduardo Saverin in order to fund his start-up costs. In too many instances, entrepreneurs are rich on ideas but not so rich where it counts. For many, the hardest part is not coming up with a business idea or a potential business to buy, but finding the cash needed to start or buy the business.

After taking an inventory of their personal finances, the next step for entrepreneurs is usually to figure out where and how they can secure the necessary funds to start their new venture. This typically causes entrepreneurs great stress and anxiety. They ask themselves, "Who can I approach for money? Could my parents or in-laws invest in the business? What about my siblings or well-off friends?"

Too often, the entrepreneur doesn't know that using retirement funds could be a viable option for investing or funding a new business venture.

This book will explore and discuss in detail a number of options available to entrepreneurs looking to start or finance a business venture with retirement funds. It is aimed at individuals who have retirement funds or are beginning to save for retirement and expect to have sufficient retirement funds available to start or buy a business.

The idea of starting a new business and leaving corporate America is becoming more and more popular. According to numerous studies, many Americans are becoming less enthusiastic about staying in corporate America and would prefer to be their own boss. In fact, half of working adults in the United States either currently own or want to own their own businesses, according to a recent study from the University of Phoenix School of Business. Among those who don't currently own a business, nearly 40 percent hope to do so in the future.[1] America has always prided itself on its individualism and has valued freedom, flexibility, and self-reliance. Yet the system of tax-deferred retirement saving in this country has shortchanged self-employed people—the very people who comprise our ranks of entrepreneurs, small-business owners, freelancers, and the like—for a long time.

Let's take the example of Ben. Ben is forty-seven years old and lives in Columbus, Ohio. He is married and has two kids, ages eleven and eight. For almost twenty years, he worked at a midsize auto-parts distribution company but was laid off in 2012 when the firm was bought by an overseas conglomerate. Although Ben is at the peak of his career, he's finding the job market extremely difficult for someone of his experience and salary expectations. He's incredibly frustrated by this until he realizes it's not the only path available to him. With his know-how and contacts, he could go out on his own. And because of Obamacare, he no longer needs to rely on employer-based health insurance to cover his family. Anxious to get back into the game, he decides to start his own auto-parts distribution company.

Or let's look at Jen, who is thirty-nine years old and lives in Sacramento, California. Jen has worked as a chef at several well-known restaurants since she graduated from culinary school at age twenty-three. She has always dreamed about opening her own restaurant and feels that the time is right to make the leap. With no kids and a strong following, she feels confident that she can open a successful restaurant.

---

1 http://www.businessnewsdaily.com/6917-owning-a-business.html

For both Ben and Jen, as well as the hundreds of thousands of other entrepreneurs contemplating the opportunities of business ownership, there are a number of factors preventing them from taking the plunge. Nearly 70 percent of those surveyed who want to own a business said a lack of adequate finances is preventing them from doing so.[2] Like everything else in the world, it's always about the money—for would-be entrepreneurs, the ability to finance their own business can make the difference when it comes to realizing their dreams and controlling their future.

Every would-be entrepreneur is aware of the risks involved in starting a business. The Small Business Administration (SBA) keeps statistics on business failures and claims that more than half of new businesses will disappear in the first five years, and only one-quarter stay in business for fifteen years or more. While you might expect this sobering reality would deter more people from launching their own businesses, according to the US Census Bureau there were 27.9 million small businesses and 18,500 firms with five hundred or more employees as of 2010. Small businesses have generated over 65 percent of the net new jobs since 1995. Approximately 543,000 new businesses get started each month.[3] Even more impressive, according to the Kauffman Index, start-up activity rose in 2015—reversing a downward trend that began in 2010 and generating the largest year-over-year increase from the past two decades.[4]

I believe

- every American should have the option to start a business;
- starting and operating a business can be the hardest thing you do in your life, but it can also be the most rewarding; and
- there are important options to consider for funding a new or existing business, including using retirement funds.

---

2 Ibid.

3 United States Census Bureau. "2011 Nonemployer Statistics." US Department of Commerce: http://censtats.census.gov/cgi-bin/nonemployer/nonsect.pl

4 http://www.kauffman.org/~/media/kauffman_org/research%20reports%20and%20covers/2015/05/kauffman_index_startup_activity_national_trends_2015.pdf

I believe that every American should have the option to start a business. Starting and operating a business can be the hardest thing you do in your life, but it can also be the most rewarding. If you are an entrepreneur looking to start a business, there are important options to consider for funding a new or existing business, including using retirement funds.

Accordingly, the companies I've built, IRA Financial Group and IRA Financial Trust Company, are designed to help you invest money for retirement through retirement savings, including investing in your own business under the right facts and circumstances.

In addition to the traditional ways you can fund your start-up business, such as personal savings, bank or SBA loans, credit cards, friends and family, or crowdfunding, there is also the option of using retirement funds. This is largely unknown to many entrepreneurs and small-business owners. The options range from using a self-directed IRA or a 401(k) loan feature to a structure known as the rollover business start-up (ROBS). This book will help you understand which business-funding option is best for you.

This book covers the following subjects:

- the many funding options available to start or fund your business
- detailed overviews of the primary business-funding options available
- advantages and disadvantages of using retirement funds to start a business venture
- Internal Revenue Service (IRS) rules governing the use of retirement funds to fund a business venture
- available options for funding a business venture with retirement funds
- how to establish a structure that allows retirement funds to fund a business venture
- the potential tax impact of using retirement funds to fund a business venture
- how to choose the best business-funding option

On its own, this book will not make your business successful or even help you determine if a potential business is right for you. But it will give you the tools you need to understand the business-funding options available to you, including the opportunity to use retirement funds to start a new business venture or finance an existing business. It is up to you to do your homework and leverage your knowledge, experience, and insight to make the best decisions for your business and retirement funds.

Retirement Funds in a Nutshell

Funding new business ventures has become a popular TV phenomenon. As the producers of the reality shows *Shark Tank* on ABC or *Crowd Rules* on CNBC know, watching would-be entrepreneurs pitch their ideas, products, or services to win money for their business has become extremely popular with the American public. By 2012, *Shark Tank* averaged over six million viewers an episode, making it the most watched program on Friday nights in the eighteen-to-forty-nine-year-old demographic.

As you may know, *Shark Tank* offers budding entrepreneurs a chance to bring their dreams to fruition. Contestants present their ideas to the "sharks"—five titans of industry who made their own dreams a reality by turning ideas into lucrative empires. The contestants try to convince the sharks to invest money in their idea.

I bet many of you feel that you have an idea, product, or service that could be very successful if you had the opportunity to pitch it to the sharks or a few wealthy angel investors. Unfortunately, being selected to appear on *Shark Tank* is quite difficult and competitive. Only a few in twenty-four thousand applicants make the cut.[5] The chances of finding a rich uncle or friend looking to make private business investments are probably much smaller.

Most would-be entrepreneurs are so focused on getting their business ventures off the ground that they are often unaware that using retirement

---

5 http://nypost.com/2012/04/25/getting-in-the-tank/

funds as an alternative business-funding option is legal and could be a viable option under the right circumstances.

I've written this book to help you examine the many different ways you can fund your business, including using your retirement funds. The book will help you decide whether using retirement funds to fund a business venture is the right choice, and, if it is, it will help you make sure that you do it the right and legal way.

I'm going to tell you how retirement saving works in general, first by describing the various types of individual retirement accounts (IRA) and defined contribution plans (401(k)) that you may already have heard of and even be using. I am then going to provide a detailed analysis of the traditional ways you can fund a business acquisition or finance an existing business, such as using personal savings, acquiring a traditional loan or SBA loan, using a credit card, approaching family or friends, or crowd-funding. Finally, I'm going to tell you a lot more about two structures you probably haven't encountered before: the self-directed IRA and ROBS. While a self-directed IRA allows you to invest in a business other than your own or that of a lineal descendant, the ROBS solution allows you to use your pretax IRA or 401(k) funds to invest in your own business venture or that of a family member.

But first let me tell you about someone who probably wouldn't appear on *Shark Tank* or *Crowd Rules*, but who may seem familiar nevertheless. I consider this person typical of the clients I talk with who are contemplating using retirement funds to buy a business. I call him Ken.

KEN'S STORY

Ken is a would-be entrepreneur struggling to make his dream of owning his own business a reality. He's fifty-two years old, and he lives in Phoenix, Arizona, with his wife and two children. Ken has been working as a salesperson at a beverage distributor in town for the last thirteen years. He likes his job but has always dreamed of owning his own business. He earns a respectable salary, and with two kids he has never felt right about jumping into the risky start-up business world. He swims regularly, enjoys watching football, and loves to do crossword puzzles. His wife, Pam, is a successful attorney at a prominent local firm.

For the past several years, Ken has thought a lot about leaving his job and starting his own business, but he just never found the right opportunity. That changed several months ago when he met his friend David at a bar to watch his favorite NFL team play on Thursday night. David owned several restaurants and had recently sold them for a handsome profit. David was smart and quite business savvy, which always impressed Ken. While enjoying the football game, a commercial appeared for a consumer home-soda-carbonation company. That got David thinking about a business opportunity he had been presented a week ago. David knew that Ken had always wanted to start his own business because they talked about it a lot whenever they got together. David asked Ken if he still had the entrepreneurship itch, and Ken nodded his head and shouted "Yes!" David laughed and started telling Ken about this potential franchise opportunity selling purified and carbonated water devices for home or business use. Ken was interested and mentioned that he had a strong knowledge of the beverage industry based on his thirteen years of work in the industry. David thought this could be a huge plus as well, and he promised to send Ken an e-mail with additional information when he got home.

Ken had a rush of excitement on his drive home and immediately went up to the bedroom to talk with Pam about his chat with David. Ken gave Pam the rundown of their conversation and a general overview of the franchise opportunity they discussed. Pam was excited for Ken. She had always known about Ken's dream of starting his own business, and she encouraged him to pursue this franchise opportunity with David in more detail. Pam also mentioned that one of the partners at her law firm, a guy named John, was a tax partner with a lot of experience in start-ups and retirement plans. Pam promised to speak with John about options and suggested setting up a meeting with him. Ken really liked this idea.

He wasn't able to sleep all night and couldn't wait to check his e-mail in the morning. Bright and early, Ken woke up and looked at his iPhone. Lo and behold, there was an e-mail from David with information and a number of attachments on the franchise opportunity. Ken took a quick shower, made some coffee, and printed out the e-mail and attachments David sent. Ken then brought the attachments he printed with him to work so he could review them on his lunch break. Ken spent his entire lunch break poring over the printed documents. The more he read, the more excited he became about this opportunity. Ken phoned Pam to share his excitement, and they made a plan to discuss it further once the kids went to bed. Ken then called David and let him know that he was reviewing the information but was really excited about the opportunity. In the meantime, Ken spent some time on the Internet researching the water franchise and trying to get a better handle on the water industry. He also spoke to a few colleagues at the beverage company to hear their thoughts on the opportunity and overall industry.

Once the kids went to bed, Ken and Pam sat down at the kitchen table and started going through the information on the franchise opportunity. Pam read all the materials while Ken provided background details on the water franchise and the water-purification industry. Pam was impressed with the opportunity and thought that this could end up being a really interesting business opportunity. Pam and Ken then went over the financial details. The price to purchase the franchise and rights to all of Arizona was $250,000. In addition, the franchisee was expected to have at least $50,000 in working capital once the business was launched. Ken assumed David would be interested in investing half the funds, so he would have to come up with just about $150,000. Pam was silent for a minute. She reminded Ken that they have close to $165,000 in savings, but those funds were tied up in the stock market and were earmarked for the kids' college tuition. Ken then mentioned that he would talk with his parents and siblings to see if they would be willing to consider investing in this opportunity, but he wasn't very optimistic because of their current financial positions. Pam said she would talk with her parents but also didn't think that it would work out. Pam mentioned that it might make sense to sit down and talk with David in detail about this and try to work out some type of financial arrangement before getting others involved. Ken thought that was a good idea.

Ken and David met a few days later to discuss the franchise opportunity. Over coffee they talked about business details and financials. David mentioned that he would be in for $150,000 to cover half the franchise fee and half the start-up working capital expense, but that was probably all he could invest now because of other investment commitments. Ken said that come hell or high water, he was going to find a way to come up with the cash to make the investment. David then suggested that they set up a meeting with the franchisor.

A few weeks later, David and Ken flew to Los Angeles to meet with the franchise owner. They came away very impressed with the company and felt even stronger about the business opportunity. Upon returning home, Ken told Pam all about their meeting and explained that he would need to find a way to come up with the $150,000 in the next few months or they could lose the opportunity. Pam understood and mentioned that they could probably invest $75,000 from their savings but that would be all. Ken thought that was probably a reasonable number. Pam then suggested that Ken call John, her law partner, to see if he could come up with any business-funding options, based on his extensive experience. Ken thought that was a great idea and promised to e-mail John in the morning.

The next day, Ken e-mailed John, and they set up a time to meet the following week.

TWO CAPPUCCINOS, TWO SCONES, AND FREE CONSULTATION

Ken met his wife's lawyer colleague John in the coffee bar located in the lobby of the law firm's building and ordered two nonfat cappuccinos and two blueberry scones. They sat at a quiet table toward the back of the coffee bar. Ken thanked John for taking the time out of his busy day to meet with him and discuss this potential business opportunity. John said, "No problem. I owe your wife a few favors after she got me out of a couple speeding tickets." Ken chuckled and said, "OK, let me get started because I don't want to waste too much of your time." Ken picked up from the beginning and explained to John that although he has a solid job and earns a reasonable salary, his dream has always been to own a business and become his own boss. Ken then mentioned his fortuitous meeting with David and how the idea of the water franchise came to be. He then showed John a printed copy of the e-mail David sent him, which included all the attachments on the water franchise. Ken explained how he had spent the past month researching the business, franchisor, and industry in great detail, and how he and David flew to Los Angeles to meet with the franchise executives. Ken wanted John to know that he was serious about pursuing this business opportunity and potentially walking away from his career in beverage sales. Ken then described his and Pam's personal financial position and their liquid assets. John thanked Ken for the recap. Ken said, "I think I forgot to add that I need to find a way to come up with $150,000 to buy the business." John laughed and said, "I've heard that before. Don't worry, you may have a few business-funding options that you are not even aware of that may help you buy your business without tapping into all of your personal savings."

John asked Ken if he and Pam had spoken to family members and friends about potentially investing in the business or lending him the necessary funds to make the investment personally. Ken replied that he and Pam had spoken to their parents and siblings, and it just wasn't going to be an option. Ken also mentioned that he spoke to a few of his well-to-do friends about investing, but wasn't successful there either. John then asked Ken if he or Pam had any retirement funds. Ken looked surprised and confused by the question. "Why would you care how much retirement funds I have? Aren't retirement funds for retirement?"

"Yes, technically," John said, "but there are some legal and IRS-approved ways that allow you to use your retirement funds to invest or fund a business venture."

"Wow," Ken said. "I guess that is why you are a tax lawyer and I am in sales."

"Actually," John said, "most attorneys and CPAs are not aware that people can use retirement funds to invest in a personal business venture legally without triggering a taxable distribution or engaging in a prohibited transaction. I can't tell you how many attorneys and CPAs I speak to about this who look at me like I am crazy when I offer them this option for their start-up business clients. The response is usually 'Is this legal? How come I've never heard about it?' It doesn't matter if it's a young attorney or a well-established attorney or CPA, the responses are all the same."

"Well, that makes me feel better," Ken admitted.

Ken told John that the last time he checked his 401(k) account with his current employer, the account was valued at approximately $135,000. "With the fluctuation in the equity markets these days I am not sure what it is worth today, but it should be close to the amount," Ken said.

"Do you have any other retirement accounts?" John asked.

"I think I have about $8,000 in a Roth IRA and only $1,800 or so in a pretax IRA," Ken said.

"I don't mean to be intrusive," John said, "but your answer to the following question will help me understand what business-funding options are available to you for your business franchise opportunity. How much does Pam have in the law firm 401(k) plan?"

"I think she has about $175,000 in her 401(k) plan," Ken answered.

"Then I think there are some good options available to you," John said.

"You certainly piqued my curiosity. Is there a way you could give me a crash course?" Ken asked.

"I'd be more than happy to fill you in," John answered, "as long as you buy the coffee and scones the next time we meet."

"That's a deal. How do we start?"

"Where everything starts. At the beginning."

Everyone has heard of a traditional IRA (individual retirement account). This is the basic way that many Americans put aside a few thousand dollars of tax-deferred or after-tax income every year for their retirement. Many are also familiar with other variations of the IRA, such as the Roth IRA, SEP-IRA, SIMPLE IRA, self-directed IRA, and rollover IRA. Don't worry if these terms and the others I am about to use are not completely familiar to you, or if you are, like most people, somewhat hazy on the differences— I will explain them simply and fully in the chapters to come.

Similarly, most of us have signed up for a 401(k) plan at some point in our working years. This retirement savings vehicle is available to employees of companies that offer such a plan. Employees' contributions to their 401(k) amount to some percentage of their total compensation and is usually deducted directly from their paycheck. That money is tax deferred, or could be after-tax in some cases, and is often matched by the employer, typically at a 3 percent rate in order to take advantage of the safe harbor 401(k) plan ERISA (Employee Retirement Income Security Act) rules.

As of 2011, there were approximately forty-seven million IRAs in the United States. As of 2012, approximately fifty-one million people participated in 401(k) plans. A lot of the people I work with have a mix of approaches in their retirement portfolio. They often have a traditional IRA and a 401(k), and they or their spouse may also have a Roth, SIMPLE IRA, or some other variation. Together, these accounts represent their retirement savings.

So if you, like Ken, want to study up on retirement accounts first, I suggest you continue to read as much or as little as you'd like. If you want to skip ahead, let's move on to chapter 2, and we can continue our conversation about potential options for using retirement funds to buy or fund a business venture.

WHAT IS AN IRA?

An individual retirement account, or IRA, is a tax-favored personal savings arrangement that allows you to set aside money for retirement. There are several different types of IRAs, which you can set up with a bank, insurance company, or other financial institution.

The original IRA is often referred to as a traditional IRA. You may be able to deduct some or all of your contributions to a traditional IRA. For 2015, you can contribute up to $5,500 annually, or $6,500 if over the age of fifty. Distributions from a traditional IRA are fully or partially taxable in the year of distribution. If you made only deductible contributions, distributions are fully taxable.

Distributions made prior to age fifty-nine and a half may be subject to a 10 percent additional tax. Unfortunately, you cannot keep retirement funds in your account indefinitely. You generally have to start taking withdrawals from your IRA or retirement plan account when you reach age seventy and a half. This is often referred to as a "required minimum distribution," or RMD. A Roth IRA does not require withdrawals until after the death of the owner.

Your RMD is the minimum amount you must withdraw from your account each year. You can withdraw more than the minimum required amount, and your withdrawals will be included in your taxable income except for any part that was taxed before (your basis) or that can be received tax free (such as qualified distributions from designated Roth accounts).

Contributions to all types of IRAs can be made only from income that the IRS determines to be "earned." You do not have to work for someone else to have taxable earned income; you can also work for yourself. Compensation from either type of employment would be considered earned income, but the complete definition is a bit broader. The IRS defines the following types of income as taxable:

- wages, salaries, and tips
- union strike benefits
- long-term disability benefits received prior to minimum retirement age
- net earnings from self-employment

However, these are examples of income that is *not* considered earned:

- pay received for work while an inmate in a penal institution
- interest and dividends
- retirement income
- social security
- unemployment benefits
- alimony
- child support

WHAT IS A ROTH IRA?

In 1997, Congress, under the Taxpayer Relief Act, introduced the Roth IRA. This is like a traditional IRA but with a few attractive modifications. The big advantage of a Roth IRA is that if you qualify to make contributions, all distributions from the Roth IRA are tax free—even the investment returns and appreciation—as long as the distributions meet certain requirements.

The rules for the Roth IRA are found in the IRC under Section 408A. Here are some of its characteristics and features:

- Contributions are not tax deductible.
- Unlike traditional IRAs, you may contribute to a Roth IRA for as long as you continue to have earned income.
- All Roth IRA contributions are made with after-tax dollars. This means that the amount of the contribution is treated as basis in the IRA.
- Earnings and gains are tax deferred and may be tax exempt. This means that all income and gains generated by a Roth IRA investment are not subject to income tax. As long as certain conditions are met and the distribution is a qualified distribution, the Roth IRA owner will never pay tax on any Roth distributions received. Essentially, if the Roth IRA account has been open at least five years and the holder is over the age of fifty-nine and a half at the date of the distribution, there should be no tax on the entire Roth IRA distribution, including contributions, income, and appreciation.
- Unlike the traditional IRA, there is no seventy-and-a-half age limit on making contributions. Individuals of any age with compensation below a certain income threshold are eligible to contribute to a Roth IRA. The total amount you may contribute to a Roth IRA for 2014 cannot exceed the lesser of $5,500 ($6,500 if over the age of fifty) or 100 percent of compensation ($11,000 for married couples and $13,000 if over the age of fifty).

The IRS has established income rules that govern who is eligible to make after-tax (Roth) IRA contributions. If your income exceeds a certain amount, you will not be allowed to contribute to a Roth IRA. Below is a table that details the Roth IRA income thresholds for 2015:

For 2015, the AGI phase-out range for taxpayers making contributions to a Roth IRA is $183,000 to $193,000 for married couples filing jointly. For singles and heads of household, the income phase-out range is $116,000 to $131,000.

For 2016, the income limit for contributing the maximum to a Roth IRA will go up by $1,000 in 2016 to $117,000 for singles and $184,000 for married filing jointly. You can't contribute anything directly to a Roth IRA when your income goes above $132,000 for singles and $194,000 for married filing jointly, both up by $1,000 in 2016.

You may ask if there a way one can still make after-tax (Roth) IRA contributions even if one has exceeded the annual income level threshold. The answer is, thankfully, yes!

THE BACKDOOR ROTH IRA CONTRIBUTION

The one way high earners can contribute to a Roth IRA is through the backdoor approach of converting a traditional IRA made with an after-tax fund, which has no income threshold, to a Roth IRA. The traditional IRA contribution made with after-tax funds may then be converted to a Roth, but may be subject to tax based on the pro rata Roth conversion rules. Note: if you maintain a traditional IRA, the maximum contribution to your Roth IRA is reduced by any contributions made to your traditional IRA.

HOW DO YOU DECIDE BETWEEN A TRADITIONAL IRA AND A ROTH IRA?

There's no right or wrong answer. The decision usually depends on a variety of factors and circumstances.

If you are not eligible to take advantage of tax-deductible contributions to a traditional IRA but qualify for after-tax contributions to a Roth IRA, then the Roth IRA is the better choice. Roth IRA contributions are made in after-tax dollars, while earnings are usually not taxable.

If contributions to a traditional IRA are tax deductible and you are also eligible to contribute to a Roth IRA, here are some considerations in making your decision:

- If you expect your retirement tax rate to be equal or higher than it is today, a Roth IRA could yield the greatest benefit.
- If you expect your retirement tax rate to be much lower than it is today, you may want to choose to make contributions to a traditional IRA.
- If you expect your investment to generate strong returns, then a Roth IRA could be a better option.

Finally, if you are younger, the Roth IRA is more attractive because you will have more time to grow your retirement without paying any tax.

NOT ALL IRAS ARE THE SAME

The majority of IRA funds are invested in traditional equity-type investments such as stocks, mutual funds, and exchange traded funds (ETFs). However, the 2008 financial crisis helped publicize and popularize the self-directed IRA and a viable investment strategy for retirement accounts.

The 2008 financial crisis resulted in many Americans asking about alternative investment options for their retirement accounts. It is believed that the financial crisis cost retirees almost 25 percent of their retirement assets, and many are still trying to get back to where they were prior to the crisis. The sudden and steep stock-market fall coupled with lack of faith in Wall Street and the global financial markets caused many Americans to seek a more balanced and diversified retirement portfolio. With this came a sharp increase in the number of Americans looking at a self-directed IRA as the vehicle for attaining a level of account diversification by making alternative-asset investments, such as real estate, precious metals, tax liens, notes, and private businesses.

Actually, the Internal Revenue Code (IRC) does not describe what a self-directed IRA can invest in, only what it cannot invest in. IRC Sections 408 and 4975 prohibit disqualified persons from engaging in certain type of transactions. The purpose of these rules is to encourage the use of IRAs for accumulation of retirement savings and to prohibit those in control of IRAs from taking advantage of the tax benefits for their personal account.

Essentially there are three different types of self-directed IRAs, each providing the IRA holder with different levels of investment and control options:

1. traditional financial institution self-directed IRA
2. custodian-controlled self-directed IRA without checkbook control
3. self-directed IRA LLC with checkbook control

Traditional Financial Institution Self-Directed IRA

The traditional financial institution self-directed IRA is by far the most popular type of self-directed IRA. The majority of all IRAs are held at traditional financial institutions such as Fidelity, Vanguard, Charles Schwab, Bank of America, Merrill Lynch, and so on. Many traditional financial institutions advertise themselves as offering a self-directed IRA, but what that really means is that you will be limited to purchasing stocks, mutual funds, bonds, and other traditional types of investments that earn the institution commission. In other words, you need the consent of your IRA custodian before making an investment.

Back to Coffee

Ken thanked John for the overview and said that he had a few questions for clarification.

"Shoot," John said.

"What's an IRA custodian?" Ken asked.

"A custodian is your IRA trustee," John said. "Basically, that's the institution that holds your IRA account. By law, every retirement account must be held at a custodian or trustee. A trustee may be a bank, trust company, credit union, or a large brokerage firm that is licensed by the IRS. IRS regulations require that either a qualified trustee or custodian hold the IRA assets on behalf of the IRA owner."

"Are there some financial custodians that will allow you to invest in areas you want to invest in?"

"Yes. A true self-directed IRA custodian is known as a passive custodian, and a passive custodian allows the IRA holder to engage in nontraditional investments like real estate. What it doesn't do is offer investment advice."

"So to get this straight," Ken said, "when you have a self-directed IRA at a traditional financial institution, you're technically able to self-direct your IRA investments. But you're probably limited to investing in the financial products offered by the financial institution."

"That's right," John answered. "For example, a financial institution such as Vanguard or Fidelity will allow you to select the type of investments for your own IRA, but your choices are usually limited to the financial products they offer. In other words, stocks, mutual funds, and bonds. They won't permit you to make alternative-asset investments such as real estate, precious metals, private business investments, foreign currency, options, and so on."

"Why won't they allow me to purchase real estate or invest in a private business with my IRA if it's permitted by the IRS?" Ken asked.

"It's just business," John said. "Financial institutions are in business to earn profit and generate strong earnings for shareholders. Like any business, they're motivated to enhance the bottom line. So they require IRA holders to invest in financial products they market and sell. That way they can earn a fee or commission and probably gain use of the funds. In fact, they make money by using the funds they have on deposit for their own investment purposes or to hold as financial reserves."

"In other words, they don't make any money by allowing you to make private business investments or other alternative-asset investments, so it doesn't make any sense to let you do that."

"Exactly," John said. "If they could make money when you bought real estate with your IRA funds, they'd probably allow you to do that. But when an IRA holder buys real estate, the parties that benefit from the investment are the seller of the property, the real-estate agent, the title-insurance company, and the closing attorney. On the other hand, if an IRA holder uses IRA assets to purchase mutual funds or stocks, the financial institution selling you those stocks benefits directly from the investment."

"So if they let you shift your IRA assets away from financial products that generate their fees and commissions to nontraditional investments such as real estate, that's going to negatively impact the financial institution's bottom line."

"Right," John said. "It'll reduce the financial institution's profits for sure, and probably put a strain on their financial reserves. So, most traditional financial institutions just don't allow it."

"So tell me about the financial institutions that allow me to make nontraditional investments with my IRA funds," Ken said.

"OK," John said. "There are two kinds of those, too. Ready?"

Custodian-Controlled Self-Directed IRA
without Checkbook Control

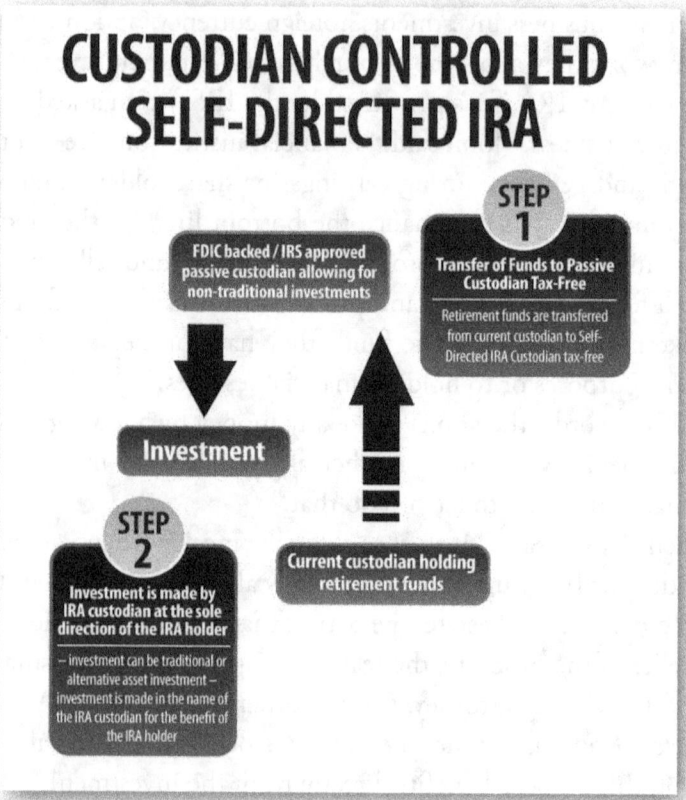

"Unlike the traditional financial institutions such as Fidelity, Vanguard, Charles Schwab, or Bank of America," John began, "there are a number of financial institutions or IRA custodians that do allow IRA holders to make nontraditional investments with their IRA funds."

"Have I heard of them?" Ken asked.

"Maybe. They include Equity Trust, Pensco Trust, and IRA Financial Trust, for example."

"Sounds sort of familiar. How are they different from the traditional IRA custodians?"

"They have a slightly different business model," John said. "Unlike a traditional financial institution, which makes the majority of its IRA-related earnings on commissions and fees associated with stocks, mutual funds, bonds, and other equity or debt type of investments, these custodians typically generate their profits through annual account valuation fees and transaction fees."

"OK, so they charge you an annual fee, a fee whenever you do something with your money, or both?"

"Exactly. They usually permit you to make alternative-asset investments such as real estate."

"I still don't like that word 'permit,'" Ken said. "It's my money, right?"

"It is," John said, "but even in this type of financial institution you still don't have checkbook control. In other words, you need custodian consent to enter into and execute any transaction."

"Sounds like a pain."

"Well, it can be. In fact, like any bureaucratic matter, it can be very inefficient. There are typically long delays between asking for consent and getting approval, and on top of that there can be high custodian fees associated with the transaction. So before engaging in an IRA investment, the IRA custodian requires you to get the consent of the custodian. You'll need to provide the custodian with the transaction documents for review as part of their transaction review process. And even upon approval, your IRA investment would be made in the name of the custodian for the benefit of (FBO) the IRA holder's IRA. So, for example, ABC Trust Company FBO Rich Smith IRA. This doesn't give the IRA owner any privacy or limited liability protection."

"Sounding less appealing by the minute," Ken said.

"And the minutes can count when you're trying to pounce on an opportunity."

"And the fees, too. I don't like the sound of that."

"You shouldn't. It's common for a moderately active investor with $1 million in assets with a self-directed IRA custodian without checkbook control to end up paying from $500 to $1,500 in aggregate annual fees, including account value fee, transaction fees, and approval letters," John said.

"And they can still say no to your investment idea?"

"They sure can. There's no guarantee that the custodian will approve your investment even though the investment would not violate IRS rules. Overall, with a custodian-controlled self-directed IRA, even though you will usually be permitted to make most alternative-asset IRA investments, time delays and high custodian fees are a major downside. For example, let's say a guy we'll call Jim wants to use his retirement funds to invest in real estate and elects to use a custodian-controlled self-directed IRA to make the investment. He selects ABC Trust Company as the IRA custodian. Before making the real-estate investment, Jim would be required to provide all real-estate transaction documents, including the purchase agreement and all ancillary purchase documents to ABC Trust Company for review and signature. Then ABC Trust Company must approve the transaction. If the transaction is approved, Jim needs to wait for ABC Trust Company to sign all documents before proceeding with the real-estate purchase. In other words, even before Jim makes an offer on a piece of real estate, he's required to seek ABC Trust Company's consent as well as receive all required signatures before the offer can be submitted. Then the funds required to make the purchase would be transferred directly from ABC Trust Company, and Jim would be required to pay an annual account fee based on the annual value of his IRA, as well as fees for each IRA transaction."

"So, for Jim to pull that real-estate deal off he's got to hope no one else snaps it up before him. ABC Trust Company has to make the purchase for him, and he's got to pay them fees on top of all the fees and costs to the transaction," Ken said.

"That's correct."

"I'm assuming there's a better way."

"You're right," John said, "there is."

Self-Directed IRA LLC with Checkbook Control

"Beginning in the mid-1990s," John continued, "a new type of self-directed IRA structure started taking shape that allowed the IRA holder to make IRA investments directly without the consent of a custodian. Unlike a custodian-controlled self-directed IRA, which requires the IRA holder to seek the consent of the custodian before making investments, with a self-directed IRA LLC with checkbook control, a limited-liability company (LLC) is established that is owned by the IRA account and managed by the IRA account holder. A passive custodian then transfers the IRA holder's IRA funds to the LLC's bank account providing the IRA holder, as manager of the LLC, with checkbook control over his or her IRA funds. So, with a truly self-directed IRA, the IRA holder has total control over his or her IRA funds."

"No need to get custodian consent?" Ken asked.

"Right. You no longer have to get each investment approved by the custodian of the account. Instead, all your investment decisions are made by you, as the manager of the LLC, or by any third-party manager you assign.

"Like the financial institutions and custodians that offer custodian-controlled self-directed IRA, there are a number of trust companies that serve as passive custodians, allowing for true self-directed IRA LLC with checkbook-control investments, such as IRA Financial Trust. The popularity of the self-directed IRA LLC with checkbook control is increasing each year. More and more custodians are getting comfortable with their clients using these types of investment structures for their IRA funds."

"Wow, that sounds really interesting," Ken said. "I would definitely like to learn more about the self-directed IRA as a potential business-funding option."

"You bet," John said. "But I think you'll see that it may not end up being a really good business-funding option for you. Here, look at these pamphlets I have on the SEP and SIMPLE IRAs and on the 401(k) plan and solo 401(k) plan."

WHAT IS A SEP-IRA?

A simplified employee pension (SEP) plan provides business owners with a simplified method to contribute toward their employees' retirement as well as their own retirement savings. A SEP is essentially an employer-sponsored profit-sharing plan. Contributions are made to a retirement account or annuity set up for each plan participant: a SEP-IRA.

A SEP-IRA account is a traditional IRA and follows the same investment, distribution, and rollover rules as traditional IRAs. Employees must be included in the SEP plan if they have

- attained age twenty-one,
- received at least $550 in compensation from your business for the year, and
- worked for your business for at least three of the past five years.

The three-of-five eligibility rule means you must include any employee in your plan who has worked for you in any three of the past five years as long as the employee has satisfied the other plan eligibility requirements. This is the most restrictive eligibility requirement allowable. You can choose to use less restrictive participation rules in your plan, such as allowing employees to participate immediately after they start work or after a shorter period of employment. If you use the three-of-five rule, you must count any work, no matter how little, in each of the prior five years. Use plan years (often the calendar year), not years based on the date the employee started working for you.

The contributions you make to each employee's SEP-IRA each year cannot exceed the lesser of

- 25 percent of compensation; or
- $52,000 for 2014.

There are no catch-up contributions for a SEP-IRA as there are for a 401(k) plan. These limits apply to contributions you make for your employees to all defined contribution plans, which includes SEPs. Up to $260,000 in 2014 of an employee's compensation may be considered. Also, contributions must be made in cash, and you cannot contribute property.

WHAT IS A SIMPLE IRA?

A SIMPLE (savings incentive match plan for employees) IRA plan allows employees and employers to contribute to traditional IRAs set up for employees. Employees may choose to make salary-reduction contributions, and the employer is required to make either matching or nonelective contributions. Contributions are made to a retirement account or annuity set up for each employee: a SIMPLE IRA.

A SIMPLE IRA plan account is an IRA and follows the same investment, distribution, and rollover rules as traditional IRAs. Any employer (including self-employed individuals, tax-exempt organizations, and governmental entities) that had no more than a hundred employees with $5,000 or more in compensation during the preceding calendar year (the "100-employee limitation") can establish a SIMPLE IRA plan. You can set up a SIMPLE

IRA plan effective on any date between January 1 and October 1 provided you (or any preceding employer) didn't previously maintain a SIMPLE IRA plan. If you're a new employer that came into existence after October 1 of the year, you can establish the SIMPLE IRA plan as soon as administratively feasible after your business came into existence.

All employees who received at least $5,000 in compensation from you during any two preceding calendar years (whether or not consecutive) and who are reasonably expected to receive at least $5,000 in compensation during the calendar year are eligible to participate in the SIMPLE IRA plan for that calendar year. Each eligible employee may make a salary-reduction contribution, and the employer must make either a matching contribution or nonelective contribution. An employee may defer up to $12,000 in 2014, subject to cost-of-living adjustments for later years. Employees age fifty or over can make a catch-up contribution of up to $2,500 in 2014, subject to cost-of-living adjustments for later years.

With respect to employer contributions, the employer is usually required to

- match each employee's salary-reduction contribution on a dollar-for-dollar basis up to 3 percent of the employee's compensation (not limited by the annual compensation limit); or
- make nonelective contributions of 2 percent of the employee's compensation up to the annual limit of $260,000 for 2014, subject to cost-of-living adjustments in later years).

If you choose to make nonelective contributions, you must make them for all eligible employees whether or not they make salary-reduction contributions. With respect to the 3 percent match, you may elect to reduce the 3 percent matching contributions for a calendar year, but only if

- the limit isn't reduced below 1 percent;
- the limit isn't reduced for more than two years out of the five-year period that ends with (and includes) the year for which the election is effective; and

- you notify employees of the reduced limit within a reasonable time before the sixty-day election period during which employees can enter into salary-reduction agreements.

Usually, the same tax results apply to distributions from a SIMPLE IRA as to distributions from a regular IRA.

THE 401(K) PLAN

The 401(k) that is so popular today was created practically by accident. It is a type of CODA, or cash or deferred arrangement. The name comes from the Revenue Act of 1978, which included Section 401(k) allowing full-time employees to fund retirement accounts with pretax dollars matched by employer contributions. In 1980, a benefits consultant named Ted Benna spotted this provision and created a 401(k) plan program for his employer. He also asked the IRS to make some changes so that the plans could be more widely adopted. Within a year, a handful of large companies had adopted 401(k) plans for their employers.

According to the most recent statistics provided by the US Department of Labor, there are 638,390 defined contribution retirement plans in the United States; 513,000 of these are 401(k) plans covering more than eighty-eight million total participants (more than seventy-three million active).[6]

Unfortunately for self-employed people, 401(k) plans can be established only through an employer. As a result, until 2002 self-employed people typically relied on SEP or SIMPLE IRAs as their retirement vehicle of choice for good reason.

In 2001, however, Congress passed the Economic Growth and Tax Relief Reconciliation Act (EGTRRA) as part of the so-called Bush tax cuts. This act, which took effect in 2002, had a tremendous impact on retirement plans in general: it increased limits, making it easier to consolidate plans and making the plans themselves more flexible, and offered a catch-up provision for older workers. Most importantly for our purpose in this book, the act provided people who

---

6 DOL Employee Benefits Security Administration, *Private Pension Plan Bulletin: Abstract of 2011 Form 5500 Annual Reports,* June 2013

were self-employed or who were small-business owners with no employees the same advantages and benefits of a conventional employer 401(k) plan.

Before the EGTRRA Act, there was no compelling reason for an owner-only business to establish a solo 401(k) plan. After all, the business owner could receive the same benefits by adopting a profit-sharing plan or a SEP-IRA. EGTRRA paved the way, however, for an owner-only business to put more money aside for retirement and to operate a more cost-effective retirement plan than a SEP or SIMPLE IRA.

Today, in 2015, the solo 401(k), also known as the individual 401(k) or self-employed 401(k) plan, allows individuals to maximize their contributions up to $53,000 ($59,000 if over the age of fifty) without burdening them with the administrative responsibilities of a conventional ERISA 401(k) qualified retirement plan. In addition, an individual participant can borrow up to $50,000, make Roth contributions, and have the checkbook control to make real-estate and other investments without tax.

It's surprising that the solo 401(k) plan is not more popular. The EGTRRA Act became law in 2002, and solo 401(k) has incredible advantages over all other IRA accounts. Yet a large number of self-employed people still adopt the SEP-IRA over the solo 401(k).

SOME INS AND OUTS OF THE SOLO 401(K) PLAN

In a way, the solo 401(k) was introduced to us in 1962 and greatly enhanced in 2002. The Keogh plan or H. R. 10 plan of 1962 was designated for self-employed business owners. But the rules for Keogh became cumbersome when the Tax Equity and Fiscal Responsibility Act (TEFRA) of 1982 removed the differences between corporate plans and Keogh plans for the self-employed, and mandated that they operate under the same rules. It wasn't until the solo 401(k) plan emerged with EGTRRA in 2002 that self-employed individuals had an easy-to-administer and flexible retirement plan tailored to their needs.

Under prior law, employer profit-sharing and matching combinations were combined with the employee deferral when determining the maximum deduction limit of 25 percent of an employee's compensation. EGTRRA increased the deductible profit-sharing contribution limit from 15 percent to 25 percent of employee compensation and changed the application of deferrals so they are not counted against the employer's maximum contribution amount. EGTRRA also increased the annual contribution limit to 100 percent of a participant's compensation. It created a Roth contribution option as well and allowed participants to designate all or a portion of their employee deferrals as after-tax (Roth) contributions. Finally, EGTRRA also modified the IRC to enable a loan feature for unincorporated businesses, which prior to that applied only to ERISA 401(k) plans.

THE SOLO 401(K) PLAN

The solo 401(k) plan has quietly become the most popular retirement plan for the self-employed small-business owner with no full-time employees, outmaneuvering the SEP-IRA. The solo 401(k) is not a term of art and you will not find it named as such in the IRC. To confuse matters even more, a number of other terms are commonly used by tax professionals to describe the same tool: individual 401(k), one-participant 401(k), self-employed 401(k), self-directed 401(k), and uni 401(k). In fact, you can call it pretty much whatever you want, because it is not, as I mentioned, defined specifically in the IRC. I like the term "solo" because it carries the sense of independence and self-reliance that I find characteristic of the people who are able to take advantage of it the most.

A solo 401(k) is perfect for sole proprietors, small-business owners, and independent contractors such as consultants. It is unique and very popular because it was designed by Congress and the IRS explicitly for small owner-only businesses—basically, any business with no employees other than the owner(s). That business can be established as a sole proprietorship, LLC, corporation, or partnership.

Here are some of the most important advantages. Don't worry if these terms and the others I am about to use are not completely familiar to you. They will be explained later.

High Contribution Limits

While an IRA allows only a $5,500 contribution limit (with a $1,000 additional "catch-up" contribution for those over age fifty), the solo 401(k) annual contribution limit is $53,000 for 2015, with an additional $6,000 catch-up contribution for those over fifty. In addition, if your spouse generates compensation from the business, he or she can also make high contributions to the plan.

Under the 2015 solo 401(k) contribution rules, a plan participant under the age of fifty can make a maximum employee deferral contribution in the amount of $18,000. That amount can be made pretax or after-tax (Roth). On the profit-sharing side, the business can make a 25 percent (20 percent in the case of a sole proprietorship or single-member LLC) profit-sharing contribution up to a combined maximum, including the employee deferral, of $53,000, an increase of $1,000 from 2014.

For plan participants over the age of fifty, an individual can make a maximum employee deferral contribution in the amount of $24,000. That amount can be made pretax or after-tax (Roth). On the profit-sharing side, the business can make a 25 percent (20 percent in the case of a sole proprietorship or single-member LLC) profit-sharing contribution up to a combined maximum, including the employee deferral, of $59,000, an increase of $1,500 from 2014.

A World of Investment Opportunities

Depending on the type of solo 401(k) plan your business adopts, you could have the option to invest in almost any type of investment opportunity that you discover, including real estate (rentals, foreclosures, raw land, and tax liens), private businesses, precious metals, hard money, and peer-to-peer lending, as well as stock and mutual funds. Your only limit is your imagination. The income and gains from these investments will flow back into your solo 401(k) plan without tax. Making an investment with your solo 401(k) plan is as simple as writing a check. As trustee of the solo 401(k) plan, you will have total control over your retirement assets to make real estate and other investments tax free and without custodian consent.

Loan Feature

While an IRA offers no participant loan feature, if the solo 401(k) plan your business adopts includes a loan option, then that solo 401(k) allows participants to borrow up to $50,000 or 50 percent of their account value (whichever is less) for any purpose at a low interest rate (the lowest is the prime interest rate, which was 3.25 percent as of January 1, 2015). This offers a solo 401(k) plan participant the ability to access up to $50,000 for any purpose, including paying personal debt or funding a business.

The Flexibility to Self-Direct Your Retirement Funds

With a solo 401(k) plan, you can serve as trustee of the plan, giving you checkbook control over its funds. To this end, making an investment with your solo 401(k) plan is as easy as writing a check. Another significant benefit of the solo 401(k) plan is that it does not require the participant to hire a bank or trust company to serve as trustee. This flexibility allows the participant to serve in the trustee role. This means that all assets of the 401(k) trust are under the sole authority of the solo 401(k) participant. A solo 401(k) plan allows you to eliminate the expense and delays associated with an IRA custodian, enabling you to act quickly when the right investment opportunity presents itself. Also, because the solo 401(k) plan trust account can be opened at any local bank or credit union (Chase, Wells Fargo, or Citibank, for example), you will not be required to pay custodian fees for the account as you would in the case of an IRA.

Flexible Contribution Options

Contributions to a solo 401(k) plan are completely discretionary. You always have the option to try to contribute as much as legally possible, but you also have the option of reducing or even suspending plan contributions if necessary. In other words, you have the ability to contribute to your solo 401(k) plan (up to an aggregate amount of $53,000 if you are under the age of fifty), but you are not required to do so.

Roth-Type Contributions

With IRAs, those who earn high incomes are disallowed from contributing to a Roth IRA or converting their IRA to a Roth IRA. Depending on the type of solo 401(k) plan your business adopts, your plan could contain a built-in Roth subaccount, which can be contributed to without any income restrictions. With a Roth solo 401(k) subaccount, you can make after-tax Roth-type contributions while having the ability to make significantly greater contributions than with an IRA: up to $53,000, or $59,000 if over the age of fifty-nine and a half.

Cost-Effective Administration

In general, the solo 401(k) plan is easy to operate. There is usually no annual filing requirement unless your plan exceeds $250,000 in assets, in which case you will need to file a short information return with the IRS (Form 5500-EZ).

Offset the Cost of Your Plan with a Tax Deduction

By paying for your solo 401(k) with business funds, you are eligible to claim a deduction for the cost of the plan, including annual maintenance fees. The deduction for the cost associated with the solo 401(k) plan and ongoing maintenance will help reduce your business's income tax liability, which will in turn offset the cost of adopting a self-directed solo 401(k) plan.

No Tax on Nonrecourse Leverage for Real-Estate Acquisition

When an IRA buys real estate that is leveraged with mortgage financing, it creates unrelated debt-financed income (UDFI), a type of unrelated business taxable income (UBTI) on which taxes must be paid. The UBTI tax is approximately 40 percent for 2015. But with a solo 401(k) plan, you can use leverage without being subject to the UDFI rules and UBTI tax. This exemption provides significant tax advantages for using a solo 401(k) plan versus an IRA to purchase real estate.

Retirement Saving Consolidation through Rollovers

A solo 401(k) plan can accept rollovers of funds from another retirement savings vehicle, such as an IRA, a SEP, or a previous employer's 401(k) plan. Thus, you can directly roll over your IRA or qualified plan funds to your new 401(k) plan for investment or loan purposes. Note that only Roth IRA funds cannot be rolled into a solo 401(k) plan.

ALL SOLO 401(K) PLANS ARE NOT CREATED EQUAL

Most people believe that all solo 401(k) plans, whether attained for free at a financial institution or provided by a specialized plan provider, are the same. But the nuances that differentiate the various plan options are important to understand. In general, there are three ways to establish and use a solo 401(k) plan for retirement and investment purposes.

1. *Financial Institution-Sponsored Solo Plan*

   This is the most common way to establish a solo 401(k) plan. Most of the major financial institutions and US banks—such as Vanguard, Charles Schwab, E*Trade, Bank of America, and CIT—provide basic solo 401(k) plan documents and investment opportunities, typically for no fee. The catch is that the solo 401(k) plan documents you adopt are very basic and usually limit your options to making pretax employee deferrals and pretax profit-sharing contributions, while also limiting your 401(k) plan investment options to the financial product offering sold by that financial institution.

   In essence, the plan will let you make basic pretax employee deferral and profit-sharing contributions but will usually restrict your investment options to stocks, mutual funds, ETFs, and other traditional financial products sold by the financial institution. In other words, this type of solo 401(k) does not permit a loan feature, or the ability to make Roth (after-tax) contributions, or the option to make nontraditional investments, such as real estate and precious metals. The advantage of adopting a solo 401(k) plan from a major financial institution or bank can be found in the price and simplicity of such a transaction.

2. *Custodian-Directed Self-Directed Solo 401(k) Plan*
This option usually offers solo 401(k) plan participants the ability to make traditional investments, including stock, as well as IRS-approved nontraditional or alternate investments such as real estate, precious metals, private lending, and private business investments through a trust company. The custodian-directed self-directed solo 401(k) plan option is generally attractive to retirement investors looking to make nontraditional investments with their solo 401(k) plan while having a third party administer the plan.

These custodians or trust companies do not offer investment advice and are essentially in business to allow you to make IRS-approved nontraditional investments. Unlike a traditional financial institution such as Bank of America or Vanguard, which make money by selling financial products, these passive custodians and trust companies make their money by opening self-directed accounts and charging an annual fee. In some cases, the fees are based on account value and/or the number of transactions done in the account in a given year.

Most of the institutions that allow solo 401(k) plans to make nontraditional investments are established as trust companies and simply let you use their plan documents and accounts to make the investments. Your solo 401(k) plan assets are usually held at an FDIC institution associated with the trust company, and all investments must go through the custodian, which is why it is referred to as a custodian-directed plan. In practice, this means that you need to go through the custodian and have the custodian send the funds.

In most cases, that custodian must also sign the necessary transaction documents to enable you to make a solo 401(k) plan investment, including real estate. In some situations, you are permitted as trustee of the plan to sign the transaction documents, including the purchase agreement, but the issuing of check payments or wires for the purchase or for ongoing expenses such as taxes or repairs, need to go through the custodian because the custodian controls the funds. The custodian-directed self-directed solo 401(k) plan option has many attractive features, such as the ability to make non-traditional investments, but it also has some limitations, including annual fees and potential time delays that can result from having to go through the trust company to make transactions.

3. *Open-Architecture Self-Directed Solo 401(k) Plan*
   The open-architecture solo 401(k) plan is quickly becoming the most popular self-directed option for the self-employed. The beauty of the open-architecture solo 401(k) plan is that it can usually be opened at most local banks, and it allows the business owner to serve as trustee of the plan with total control over the investments made. Self-directed solo 401(k) plans are usually provided by specialized plan-provider companies, which are able to customize the plan based on the individual's retirement and investment goals. Most of the companies that offer self-directed open-architecture solo 401(k) plan documents are not typical financial institutions that sell financial products or house the solo 401(k) plan account. These companies essentially make money by selling the plan documents and offering advisory services regarding the features of the plan.

   Major financial institutions usually do not include the self-directed features in their solo 401(k) plan documents because that does not serve their financial interests. That has not stopped a number of specialized self-directed retirement facilitators from emerging as firms that specialize in helping to set up self-directed retirement solutions. This includes the self-directed solo 401(k) plan, which has become more popular because of growing demand for the diversification of nontraditional investments, such as real estate.

The open-architecture self-directed solo 401(k) plan has started to overtake the custodian-directed solo 401(k) plan as the most popular self-directed solo 401(k) plan option for a number of reasons:

- The plan can be opened at most local banks, which gives the plan participant more control and comfort than having the funds sit with a trustee in another state or at an unfamiliar bank.
- Once the documents have been purchased, there are typically very small annual compliance fees, since a solo 401(k) plan has very few administrative requirements—usually none if the plan's assets are under $250,000.
- You will have checkbook control, which means that as the trustee, you can make investments from your solo 401(k) account by simply writing a check or executing a wire.
- You can also customize the plan documents to include all available options allowable by the IRS.

The following information will help you decide which solo 401(k) plan options best suit your needs.

WHO'S ELIGIBLE TO USE A SOLO 401(K)?

It's important to understand who is eligible to create a solo 401(k), since that will determine whether you will be interested in digging deeper or just contemplating the big picture to get a better sense of how your career, work, and retirement savings options might unfold.

There are two specific eligibility requirements for the solo 401(k):

1. the presence of self-employment activity
2. the absence of full-time employees

As with anything drafted by the IRS, in between these dry declarations is a world of variety and possibility.

Who is a self-employed person? The obvious answer is that she works for herself. Think of a self-employed contractor, an independent consultant, a primary care physician, or a freelance graphic designer. I have come to believe that the variety of ways a person can make a living are nearly limitless.

Notice that there is no stipulation that such a person has to own his or her own business or be incorporated in any way. Some people take the formal approach when they work independently by creating a corporation, LLC, or partnership, and some people don't, which means they have a sole proprietorship. In general, any person who is self-employed or performing some activity that generates self-employment income not through an entity is automatically treated as a sole proprietorship.

Regardless, the solo 401(k) is still a fit so long as the person doesn't have any full-time employees, defined as people who work over a thousand hours for them annually. This means the independent contractor can still hire electricians, laborers, or architects to do a housing job, but can't employ such people full time. Or the graphic designer can pay an editor or a web designer or a videographer as an independent contractor, for example, but not as full-time employees.

However, the spouse of a small-business owner is not counted as a full-time employee even if the spouse's full-time income comes from the business. This is because spouses are not considered employees for ERISA purposes when it comes to determining 401(k) plan eligibility. Additionally, people under the age of twenty-one are not considered full-time employees, so you can feel free to put your children to work in the family business.

Finally, there's nothing in the eligibility requirements of the solo 401(k) that stipulates how much of your income must come from self-employment activity. In other words, you do not have to be just a contractor, or a primary care physician, or a graphic designer. You can, in fact, be an endless variety of other things in addition. For instance, you can be a radio talk-show host who also sells real estate, or a physician who works for a hospital and also provides medical consultations for a local sports team. You might be a graphic designer for a major advertising firm who also does graphic design work on a freelance basis, or the manager of a flower shop who also sells antiques on eBay. Whatever portion of your income arises through self-employment activity can be used to build savings through a solo 401(k). In essence, as long as there is the anticipation or expectation of earned income, the activity can be treated as self-employment activity.

This is the real magic of the solo 401(k). Rather than discouraging us from earning income in ways that are outside traditional lines, the solo 401(k) allows us to leverage those interests and activities to save a significantly higher portion of our money for retirement and at the same time reduce a large percentage of the tax due on the income earned through the activity.

DEFINED BENEFIT PLAN

Other than the solo 401(k) plan, a defined benefit (DB) plan is often considered to be the best retirement plan for the self-employed or small-business owner. The one major advantage of establishing a DB plan is that you can sock away a whole lot of money for retirement—far more than with any other retirement plan. For example, in 2015 the annual benefit cannot exceed the lesser of

- 100 percent of the participant's average compensation for his or her highest three consecutive calendar years; or
- $210,000.

A DB plan identifies the specific benefit that will be payable to you at retirement. Your basic retirement benefit is usually based on a formula that takes into account such factors as the number of years a participant works for the employer (years of service) and the participant's salary. Your retirement benefit is provided in the form of regular payments over your lifetime beginning at what the plan calls "normal retirement age," which is typically age sixty-five.

While it is really nice to know how much money you will have at retirement or payout, some DB plans do not adjust your future payouts to keep pace with inflation. In addition, you usually don't have much say in how the money is invested. Moreover, you can't choose to invest more in the plan, and the yearly maintenance fees for the plan can become significant. That being said, one of the major advantages of a DB plan is that there is no effort required on your part. The company that provides the DB plan is responsible for making all contribution and investment decision, which, when you are self-employed, is *you*. However, the DB plan sponsor bears the investment risk associated with the plan. In a weak market, higher contributions will be required to compensate for lower-than-expected investment return to satisfy the defined contribution requirement.

In sum, most business owners who elect to adopt a DB plan are doing it because substantial benefits can be provided and accrued within a short time, even with early retirement, and the plan provides a predictable benefit.

I won't go into more detail about DB plans for a simple reason: they are increasingly uncommon. Today, there are about 38,000 insured DB plans in the United States, compared to 114,000 in 1985. DB plans offer substantial tax-deductible retirement contributions and a significant and predictable future retirement income. They appeal to business owners who would like to shelter the largest percentage of their income or make the largest retirement plan contribution possible under IRS rules. However, the DB is one of the most costly types of retirement plans to adopt and administer, and has rigid annual funding requirements. Generally speaking, it is falling by the wayside.

THE POWER OF TAX DEFERRAL

Tax deferrals are wildly underappreciated. The concept is premised on the notion that all income and gains generated by a pretax retirement account investment flow back into the retirement account tax free. So instead of paying tax on the returns of a solo 401(k) plan investment such as real estate, tax is paid only at a later date, leaving the investment to grow unhindered. For example, if a 401(k) plan participant invested $100,000 from a solo 401(k) plan in 2013 and the account earned $10,000 in 2013, the investor would not owe tax on that $10,000 in 2013. Instead, the 401(k) plan participant would be required to pay the taxes when he or she with-draws the money from the 401(k) plan, which could be many years later. Assuming the 401(k) plan participant mentioned above is in a 33 percent federal-income-tax bracket, she avoided paying $3,333 in federal income taxes on the $10,000 earned on the 401(k) plan investment in 2013. That would have left $6,667 in the account. Instead, at an 8 percent annual return, those earnings actually go on to produce $533.36 in 2014, but would be over 40 percent more: $800 in total if we go back to the original account balance of $10,000. The beauty of tax deferral is that the deferral compounds each year.

Take the example of Joe. Joe was thirty years old when he decided to start a solo 401(k) plan and had a retirement account balance of zero at that time. Assuming that Joe decides to make annual 401(k) contributions of just $3,500 each year until he reaches the retirement age of seventy and that he is able to generate an average annualized rate of return of 9 percent with a prevailing tax rate of 25 percent, at age seventy, Joe will have $1,289,022 of tax-deferred income in his 401(k) plan. In contrast, if that money had been invested outside of a retirement account as personal funds, the same assumptions produce just $699,475.

In other words, a solo 40(k) plan allows Joe to accumulate an additional $589,547 of wealth. While Joe is not rich, he is able to put about $67 a week away for his retirement account every year. This small amount of money could turn into a million dollars plus for Joe by the time he retires. Now, imagine if Joe could put away $10,000 a year starting at age forty, with an average rate of return of just 7 percent. At age seventy, Joe would have over $1 million versus just over $730,000 in a taxable account. The numbers don't lie, saving for retirement and continuing to do so diligently throughout the years can help one build wealth fast while also benefiting from tax deductions and a reduction of taxable income.

Ken looked up after reading through the pamphlets. "Wow, that was a really helpful and clear way of summarizing all the main retirement accounts. I wasn't even aware of the self-directed IRA or solo 401(k) plan," he said.

"Thanks. When I wrote them, I tried to keep things simple and just focus on the important aspects of the many different types of retirement accounts available," John said.

"You did a great job," Ken said. "Do you think we can meet again next week to continue talking?"

"You bet," John said. "Next time we get together, I want to tell you about some of the most common options available for starting or funding a business. I think you'll find it very helpful especially since you're still trying to find the best way to finance your new water franchise."

"Perfect," Ken said. "I can't wait."

2

The Most Common Business-Funding Options

Ken's head was spinning in a good way when he got home that night. He felt like the weight of the world had been lifted from his shoulders and that there were funding options available to him. Not only could he now start preparing to buy the water franchise with David, but he could finally begin to pursue his dream of becoming his own boss. He was beginning to understand how he could leverage his retirement funds (while continuing to grow them) to do so. He explained the gist of all that to Pam, knowing that there was a lot more he needed to learn before he got started. Even so, he and Pam enjoyed one of their most relaxed and pleasant nights in a while, drinking some wine on the couch while they talked about the future with a sense of hope rather than dread.

Ken e-mailed John the next morning, thanked him for their initial meeting, and confirmed their next date and time. John and Ken met again at the coffee bar. Ken picked the same table and paid for the cappuccinos and scones. Ken felt both full of knowledge and full of questions and was eager to get started.

John was more than happy to help Ken begin exploring his options for using retirement funds to fund a business venture, as he really enjoyed helping would-be entrepreneurs. John had advised thousands of clients on the process of establishing new businesses, including helping establish the corporate entities and preparing all necessary corporate documentation. In addition, John was one of the few attorneys nation-ally who had experience advising clients on the taxation of retirement funds and the rules surrounding retirement account investments. Because he respected Ken's wife, Pam, so much and enjoyed working with her, he was excited to help Ken out.

John began the meeting by making sure Ken understood the risks involved in establishing a new business, especially given the fact that he was going to be leaving a successful career and a company he had worked at for over thirteen years. In addition, he wanted Ken to know that if he elected to use retirement funds to buy the business, he would potentially be putting those funds in jeopardy, which could certainly impact Pam, their children, and their retirement. The goal of their meeting was not to tell Ken whether or not his business would be successful or how to run a successful business, but rather the conversations would focus on the more popular start-up business funding options available, including the use of retirement funds.

STARTING A NEW BUSINESS—THE FACTS

"According to the Small Business Association," John said, "only about half of all new establishments survive five years or more, and only about one-third survive ten years or more."

"Those are scary statistics for someone starting a new business," Ken agreed.

"Right," John said. "I'm not telling you this to dissuade you from investing in your new business, but I think it is only right that I lay out all the facts. The key is to complete your due diligence and homework about the business you want to start before you buy it. I have seen too many entrepreneurs jump into buying a business only to fail within a year because they didn't really understand what it took to run the business and the costs involved."

John handed Ken a list of some items he should consider doing before signing on the dotted line to purchase the franchise.

- **Research the business concept.** Investigate the economics of the business. Is there a good business case or model? Are other people who are pursuing the same concept making money?
- **Create a business plan.** Many people skip this step and end up backtracking. Creating your business plan at the beginning will help guide your vision and direction as you continue along you entrepreneurial journey. Think of your business plan as an airplane flight plan. Would you get on a plane if you weren't sure the pilot knew where she was going?
- **Create a marketing plan.** A marketing plan is an essential planning element for a new small business. The marketing plan describes the products and services of the business, identifies the customers, and creates a strategy by which to market the business. A marketing plan usually covers the business one year at a time, though it is an ever-evolving document that changes as industry circumstances merit. In order to write a marketing plan for a new business, you will need a real handle on the ins and outs of the business.
- **Project your budget and estimate cash flow.** Financial projections and cash flow analysis are among the most critical elements to determine whether the new business makes financial sense. If you're like most start-up businesses, you are probably going to experience at least some time during which expenses exceed revenue. Without plans for adequate cash reserves, borrowing capacity, or other means of meeting those expenses, a cash shortfall can cause the early demise of your new business. It doesn't matter that the idea behind the business is fundamentally sound; without adequate capital, you won't make it.
- **Get to know your business partner.** If you are going to have a partner in your business make sure you know him or her very well. Make sure you have the same goals and work habits; as with any team, chemistry can be the key to winning or losing.

- **Understand your financing options.** How will you fund your business? This is an extremely important question for any new business owner. You must also carefully think through how much it will cost to run the business and how much ongoing working capital is needed.
- **Size up the competition.** Who else is doing what you're planning to do? How well do they do it? By examining your potential competitors, you can learn from others' mistakes—or even what their customers appreciate. Learn how much people are willing to pay for your product or service and how you could enhance the current offerings.
- **Know how you will pay yourself.** You need to think about this up front. With the best intentions of reinvesting profits straight back into the business, how are you going to put food on the table?
- **Talk to other franchisees or people in the industry.** Sometime the best way of getting a true handle of the viability of an existing business or franchise is to talk with other franchise owners or people in the industry. In most cases, you will get honest answers to your questions, but you can usually get a better idea of the financial potential of the business by talking to the franchisor or doing research online.

"This list is not meant to be exhaustive," John said, "but its goal is to get you thinking of items you should probably review in detail before purchasing a new business."

"Got it," Ken said.

"However, there's no guarantee that if you do everything on the list your business will be a smashing success or even mildly successful," John said. "The list is a good starting point and will hopefully help you make a reasonable determination whether the business you are looking to purchase makes financial sense."

"I understand there is no guarantee when starting a business that it will be successful, but I think I'm ready to take that risk," Ken said.

"OK," John replied. "I just want you to be clear. Again, I'm not trying to scare you into staying at your job and giving up your dream of owning your own business, but facts are facts. With almost half of new businesses failing within five years, there are real risks involved. I can't tell you how many smart engineers, doctors, lawyers, and professors I have seen fail in their business venture and, trust me, some of the business ideas were ingenious, but for whatever reason it just did not work out."

"Thanks for your candor. I appreciate it," Ken said.

"Does the fact that I am thinking about buying an existing franchise reduce my risk of failure compared to starting a new business from scratch?" Ken asked.

"That's a great question," John responded. "I am not an expert on franchises but have certainly helped a number of clients buy them with personal and retirement funds, and helped them structure their deals. Let's start with the different risks involved between buying an existing business and a start-up. Unlike a start-up business, an existing business has a location, where you often take over the seller's existing lease, or you may have to negotiate a new lease. An existing business may also have employees in place, if you elect to keep them, as well as equipment that you can use immediately. But best of all, most existing businesses have customers—many of whom will hopefully continue with the business after it changes ownership. An existing business also usually has some level of goodwill, which includes the business's reputation, brand name, customer lists, unique market position, knowledge of new technology, good location, and special skills or operating methods. Also, because the existing business has a history, you can review financial statements, tax returns, and other data to better determine the financial health of the business, how long it will take you to recoup your investment, as well as how much you will be able to take out of the business each month as compensation."

"So it would seem that buying an existing business has less risk than a start-up?" Ken asked.

"Yes and no," John answered. "Don't you hate lawyers; we can never give you a straight answer. It's true, if you start a business from scratch, you usually have no customers, equipment, infrastructure, employees, cash flow, or even a good idea of the financials involved in operating the business. All you have to go by are projections, estimates, and assumptions, which sometimes don't pan out. I've helped hundreds of clients start businesses and buy existing businesses, and the success rate is a little bit higher when buying an existing business, but not by much. Many times, when you buy an existing business, market conditions or customer behavior changes over time, and the financials you were shown from years past before buying the business are no longer accurate. Overall, the clients who ended up having success with their business acquisitions are the clients who spent considerable time and energy conducting due diligence on the business, working with an accountant or tax professional to prepare projected financials or review existing ones, and had a solid understanding of the industry and market they were entering. I wish I had a secret for business success, but I don't. Trust me, if I did, I would not be practicing law any longer," John said.

"OK," Ken said, "what about if I buy a franchise? What are my risks?"

"Well, like an existing business, a franchise usually has some goodwill and track record, but if you are opening the franchise in an area where it has not previously operated, there are certainly some similar risks to a start-up. The nice thing about a franchise is that the business probably has a solid track record and does have the infrastructure in place to help you get the new franchise off the ground. The franchise hopefully has a solid product or service that will be attractive in the market you are in. However, one of the biggest pitfalls of starting a new franchise is having sufficient working capital on hand. It all starts with doing your homework and conducting due diligence. I have had a number of clients who purchased a franchise they thought was a can't-lose opportunity, and they failed because they didn't do their due diligence to find out all the working capital they would need. A new business, which does not have proper capital to start a franchise, is a huge risk. In general, the Franchise Disclosure Document (FDD) has language that details the initial investment required for a franchise but typically lays out only three months of investment. Unless you are successful in that first three months, which most businesses are not, you will likely need more cash flow to keep your business running. Another common mistake among new franchise owners is that they don't spend enough time talking to existing franchisees and really listening to what they are saying about the business. A good idea is to ask them questions about the business beyond what the franchisor has provided you. Ask them what has made them a successful owner. What were their pitfalls and mistakes? Don't be afraid to talk to every franchisee in your area or surrounding areas, even if you have to ask the same questions over and over. Don't just listen to their words; listen to their tone. Do they seem happy? Are they satisfied with the support the franchise is giving them? Are they still as excited about the franchise as they were when they first bought into it?"

"I assume I should read all the franchise-related legal documents," Ken said.

"Hey, you're asking a lawyer, so of course you should," John said. "You should definitely hire a franchise attorney, who will better be able to negotiate on your behalf because he or she understands the franchisor/franchisee relationship. A franchise attorney will look for things outside the norm of franchising in the FDD and franchise agreement. Most agreements are standard, and experienced franchise attorneys will be able to detect anything unusual. You should already know the documents yourself and make sure you understand everything in the agreement and what is being asked of you."

John handed Ken a chart, which detailed some of the items to consider before starting a business, buying an existing business, or buying a franchise. John also suggested that Ken spend some time on the SBA website because it has some great free information and tools that would help him better prepare himself for becoming a small-business owner.

Items to Consider Before Starting a Business

STARTING A NEW BUSINESS	BUYING AN EXISTING BUSINESS	BUYING A FRANCHISE
Do your research and due diligence	Do your research and due diligence	Do your research and due diligence
Evaluate your finances	Evaluate your finances	Evaluate your finances
Seek professional and legal guidance	Seek professional and legal guidance	Seek professional and legal guidance
Strategize and plan	Strategize and plan	Strategize and plan
Develop a business and marketing plan	Develop a business and marketing plan	Develop a business and marketing plan
Generate projected financial statements (balance sheet, cash flow, etc.)	Review existing financial statements (balance sheet, tax returns, etc.)	Review financial information made available by franchisor
Estimate your costs	Understand your costs	Understand your costs
Estimate the amount of working capital needed after first three months of business operations	Estimate the amount of working capital needed after first three months of business operations	Estimate the amount of working capital needed after first three months of business operations
Decide on your business structure (LLC, S Corporation, or C Corporation)	Decide on your business structure (LLC, S Corporation, or C Corporation)	Decide on your business structure (LLC, S Corporation, or C Corporation)
Talk to business owners in the area involved in the same industry	Talk to business owners in the area involved in the same industry	Talk to existing franchisees in your area if buying a franchise
Determine location of your business	Determine location of your business	Determine location of your business
Find out what registrations or licenses you need, if any	Find out what registrations or licenses you need, if any	Find out what registrations or licenses you need, if any
Registering business and name with appropriate government agencies	Registering business and name with appropriate government agencies	Registering business and name with appropriate government agencies
Find out what insurance is needed	Find out what insurance is needed	Find out what insurance is needed
Identify technology that is needed	Identify technology that is needed	Identify technology that is needed
Is there demand for the product or service?	Does the existing business owner have a good reputation	Does the franchisor have a good track record
Does the new product or service fare well against competitors' offerings?		Is the franchisor's financial condition strong?
Is there potential for growth in the industry	Was the existing business profitable? Is there demand for the product or service?	Are the franchisor and its franchisees profitable? Is there demand for the product or service?
	Does the existing business product or service fare well against competitors' offerings?	Does the franchise's product or service fare well against competitors' offerings?
	Is there potential for growth in the industry	Is there potential for growth in the industry
	What are the terms of the business purchase agreement? Can you live with them?	What are the terms of the franchise agreement? Can you live with them?
	What type of support can you expect from the existing business owner	What type of franchisor support can you expect?

"Thanks so much. This list is great, and I am sure will really help me out in making a final determination about the water franchise I am looking to invest in," Ken said.

"Now that we've spent some time on the items to consider when looking to starting a business, buying an existing business, or buying a franchise, let's spend some time going through the financing options available to you," John said. "I'll go through these options generally right now, and then we can touch on each of them in greater detail the next time we meet."

"That would be perfect," Ken said.

1. All-Cash Purchase

"The first and most basic way to buy a business is with cash," John said. "Simply put, this means the buyer is paying cash for the new business's assets or stock. No loan is used, and at closing, cash is transferred from the buyer to the seller either by check or wire. Using cash to acquire a business is also the quickest and easiest way because there is no need to look for financing options such as a bank loan or SBA loan, which can take time to get approved. Clearly, if you are Warren Buffet or Bill Gates and you want to start a new business, buy an existing business, or buy a franchise, an all-cash purchase would probably make the most sense. Unless you were acquiring a large company valued at tens of millions of dollars, seeking financing for a small-business acquisition would likely not be required. The same goes for using retirement funds as a business-funding option. For people like Warren Buffet or Oprah Winfrey, who are cash rich, there is really no need to even explore the use of retirement funds to finance a business. We'll soon chat about the advantages and disadvantages of using retirement funds to buy a business, but for the wealthy, who can afford to pay for the business with cash without impacting their personal financial position, an all-cash purchase generally makes the most sense," John said.

"I always thought that the super rich were good at using leverage when making investments and taking advantage of the principal of other people's money," Ken said.

"You make a good point," John said, "and we'll talk next about the option of getting a bank loan or SBA loan to buy a business. But in today's world, being able to acquire these types of loans is no sure thing. Of course if you are super wealthy and have assets worth millions of dollars, securing a small-business loan would be a solid option, but for many would-be entrepreneurs acquiring either a bank loan or SBA loan for the purchase of a business is not a sure thing. The use of leverage to buy a business could make financial sense. For example, by borrowing funds, you incur a debt that must be paid. But this debt is paid in small installments over a relatively long period of time. This frees funds for more immediate use. Also, interest rates today are low, so borrowing money is actually much cheaper than it was fifteen or twenty years ago. In addition, another advantage of using leverage to finance business operations is that it provides tax breaks. When you have to pay interest for business purposes, the IRS allows the company to get a tax deduction for the interest paid. I'll go through the entire process for acquiring a loan shortly, so don't worry. In your case, and based off your and Pam's financial position, a bank loan or SBA loan may prove to be a good option."

"OK, great," Ken said. "You talked before about buying a business's assets or stock. Is there a difference?"

"I'm happy you brought up this point because it's important for someone buying an existing business. In your case, if you will be buying a franchise from the franchisee or doing a start-up, you would not have to worry about a business purchase but would likely be more focused on determining what business entity to use to buy the business. Of course, we will cover this topic in detail shortly," John said.

"When it comes to making the decision to buy an existing business, one of the first things the buyer and his or her attorney will likely discuss is whether the transaction will be a stock or an asset purchase. The asset purchase means the buyer is buying the business assets agreed to by the parties, such as facilities, vehicles, equipment, accounts receivable, machinery, or inventory. A stock purchase transaction involves the purchase of the selling company's stock or membership interests only. Most buyers prefer an asset sale, and many sellers would prefer a stock sale."

John handed Ken a chart that outlined advantages and disadvantages of an asset purchase as compared to a stock purchase.

ADVANTAGES of an Asset Purchase Compared to a Stock Purchase	DISADVANTAGES of an Asset Purchase Compared to a Stock Purchase
In an asset acquisition, the buyer is able to specify the liabilities he or she is willing to assume, while leaving other liabilities behind. In a stock purchase, the buyer purchases stock in a company or interests in an LLC that may have unknown or uncertain liabilities.	It is necessary for the selling company's assets to be retitled in the name of the buyer. This is not required in a stock transaction.

If the purchase price exceeds the aggregate tax basis of the assets being acquired, the buyer receives a stepped-up basis in the assets equal to the purchase price. In other words, the basis in the assets acquired will equal the purchase price, which can help for depreciation purposes.	In a stock transaction, the buyer can normally obtain the selling company's nonassignable contracts, permits, and licenses without the consent of the other party to the contract, permit, or license.
By purchasing assets rather than stock, the buyer avoids the problems presented by minority shareholders who refuse to sell their shares.	If the selling company does not have a large number of shareholders, a stock transaction may be less complicated.
Purchasing a business through an asset acquisition is less complicated from a securities law perspective because the parties are not normally required to comply with state and federal securities laws and regulations.	Buyer and seller would have to agree and list all assets being purchased and agree on the value of each asset as required by the IRS for purposes of completing IRS Form 1060. This can cause some disagreement between buyer and seller in terms of assigned goodwill value.
Goodwill can be amortized by the buyer for tax purposes over a period of fifteen years.	In states that impose sales or transfer taxes on the sale of assets, a stock transaction can avoid some or all of these taxes that apply in the event of an asset transaction.

"Overall, I advise clients who are looking to buy a business to buy the assets and not the stock. The main reason is that I don't want my clients potentially stuck with any liability of the company they acquired, which would be the problem of the buyer upon stock sale. Now, one way to minimize the risk of a stock sale is for the stock purchase agreement to have very strong seller representation and a solid seller identification provision, which includes a large holdback of sale proceeds for a period of time to cover any undisclosed liabilities and protect the buyer from having to chase down the seller to cover these liabilities that arose prior to the sale. However, I've had some clients agree to a stock purchase because of the difficulty of retitling some business licenses, such as a liquor license, which would have to be retitled in the case of an asset purchase. The same goes for clients I represented who were selling their business. There is really no 100 percent right or wrong way to buy or sell a business. What is important is to work with an attorney and a CPA who can help you navigate all the corporate and tax issues that go along with a corporate transaction. A lot depends on the facts and circumstances involved," John said.

"Got it," Ken said.

"Again, in the case of a start-up or franchise acquisition, choosing between a stock and asset sale is not very relevant. What is more relevant is what type of entity you should use to start the business." John said.

"OK, now that you brought this topic up, do you mind expanding on it?" Ken said. "I have always heard that an LLC or S corporation is better than a C corporation, but to be honest, I never really understood the difference."

"You're not alone," John said. "Most attorneys don't even know the difference. Despite the emphasis on establishing an entity to operate your business, the IRS doesn't really have an issue with how you legally establish your business. There is actually no requirement that you establish an entity, such as an LLC or a corporation. In fact, you do not have to take any formal action to form a sole proprietorship. As long as you are the only owner, this status automatically comes from your business activities. But, as we will soon see, that may not be your best option. However, in your case, Ken, the franchisor agreement will likely require you to establish an entity to operate your business."

Ken nodded.

"While an LLC, C corporation, or S corporation are all business structures that offer liability protection to owners of a company," John continued, "they differ in several important ways. C corporations make up almost all public companies, such as Apple and IBM, as well as the majority of large corporations in the United States, but are not as popular among small businesses. Over the last ten or so years, the majority of all new businesses being formed are LLC or S corporations."

The C Corporation

A C corporation (sometimes referred to as simply a corporation) is an independent legal entity owned by shareholders. This means that the corporation itself, not the shareholders that own it, is held legally liable for the actions and debts the business incurs.

Corporations are more complex than other business structures because they tend to have costly administrative fees and complex tax and legal requirements. Because of these issues, corporations are usually suggested for larger, established companies with multiple employees.

Forming a C corporation allows the company to have an unlimited number of shareholders. This is beneficial to companies that will require many investors, as well as companies that envision offering stock publicly. An inherent benefit of all corporations and LLCs is that they shield their shareholders from personal liability arising from business debts and business lawsuits.

A C corporation is formed by filing for incorporation at the state level. To become a C corporation, the business must have management and a board of directors and must file any required documents yearly. Businesses are taxed twice in C corporations: once for corporation revenue and again when that income passes through to C corporation owners (shareholders). This is known as double taxation.

To form a corporation you'll need to establish your business name and register your legal name with your state government. If you choose to operate under a name different than the officially registered name, you'll most likely have to file a fictitious name (also known as an assumed name, trade name, or DBA name, short for "doing business as"). State laws vary, but usually corporations must include a corporate designation (corporation, incorporated, limited) at the end of the business name.

To register your business as a corporation, you need to file certain documents, typically articles of incorporation, with your state's secretary of state office. Some states require corporations to establish directors and issue stock certificates to initial shareholders in the registration process.

One of the major disadvantages of a C corporation is taxation. C corporations are required to pay federal, state, and in some cases, local taxes. Most businesses must register with the IRS and state and local revenue agencies, and receive a tax ID number or permit.

When you form a corporation, you create a separate tax-paying entity. Unlike sole proprietors and partnerships, C corporations pay income tax on their profits. In some cases, corporations are taxed twice—first, when the company makes a profit, and again when dividends are paid to shareholders on their personal tax returns. C corporations use IRS Form 1120 or 1120-A, US Corporation Income Tax Return, to report revenue to the federal government.

Shareholders who are also employees pay income tax on their wages. The corporation and the employee each pay one-half of the Social Security and Medicare taxes, but this is usually a deductible business expense.

Prior to the 1990s, almost all new businesses were established as a corporation. However, the LLC as entity of choice for the small-business owner became commonplace in the 1990s.

"The LLC was invented in 1977," John continued, "when Wyoming became the first state to enact an LLC statute. In 1982, Florida enacted the second LLC act to attract new business to the state. Today, all fifty states and the District of Columbia have enacted statutes that provide for the creation and governance of LLCs. Generally, the statutes contain similar basic procedures and elements that are required to establish the LLC. As a result, most businesses can be organized as an LLC in any of those jurisdictions, but laws governing LLCs can vary by location. LLCs are a creation of state law. An LLC is somewhat of a hybrid entity in that it can be structured to resemble a corporation for owner liability purposes and a partnership for federal income tax purposes. An LLC offers the limited liability benefit of a corporation and the single level of taxation of a partnership. The owners, not the entity, are then responsible for the payment of the tax, if any. LLCs are owned by investors known as members. An LLC is typically managed by a designated member or group of members. Like shareholders of a corporation, the members' liability is limited to the amount of their investment. For tax purposes, LLCs with more than one owner are treated as partnerships, and LLCs with one owner are disregarded. In both cases, the LLC income is taxed to the owner directly without any entity-level tax."

John handed Ken a piece of paper that outlined the advantages of forming an LLC:

- easy and inexpensive to form
- recognized by all states
- limited liability for all members
- one level of tax for federal income tax and state income tax purposes (in most cases)
- pass-through of business losses to the member or members
- can utilize a corporate management structure
- can have one member or multiple members
- flexibility in distributing cash to the members
- flexibility in allocating profits/losses to the members
- flexibility in conducting business affairs
- can exist indefinitely

"The LLC looks like a really good option. Can you explain more?" Ken asked.

"Of course," John continued. "An LLC is formed under, exists, and is governed by a state statute that determines how an LLC in that state is formed, registered, and terminated. The statutes also usually provide that either the LLC adopt articles of organization, an operating agreement, or use the default provisions of the statute to determine other matters that impact the operation of the LLC."

"Are they as common as they seem?" Ken asked.

"They're very common," John answered. "According to some reports, there are close to four million LLCs in the United States. And probably a significant majority of all new entities formed in the United States are LLCs. They've really taken over from the C corporation and S corporation to become the most widely established entity in the United States, and everything I've read suggests the trend will accelerate as more and more people get comfortable with the LLC."

"So what are the advantages?" Ken asked.

"Initially, there was a question as to whether LLCs would be classified as partnerships and receive favorable pass-through tax treatment, or be classified and taxed as corporations for federal income tax purposes."

"How did it turn out?" Ken asked.

"The best of both worlds," John answered. "The Treasury and the IRS enacted Treasury regulations Section 301.7701, which entitled the LLC to elect to be treated for federal income tax purposes either as a partnership or a corporation. The regulation also contained certain default provisions for a situation in which no election was made. Usually, an LLC with two or more members that does not make an election will be treated as a partnership and receive pass-through tax treatment, and an LLC with only one member will be disregarded as a separate entity from its owner, meaning it is treated as a sole proprietorship and not taxed as a corporation."

"Sounds flexible."

"Yes, very," John agreed. "And an LLC has broad possibilities for its structure, operation, management. But each state has certain mandatory and default provisions. Mandatory provisions are those rules that must be complied with, and default provisions are rules that take effect if the LLC's certificate of formation or operating agreement do not address them. In general, LLC statutes are interpreted liberally in order to give maximum effect to the freedom of contract and the enforceability of the operating agreement.

"Now you can see why the LLC has become the entity of choice for most small-business owners. It is easy to set up and maintain, it offers great flexibility with little corporate formality, and it is far more tax efficient than a C corporation.

"Basically, the only business owners establishing C corporations are owners who either expect the business to go public, have been required to do so by private equity investors, or have retirement accounts as owners, which we will spend considerable time discussing," John said.

"OK, can't wait," Ken responded. "So what about the S corporation? I have heard some of my friends have set up S corporations to run their business. What is the deal with the S corporation versus the LLC or C corporation?"

"According to the IRS, S corporations are corporations that elect to pass corporate income, losses, deductions, and credits through to their shareholders for federal tax purposes. Shareholders of S corporations report the flow-through of income and losses on their personal tax returns and are assessed tax at their individual income-tax rates. This allows S corporations to avoid double taxation on the corporate income. S corporations are responsible for tax on certain built-in gains and passive income at the entity level. To qualify for S corporation status, the corporation must meet the following requirements":

- It must be a domestic corporation.
- It must have only allowable shareholders.
  - These may be individuals, certain trusts, and estates.
  - These may not be partnerships, corporations, or nonresident alien shareholders.
- It must have no more than one hundred shareholders.
- It must have only one class of stock.
- It must not be an ineligible corporation (i.e., certain financial institutions, insurance companies, and domestic international sales corporations).

"In order to become an S corporation, the corporation must submit Form 2553 Election by a Small Business Corporation (PDF) signed by all the shareholders. S corporations are corporations that elect to pass corporate income, losses, deductions, and credit through to their shareholders for federal tax purposes. Shareholders of S corporations report the flow-through of income and losses on their personal tax returns and are subject to tax at their individual income-tax rates. Unlike a C corporation, which is subject to a double level of tax, the pass-through tax treatment of an S corporation allows S corporations to avoid double taxation on corporate income. S corporations are responsible for tax on certain built-in gains and passive income." John said.

"I follow," Ken said.

"Believe it or not, the main reason many small businesses establish an S corporation versus an LLC is to potentially minimize the impact of self-employment tax," John said.

"Do you mind expanding on that?" Ken asked.

"Sure," John said. "S corporations are essentially partnerships, except that they enjoy limited liability like regular corporations. The owners of an S corporation or LLC will be subject to income tax on their share of the profits, and there is no corporate level tax. But the tax laws treat owners of S corporations quite differently from partners in a partnership or members of an LLC when it comes to Social Security and Medicare taxes. Partnership partners or members of an LLC are subject to these taxes on all of their 'active' income, while active S corporation owners are supposed to determine what salary they would pay themselves if they treated themselves as employees. Social Security taxes are paid on 'wages' up to an inflation-adjusted maximum ($118,500 in 2015). Medicare taxes are also paid on wages, but there is no upper limit. For decades, taxpayers have used S corporations to reduce these 'payroll taxes.' Taxpayers have the S corporation pay only a limited amount of its income as wages, or none at all. The rest of the income is either kept in the S corporation or, more likely, paid in a shareholder distribution, which is not subject to payroll tax. John Edwards, who ran for vice president, made the technique famous. For the years 1995–1998, Edwards had his S corporation pay him an aggregate salary of $1.26 million per year. The salary was said to have been based on what the average personal injury lawyer in North Carolina made. The issue was that John Edwards's corporation's total net income for the three years was $25.5 million. He saved about $600,000 in Medicare taxes."

"Wow, that seems really interesting," Ken said.

"Don't get too excited—the IRS is all over this and pays extra special attention to S corporation returns (IRS Form 1120S) in relation to the W-2 income taken by the shareholders," John responded.

"I think it would be helpful to spend some time discussing the advantages of using an LLC over the other entities we discussed," Ken said.

"Most franchisors will allow you to establish the franchise as an LLC. Because of its flexibility, lack of corporate formality, and tax efficiency, I usually recommend the LLC for my would-be entrepreneurs and new business owners," John said.

The Advantages of Using an LLC over a Sole Proprietorship

If you currently operate a business by yourself and report your income on a Schedule C, then you are a sole proprietor. Even though a sole proprietorship is the cheapest form of business, the risks of using a sole proprietorship can end up making it the most costly business structures over the long term.

As a sole proprietor you put your personal assets at risk for liability. You also will not receive the benefit of considerable tax savings and will likely have fewer options for growing your business. Sole proprietorships are also much more likely to come under examination by the IRS. And finally, when it comes time to sell or transfer your sole proprietorship, you'll find that the process is difficult, time consuming, and expensive.

As a sole proprietor, you and your business are one and the same. In other words, your company's debts are legally your debts—a legal claim or a lawsuit brought against your business is also a lawsuit brought against you. This means that your personal savings, including your home, car, and investments, can be taken from you if your business were to be sued or become insolvent.

By contrast, an LLC is viewed as a legally distinct entity. An LLC provides limited liability for all members. If your business is sued or becomes insolvent, its members will usually not be held personally liable for the debts and liabilities of the LLC.

The Advantages of Using an LLC over a C Corporation

An LLC enjoys many of the same advantages of a C corporation, as well as retaining many of the characteristics of unincorporated entities such as partnerships and sole proprietorships. Like a C corporation, the LLC offers its members limited liability protection (a member is usually liable only up to the amount contributed to the LLC), and like a partnership, the LLC's earnings are not subject to an entity level of tax (only one level of tax imposed directly to the member), whereas a C corporation imposes a double level of tax (entity level and shareholder level) on distributable income.

For example, an LLC generates $100 of profits and let's further assume that the individual and corporate tax rate is 20 percent. In the case of an LLC, the LLC would not pay tax, and only the owner would be subject to tax on the net profits allocated. In this case, the individual would receive $100, would pay 20 percent tax, and would have a net of $80. On the other hand, if that individual used a corporation to make an investment that generated $100 of profits, the corporation would pay tax on $100, which would be $20 (20 percent of $100). Then if the corporation wanted to distribute the $80 of earnings to the individual shareholder, that individual shareholder would then be required to pay tax on the $80 received, which would be another $16 of tax paid, leaving the individual shareholder with just $64. Thus with an LLC, the individual would be left with $80; with a C corporation that person would be left with just $64.

Usually the LLC entity form should always be used over the C corporation form, unless the entity is anticipating an initial public offering.

Like the shareholders of a C corporation, the owners/members of an LLC are usually not liable for the debts of the business beyond the extent of their investment. The owners can operate the business with the security of knowing that their personal assets are protected from the entity's creditors. There are exceptions, such as an instance when an individual member personally guarantees the debts or liabilities incurred by the LLC.

Unlike a C corporation, an LLC is treated as a partnership for federal income tax purposes. This can provide a number of important benefits to the owners. Partnership earnings are not subject to an entity-level federal income tax; instead, they "flow through" to the owners, in proportion to the owners' respective interests in profits, and are reported on the owners' individual tax returns (one level of tax). Thus, earnings of an LLC are taxed only once. An LLC that is taxable as a partnership can also provide special allocations of tax benefits to specific members.

The Advantages of Using an LLC over an S Corporation

LLCs and S corporations are similar in many ways. From a tax perspective, both are treated as pass-through entities (no double taxation). Both entities provide limited liability to the owners of the business.

The LLC offers far more flexibility than an S corporation. In order to be considered an S corporation, a company must meet the following requirements:

- The entity must not have more than one hundred shareholders.
- Shareholders must be US citizens or residents, and must be natural persons, so corporate shareholders, partnerships, and multimember LLCs are excluded.
- The entity must have only one class of stock.
- Profits and losses must be allocated to shareholders proportionately to each one's interest in the company.
- Corporate formalities must be followed.

The LLC Entity Form—the Right Entity Choice for Most of Us

"By now you can probably tell that I am a big fan of the LLC," John said. "Under current law, unless a start-up company wants to go public or a company will be engaged in a complex cross-border transaction, there is very little reason to choose to operate as a C corporation or an S corporation. Most of the nontax advantages of operating in corporate form are now available in all states in the form of the LLC, and the double tax creates a clear tax bias against the corporate form. An LLC offers all of its members limited liability without restrictions on their participation in the venture. Furthermore, ownership interests in the LLC can be freely transferable if its members so choose. For these reasons, it is significantly more common for a new business to select the LLC entity form and not a C or S corporation."

"OK," Ken said, "the LLC will probably make the most sense for me, but I know you mentioned that it may not be an option if I want to use retirement funds, so I will hold off on making a decision for now. One additional question, I always hear about single-member and multiple-member LLCs. What do they mean?"

Single-Member LLC

"Like the name suggests," John said, "a single-member LLC is an LLC owned by one person or entity. The member of a single-member limited-liability company (SMLLC) will benefit from the limited liability associated with a limited-liability company (LLC) as well as the benefit of a single level of tax and the flow-through of business losses."

"I see," Ken said.

"For tax purposes, a SMLLC is treated as a sole proprietorship and will not require a separate federal income tax filing. The income tax can be reported on Schedule C of the member's personal income tax return (Form 1040). For federal income tax purposes, a SMLLC is disregarded. Therefore, if a SMLLC is treated as a disregarded entity for federal income tax purposes, the income of the LLC is taxed to the owner directly, without any entity-level tax. In addition, LLC losses would "flow through" to the member, and the member could deduct his, her, or its ratable share of the losses generated."

Multiple-Member LLC

"A multiple-member LLC," John continued, "is an LLC that is owned by two or more persons or entities. Members of a multiple-member LLC will benefit from the limited liability associated with an LLC as well as the benefit of a single level of tax and the flow-through of business losses."

Ken nodded.

"For tax purposes," John said, "a multiple-member LLC is treated as a partnership and is required to file a US partnership tax return (Form 1065). If an LLC is characterized as a partnership for federal income tax purposes, the LLC's earnings would not be subject to an entity-level tax; instead, they would "flow-through" to the members usually on a pro rata basis. Thus, earnings are taxed only once. In addition, LLC losses would flow through to the members, and the members could deduct their ratable share of the losses generated."

"Is it possible for a multiple-member LLC to elect to be taxed in the same manner as a C corporation, with double taxation?" Ken asked.

"Yes, but this is usually not advisable, as this election will last for a minimum of five years, and as there may be tax consequences for switching back to pass-through taxation."

"OK," Ken said, "makes sense, but should these LLCs be member or manager managed?"

"That is a really good question. For a single-member LLC it doesn't really matter, since in almost all cases, the owner of the LLC will be the same person running the LLC. For example, if you establish ABC, LLC for your water business, and you will be the only owner and manager of the business, then it would not matter whether you are considered a member- or manager-managed LLC. Whereas, if the LLC was owned 100 percent by you but your friend was going to run it, then you would probably want to make the LLC a manager-managed LLC since your friend, not you, will be running the business on a day-to-day basis. The same goes for a multiple-member LLC: if all the owners of the LLC will be managing the LLC as board of management, it would not matter if the LLC is considered member or manager managed, But if not all of the owners of the LLC will be managing the LLC, then you would likely want to elect manager managed."

"Where do I make this election?" Ken asked.

"Some states will give you this option when you form the LLC by filing the articles of organization. Otherwise, the LLC operating agreement will demonstrate if the LLC is member or manager managed," John responded.

"OK," Ken said. "You've mentioned the term "operating agreement" a few times. Is it like a shareholder agreement?"

"It is extremely important that every LLC have an LLC operating agreement. The LLC operating agreement is the core document that is referred to when issues concerning the LLC need to be resolved. The LLC operating agreement is the most important document for your LLC. The LLC operating agreement reflects the agreement among the members with respect to the affairs and management of the LLC, and it governs the relationship among the members of the LLC. By having an LLC operating agreement, members will be provided with a clear set of rules that all members have agreed upon, greatly reducing the likelihood of disagreement in the future. An LLC operating agreement will also greatly reduce financial and management misunderstandings, and make sure your business is governed by your own rules, not default rules created by your state," John said.

"I assume every LLC should have an operating agreement?" Ken asked.

"Many state LLC statutes, for example, have default rules that govern how certain business decisions should be made, such as how the LLC will be managed, how meetings will be held and votes will be taken, how the LLC will be sold, how profits and losses should be allocated, how the operating agreement could be amended, how a new member can be admitted, and how the LLC would be dissolved. Defaulting to state law for important LLC decisions could jeopardize your business. If you don't want the state to tell you how to run your LLC and don't want to default to state law for important business decisions, it's important that you have a well-drafted LLC operating agreement. By having an operating agreement, you can make the rules that will govern your LLC's inner workings, rather than having to follow state default rules that may or may not be right for your LLC," John said.

"So the LLC operating agreement will let me run the LLC business the way I want to as the owner?" Ken asked.

"Yes. The operating agreement governs the operation and management of the LLC. It describes the business and economic arrangement of the members. LLCs need to document important and material issues that could impact the members, such as profit-sharing and decision-making rules as well as procedures for handling the departure/addition of members, and the dissolution/termination of the LLC. Without an operating agreement, the owners will be poorly equipped to settle misunderstandings over the operations, finances, and management of the LLC. In addition, without an operating agreement, the LLC will be subject to the default operating rules created by state law. The LLC operating agreement usually specifies, among other things, the business name, the official business address, the identities of the members, the way in which cash is distributed to the members, the way in which profits and losses are to be divided between the members, and how the company will be managed. The operating agreement should also reflect each member's financial contributions to the LLC and the member's ownership interests," John said.

"What about single-member LLCs? Do they need an operating agreement?" Ken asked.

"Good question. Even though the LLC operating agreement is not required to be filed with any state agency, it is unwise to operate an LLC without one, even if you're the sole owner of your LLC. It is extremely important that you create an operating agreement to separate yourself as an individual from your LLC, even if you are the sole owner. Without the formality of an operating agreement, the LLC can closely resemble a sole proprietorship, which does not limit your personal liability for business debts of the LLC. Without an LLC operating agreement, the basic operation of the LLC would then be governed by state law, which may not be advantageous for the LLC, it members, or the business it conducts." John said.

"I assume I need an attorney for the LLC operating agreement?" Ken asked.

"Yes. It's vital that you work with your attorney to draft the operating agreement for your water company if you elect to use an LLC. This is especially the case because you will have a partner, and you want to make sure that the business deal you and David agreed to is properly documented. This will help protect you and your partner in case of any misunderstanding. It will also give you the peace of mind that the business deal you both agreed to is actually what is going to govern the business relationship," John responded.

"OK, thanks. Can you briefly explain how one can form an LLC?" Ken asked.

"An LLC is a separate legal entity that is formed under the authority of a state statute. All fifty states and the District of Columbia have enacted limited-liability company statutes. An LLC is formed under, exists, and is governed by a state statute. In general, the state statute provides how an LLC in that state is formed, registered, and terminated. The statutes also provide that either the LLC adopt articles of organization, an operating agreement, or use the default provisions of the statute to determine the other matters that impact the operation of the LLC. In most cases, forming an LLC is as simple as filing a one-page form, often called the articles of organization, with the state along with the state filing fee. You can form the LLC yourself, or hire an attorney or a formation company to do it for you. It's actually quite simple, and many states will actually allow you to do it online," John said.

"What about timing?" Ken asked.

"That depends on the state, but it can take anywhere from a few hours if done online to a few weeks."

"And cost?" Ken asked.

"I knew you were going to ask about fees, so I had my assistant print out a chart for you."

John handed Ken a chart that provided the establishment fees to form an LLC in all fifty states and the District of Columbia, as well as the annual fees (See Exhibit A).

"As you can see, it costs anywhere from $50 to $600 to form an LLC. The average LLC establishment fee is probably around $200. According to the LLC annual report on franchise fees, the fees range to $0 all the way to $800, for a California LLC."

"OK, seems pretty fair. That is kind of what I was expecting."

"I bet your next question is going to be 'Where should I form my LLC? Should I set up in Delaware or Nevada?'"

"How did you know?" Ken said with a laugh.

"Like I said, I have done this a few times. Since all fifty states and the District of Columbia have LLC statutes, most businesses can be organized as an LLC in any of those jurisdictions, but laws governing LLCs can vary by location. In deciding where you should form an LLC, you should consider factors such as the formation cost, state tax laws and business laws, and whether it will be necessary for the LLC to qualify/register to conduct business in one or more states. Forming an LLC in a state different from where the LLC will operate is permissible since every state will recognize a foreign LLC—an LLC formed in another state—and will allow the LLC to conduct business within the state. However, each state will typically require the foreign LLC to register with the state by filing an application for certification of authority, maintain a registered agent, and pay certain fees."

"What are the considerations?" Ken asked.

"Organizing in a state different from where the LLC will operate could lead to additional problems and costs. Typically, additional organizational and registration costs and fees will apply, such as 'foreign qualifications' if you form your LLC in a state different from where the LLC will operate. For example, if an LLC operates a business in the state of Colorado but was organized in the state of Delaware, the LLC will incur dual costs—formation costs in Delaware and the cost of qualifying the LLC to do business in Colorado. In addition, by forming your LLC in a state different from where the LLC will operate you may be become subject to franchise taxes and other government fees in more than one state. Usually, LLCs must file separate tax returns for each state in which they do business based on the income generated in each state, regardless of where the LLC was formed. In addition, several states will impose other types of taxes on the LLC, such as annual fees, filing fees, franchise fees, and others. In most cases it is far more cost effective and efficient to form your LLC in the state in which you will conduct the majority of your business."

"So what's the deal with Delaware or Nevada?" Ken asked.

Delaware

The state of Delaware is the most commonly selected state for LLC formation largely for the following reasons:

- Delaware law has been tested and provides predictability.
- Delaware has a separate court of chancery that handles corporation law cases quickly and competently.
- Delaware is perceived as an easy and reliable state in which to form an LLC.
- Delaware allows the owners and managers of an LLC to remain anonymous.
- Delaware has no sales tax or intangible personal property tax.
- No Delaware income tax has to be paid, and a business license is not required if the LLC does not do business in Delaware. However, Delaware imposes a $250 annual fee on LLCs.

Nevada

The state of Nevada is a popular state for LLC formation largely due to the following reasons:

- The state of Nevada does not tax LLC profits. Nevada also has no personal income tax or annual franchise tax.
- As long as a company remains in good standing, its owners and executives have protection from personal liability in a Nevada LLC.
- Nevada does not require a minimum capital investment for LLCs or corporations.

"Gotcha. Seems like it makes the most sense to form the new water franchise in Arizona, since that is where we will be physically located," Ken said.

"Yes. I think that is probably your best bet," John said.

"Can I serve as my own registered agent?" Ken asked.

"Yes, so long as you have an address in the state, which you do since you live in Arizona. A registered agent acts as the representative for receiving service of process served upon the company within the jurisdiction of any state where the company conducts business. Service of process is broadly construed to include any legal proceeding, legal notice, or official government communication presented to the company while it is within the jurisdiction of a state. I recommend that my clients serve as their own registered agent if they are forming an entity in a state where they have a physical address. No need to spend additional funds for a company to serve as the registered agent."

"OK, once my LLC has been formed, do I need a tax ID for the entity?"

"If your LLC will be owned by more than one person, then yes. An employer identification number (EIN) is also referred to as a federal tax identification number. The EIN is used to identify a business entity. In general, every business must have an EIN. There are several ways to obtain one."

You will need an EIN if you answer yes to any of the following questions:

- Do you have employees?
- Do you operate your business as a corporation or a partnership?

- Do you file any of these tax returns: employment; excise; or alcohol, tobacco, and firearms?
- Do you withhold taxes on income, other than wages, paid to a nonresident alien?
- Do you have a Keogh plan (A tax-deferred pension plan available to self-employed individuals or unincorporated businesses for retirement purposes)?
- Are you involved with any of the following types of organizations?
  - trusts (except certain grantor-owned revocable trusts), IRAs, exempt organization business income tax returns
  - estates
  - real-estate mortgage investment conduits
  - nonprofit organizations
  - farmers' cooperatives
  - plan administrators

"Essentially you will need the EIN in order to open a bank account for your LLC. Most banks require at least the LLC articles of formation and LLC EIN to open a bank account for the LLC. Some banks actually ask for the LLC operating agreement, but this is not common."

"Do I need an employee identification number if I'm a single-member LLC?" Ken asked.

"No. The sole member of a single-member LLC will not need a separate EIN for the LLC if he or she is the sole owner and the LLC has no employees. The sole member of a single-member LLC can use his or her Social Security number instead of applying for an EIN."

"Great," Ken said.

"Before we move on to discussing the next business-funding option, using a business loan, I want to give you a chart that summarizes the features of the business forms we discussed: sole proprietorship, C corporation, LLC, and S corporation."

John handed Ken a chart. (See Exhibit B).

"I know you haven't had much of a chance to examine our financial position, and maybe this question is best saved for my CPA, but do you think a cash deal could make sense for me?" Ken asked.

"You're right. I haven't spent much time focusing on your personal finances, but I do remember you mentioning that the $175,000 in savings you have is mainly earmarked to pay for your kids' college, and that you both were comfortable using approximately $75,000. So without securing a loan or using retirement funds, I am not sure an all-cash deal will work for you."

"Got it," Ken said.

"Let's move on and talk about combining the $75,000 you are looking to use personally with a loan option," John said.

2. Using a Credit Card to Fund a Business

"Let's look at probably the most popular option for funding a new business: using a credit card. I think you can probably guess why credit-card financing has become so popular as a vehicle to finance a business."

"Yes, they are so easy to get and so easy to use," Ken said.

"That pretty much sums it up. Using a credit card to fund a business is certainly convenient and easy to accomplish. Using a credit card to buy business assets or help get the business off the ground is much less stressful than approaching friends and family about investing or trying to get a bank loan. But of course there are some downsides. As we discussed in great detail, start-ups are inherently risky, so when you use a credit card to finance the business, you are gambling with your personal credit score," John said.

"Is this true even if I use a business credit card?" Ken asked.

"Typically, as a start-up, if your business receives a credit card, you as the business owner will be required to personally guarantee any credit-card debts or obligations, so using a personal or business credit card could potentially have a negative impact on your personal credit score if you get into a nonpayment situation. Also, if the credit-card debt proves to be the downfall of your company, debt collectors will likely be able to come after both your company and your personal income/assets to recoup what you owe," John said.

"I suppose there is no guarantee I can even get a business credit card," Ken said.

"That is true. Because business credit-card underwriting has more to do with *your* personal credit standing than that of your business, that might help you get a better credit card because your business will be a start-up, but it could also have the opposite effect. However, past personal credit problems could keep you from getting a business credit card."

"If I did elect to use a credit card as a business-funding option, what are the typical credit-card limits?" Ken asked.

"Since credit cards are usually unsecured, they provide lower spending limits than alternative lending options. You could typically get up to tens of thousands of dollars to use, but there is usually an invisible ceiling around the $50,000 mark." John said.

"What about the interest rates on a credit-card loan?" Ken asked.

"The average annual percentage rate on credit cards is just below 15 percent as of early 2013, while interest on loans up to $25,000 that are backed by the SBA can't exceed the prime rate—3.25 percent as of September 1, 2015—plus 4.25 percent, which brings the total to 7.5 percent. The Marion Kauffman Foundation has found that for every $1,000 in credit-card debt that a small business takes on, its chances of long-term survival fall by more than 2 percent," John said.

"What if I didn't do a credit-card loan but just used the credit card to make business-related purchases and now can't make the monthly payments on time?" Ken asked.

"You are probably looking at between 13 percent and18 percent interest on the card's outstanding balance, which can significantly impact the business's cash flow as well as your personal credit score. The interest rate does hurt if you fail to make timely payments on the card. However, having a business credit card can help improve your credit scores and the credit score of the business—as long as payments are made on time. There are also special rewards and perks such as airline miles, discounted gas, or even cash," John said.

"OK, that is helpful. I can't rule out using either my personal credit card or a business credit card for my start-up funding, but I am anxious to hear about some other financing options that may prove to be a bit less costly," Ken said.

"I totally understand. First, let me say unequivocally, the use of personal credit cards can be a very risky means of financing business operations. It can hurt your personal and business credit score and could also negatively impact the cash flow of the business if payments are not made on time. We all know MasterCard and American Express are in the business of making money, and the high interest they receive from outstanding credit-card balances is obviously quite profitable. On the other hand, using a credit card offers quick and easy access to funds that can help launch or finance a start-up. Let's now move on to discuss the traditional business loan option, which may be more difficult to attain than a credit card but comes with much better payment terms," John said.

3. Securing a Business Loan

"As you and I both know, without money it is almost impossible to start any business. Even a software developer whiz needs some money to launch a website or smartphone application. It can be said that money is the sustenance of any business, so whether you're starting a business or running an existing one, securing financing is vital, especially for small businesses. Most of my clients find the undertaking of securing financing scary, stressful, and intimidating, and most don't even know where to start," John said.

"Good. I am not alone," Ken said with a chuckle.

"No, you are not. In fact the US Small Business Administration (SBA) understands this and has extensive information and tips on their website. I encourage all my would-be entrepreneur clients to spend a considerable amount of time reviewing the website, especially as it pertains to the loan process," John said.

"Great," Ken said.

"I hope you don't mind, but I am going to outline many of the tips the SBA suggests on their website for applying for a small-business loan."

What criteria do banks look for in making small-business loans?

Different banks or lending institutions may have different standards, but in general, in order to consider your application for a small-business loan, banks will require the following.

"I am going to focus on traditional bank loans and then will move to the SBA loan process, which has somewhat different requirements." John said

Bank requirements

- The loan must be for a sound business purpose.
- You and your partner(s) must be of good character, have experience, and have good personal and/or business credit history.
- You must be able to pay back the loan—reasonable to strong collateral (personal and business assets) is very important. And of course, owners must have personal equity investment in the business.

"So how hard is it to actually get a bank loan?" Ken asked.

"Well, like so much in the financial world, everything changed after the 2008 financial crisis. Increased regulatory scrutiny has caused banks to boost lending standards, lowering the fraction of creditworthy borrowers. Bank consolidation has reduced the number of banks focused on the small-business sector, and small-business lending has become relatively less profitable than other types of lending, reducing bankers' interest in the small-business credit market."

"I've noticed," Ken said.

"The evidence indicates that now it's easier than it's been in quite some time, at least going back to the financial crisis in 2008 and 2009. This is not to say that every single loan application will be approved, but it does show that the struggle to find capital to fund small businesses is easing."

"OK, that is helpful. Clearly I will need to have some personal investment, so the $75,000 should help. I assume we will talk in detail about using retirement funds as an option, so that may also help me out," Ken said.

"Yes, that is correct—the bank will look at your financial position, your level of education and experience, the business idea, your business plan, and financial projections. Also, it is helpful to build a relationship with the people at the lender before the business actually needs the loan. If you have a relationship with anyone at your local bank, or at any bank for that matter, that is something you may want to take advantage of. People like doing business with people they know. That is just a reality," John said.

"One more thing," he continued, "that I probably should have mentioned at the top. Your credit score is critical for securing a bank loan. Banks still look at personal credit scores as a way to judge the reliability of the principals who are borrowing the money. It is important to know what lenders look for and how the scores compare to those expectations."

"So what is considered a good credit score?" Ken asked.

"Based on my experience, a credit score of above 650–700 is acceptable but does not guarantee a loan. Most lenders will look for a credit score that is at least in the 700–800 range," John said.

"OK, I better get my credit score," Ken responded. "I know we are focusing on banks as a lending option right now, but real quick, what type of lenders will typically lend to a small business or would-be entrepreneur?"

John handed Ken a document that summarized the common lenders willing to lend to small businesses or budding entrepreneurs.

i. Commercial banks: This is best for traditional loans that fall into the strict parameters discussed.

ii. Nonbank lenders: These are increasing in record numbers for lenders looking to get a higher return. There are fourteen SBA-licensed preferred nonbank lenders nationwide. Because the SBA, rather than financial regulators, oversees these nonbank lenders, they can approve loans that many banks cannot. Two popular nonbank lenders are GE Capital Small Business Finance and CIT Small Business Lending Corporation.

iii. Region-specific lenders: Local community banks and other lenders that have an interest in economic development in a certain geographic or industry area.

iv. Micro and alternative lenders: Crowdfunding sites like Kickstarter can be helpful for capital needs under $10,000. Personal loans can also be sourced from peer-to-peer sites like Prosper and The Lending Club.

v. SBA loan: The SBA participates in a number of loan programs designed for business owners who may have trouble qualifying for a traditional bank loan. The most popular type of SBA loan is the basic 7(a) loan program. The program gives 7(a) loans to eligible borrowers for starting, acquiring, and expanding a small business. Borrowers must apply through a participating lender.

"Don't worry, we will go through the SBA loan process in greater detail shortly," John said.

"OK, so what information would I need to apply for a traditional bank loan?" Ken asked.

"Different lenders may require more or fewer documents, but in general, you will need these items":

- personal and business credit history
- personal and business financial statements for existing and start-up businesses and a projected financial statement
- strong, detailed business plan (including personal information such as bios, education, etc.)
- cash-flow projections for at least a year
- personal guaranties from all principal owners of the business

"The key is being prepared and starting the preparation early. I always refer to the SBA.gov website when advising clients on how to best prepare for a small-business loan application. This is what the SBA suggests":

- Choose your lending institution carefully. Larger banks tend to shy away from small loans, as they are less profitable and take the same amount of underwriting and servicing. That doesn't mean large banks do not make small loans; it is just more difficult to secure one.
- Approach banks or lending institutions you have worked with or where you have an account.
- Explore community banks and credit unions.
- Talk to a lending officer and find out exactly what documentation they require.
- Be thorough and bring everything they ask. Many loan applications are denied or face unnecessary hurdles because of incomplete applications.

"Even before you start gathering and organizing the information required by lenders to consider your application, you should educate yourself so you can understand and discuss business loans intelligently with the lending officers when the time comes."

"Does the size of the loan matter? In my case, I only need probably $100,000 or so. Is that too much or too little?" Ken asked.

"Good question. According to the SBA.gov website, in the banking industry the median small-business loan is about $130,000–$140,000, with the highest around $250,000. SBA small-business loans range from about $5,000 (microloans) to $5 million (largest guaranteed), with the average loan around $371,000," John said.

"OK. So it looks like I would use less personal funds and get a bigger loan if I go with a bank loan, whereas an SBA loan will allow me to use more personal funds. Is the fact that I am buying a franchise good for securing a small-business bank loan?" Ken asked.

"Based on my experience, start-ups are probably the most difficult ventures when it comes to securing financing. That is the main reason many start-up businesses seek financing from family, friends, and credit cards. If the credit is sound, the business plan is strong, and you have enough personal resources to invest and collateral to guarantee, smaller community banks, other community financial institutions, and credit unions may consider lending you money. For start-ups, if friends and family are not an option, and neither is using a credit card, then the SBA loan maybe an option. Of course, if you have retirement funds, that may be an option as well, which we will soon see."

"What should I be thinking about?" Ken asked.

"Well, in general, many banks favor businesses with brand names and long track records of consistent cash flow, so your choice of a franchise system can help or hurt you. Newer franchises are somewhat less attractive to banks in part because they lack a proven track record," John said.

"What about getting some financing from the franchise—is that an option?" Ken asked.

"A few franchisers offer internal financing. For example, the franchisor may defer a portion of the initial franchisee fee, essentially financing the deal. However, interest rates could be high, and this option is not always available. You can certainly ask the franchisor if it is something they would entertain—can't hurt," John answered.

"I might do so," Ken said. "What about a personal guarantee—is that a must for most lenders?"

"In general, bank loans unsecured by collateral are relatively rare, even for those with good credit. In addition to securing a loan with a mortgage on your home or other asset, be ready to be asked to put your own money into the deal, typically about 20 percent of the amount needed. Even with healthy businesses and solid collateral, most bank loans to new franchisees occur when a borrower has established relationships with a banker, has previous experience, or is a figure in the community," John answered.

4. SBA Small-Business Loan

"What about SBA loans?" Ken asked.

"SBA loans are partially guaranteed by the government, making them less risky. In fact, the SBA does not actually make direct loans; instead, it provides loan guarantees to entrepreneurs, promising the bank to pay back a certain percentage of your loan if you are unable to. Banks participate in the SBA program as regular, certified, or preferred lenders. The SBA can help you organize your loan package, which you then submit to banks. If the bank approves you, it submits your loan package to the SBA. Applications submitted by regular lenders are reviewed by the SBA in ten to fourteen days, whereas certified lender applications are reviewed in three days, and approval through preferred lenders is even faster."

"Sounds clear," Ken said.

"The most basic eligibility requirement for SBA loans is the ability to repay the loan from cash flow, but the SBA also looks at personal credit history, industry experience or other evidence of management ability, collateral, and owner's equity contributions. If you own 20 percent or more equity in the business, the SBA asks that you personally guarantee the loan. The SBA offers a wide variety of loan programs for businesses at various stages of development. Here's a closer look":

7(a) Guaranty Loan Program

The standard SBA loan for franchisees is known as the 7(a), which is issued by a bank or other qualified lender and partly guaranteed against default by the US government. The SBA does not lend money itself but provides maximum loan guarantees of up to $5 million or 75 percent of the total loan amount, whichever is less. For loans less than $150,000, the maximum guarantee is 85 percent of the total loan amount. SBA policy prohibits lenders from charging many of the usual fees associated with commercial loans. Still, you can expect to pay a one-time guaranty fee, which the agency charges the lender and allows the lender to pass on to you.

A 7(a) loan can be used for many business purposes, including real estate, expansion, equipment, working capital, and inventory. The money can be paid back over as long as twenty-five years for real estate and equipment and ten years for working capital. Interest rates vary with the type of loan you apply for.

SBA Express Program

A general 7(a) loan may suit your business's needs best, but the 7(a) program also offers several specialized loans. One of them, the SBA express program, promises quick processing for amounts less than $350,000. SBA express can get you an answer quickly because approved SBA express lenders can use their own documentation and procedures to attach an SBA guarantee to an approved loan without having to wait for SBA approval. The SBA guarantees up to 50 percent of SBA express loans.

CAPLines

For businesses that need working capital on a short-term or cyclical basis, the SBA has a collection of revolving and nonrevolving lines of credit called CAPLines. A revolving loan is similar to a credit card on which you carry a balance that goes up or down depending on the payments and amounts you borrow. With nonrevolving lines of credit, you borrow a flat amount and pay it off over a set period of time.

CAPLine loans provide business owners short-term credit, with loans that are guaranteed up to $2 million. There are five loan and line-of-credit programs that operate under the CAPLines umbrella:

1. A **seasonal line of credit** is designed to help businesses during peak seasons, when they face increases in inventory, accounts receivable, and labor costs.
2. A **contract line of credit** is used to finance labor and material costs involved in carrying out contracts.
3. A **standard asset-based line of credit** helps businesses unable to meet credit qualifications associated with long-term credit; provides financing for cyclical, growth, recurring, or short-term needs.
4. A **small asset-based revolving line of credit** provides smaller, asset-based lines of credit (up to $200,000), with requirements that are not as strict as the standard asset-based program.

5. A **builder's line of credit** is used to finance labor and materials costs for small general contractors and builders who are constructing or renovating commercial or residential buildings.

Each of the five credit lines has a maturity of up to five years but can be tailored to the borrower's needs.

Microloan Program

SBA financing isn't limited to the 7(a) group of loans. The microloan program helps entrepreneurs get very small loans, up to $35,000. The loans can be used for machinery and equipment, furniture and fixtures, inventory, supplies, and working capital, but they cannot be used to pay existing debts or to purchase real estate. This program is unique because it assists borrowers who do not meet traditional lenders' credit standards.

Microloans are administered through nonprofit intermediaries. These organizations receive loans from the SBA and then turn around and make loans to entrepreneurs. Small businesses applying for microloan financing may be required to complete some business-skills training before a loan application is considered.

The maximum term for microloans is six years, and the interest rates vary.

CDC/504 Loan Program

For more long-term lending, the 504 loan provides long-term, fixed-rate loans for financing fixed assets, usually real estate and equipment. Loans are most often used for growth and expansion.

504 loans are made through certified development companies (CDCs)—nonprofit intermediaries that work with the SBA, banks, and businesses looking for financing. There are CDCs throughout the country, each covering an assigned region.

If you are seeking funds up to $5 million to buy or renovate a building or put in some major equipment, consider bringing your business plan and financial statements to a CDC. Typical percentages for this type of package are 50 percent financed by the bank, 40 percent by the CDC, and 10 percent by the business.

In exchange for this below-market, fixed-rate financing, the SBA expects the small business to create or retain jobs or meet certain public policy goals. Businesses that meet these public policy goals are those whose expansion will contribute to a business district revitalization, such as an empowerment zone; a minority-owned business; an export or manufacturing company; or a company whose expansion will contribute to rural development.

"For you, Ken," John said, "I would think the 7(a) guaranty loan program or SBA express program would be your best SBA loan option if you went that route. Unless you have a contact with a local bank, the SBA loan is probably your best bet in terms of getting through the loan application process, loan terms, and fees."

"The SBA loan is really neat. It is a really great thing that the government is doing to help the business community," Ken said.

"The SBA has been making loans to businesses since the 1950s. In fact, with the Small Business Act of July 30, 1953, Congress created the Small Business Administration, whose function was to "aid, counsel, assist, and protect, insofar as is possible, the interests of small-business concerns." The charter also stipulated that the SBA would ensure small businesses a "fair proportion" of government contracts and sales of surplus property. Because of that backing, such loans are seen as relatively low risk. SBA loans of five- to six-year maturities can provide short-term working capital and equipment. Real-estate loans can run for twenty years or more. About 10 percent of all SBA loans go to franchisees, with the size running between $250,000 and $500,000, and a maximum of $2 million. Most of that money is for franchise entry fees, improvements, or working capital. Borrowers must be creditworthy, typically must contribute some equity, and are expected to repay the SBA loan out of the franchise's cash flow. Also, many SBA loans carry fluctuating interest rates. While the actual rate is negotiated between the bank and the borrower, it's subject to SBA maximums, which are tied to the prime rate. While a low rate may be attractive initially, it is important that you make sure you can create enough cash flow to cover the payments if the rate rises."

"Great," Ken said.

"I am not sure this if relevant to you, but the Department of Veterans Affairs also has a lending program. The program, called Patriot Express because of its relatively fast approval time, makes loans up to $500,000 to active-duty military preparing to transition to civilian life, as well as to spouses and survivors of veterans. The loans come with the SBA's lowest rates," John said.

"How do I apply for an SBA loan?" Ken asked.

"Again, the best resource is the SBA.gov website. It has detailed information on the entire loan application process."

John handed Ken a printout of the SBA loan application checklist he found on the SBA.gov website.

"Let me just briefly review it with you," John said. "First, once you have decided to apply for a loan guaranteed by the SBA, you will need to collect the appropriate documents for your application. The SBA does not provide direct loans. The process starts with your local lender and working within SBA guidelines. Use the checklist below to ensure you have everything the lender will ask for to complete your application. Once your loan package is complete, your lender will submit it to the SBA."

1. SBA loan application. To begin the process, complete an SBA loan application form (See Exhibit C).
2. Personal background and financial statement. To assess your eligibility, the SBA will require a statement of your personal history and personal financial statement.
3. Business financial statements. To support your application and demonstrate your ability to repay the loan, prepare and provide your P&L and projected financial statements.
   - Profit and loss (P&L) statement: this must be current within ninety days of your application and include supplementary schedules from the last three fiscal years.
   - Projected financial statements: include a detailed, one-year projection of income and finances, and attach a written explanation as to how you expect to achieve this projection.

4. Business ownership. Provide a list of the owners of the business as well as other businesses you or your partner(s) own or have an interest in.
5. Business formation documents. Provide your LLC or corporate articles of formation or incorporation, as applicable, including your corporate seal on the SBA loan application form if your business is a corporation.
6. Loan application history. Include records of any loans you have applied for in the past.
7. Income tax returns. Include signed personal and business federal income tax returns of your business's principals for the previous three years.
8. Résumés. Provide personal résumés for you and your partner(s).
9. Business overview and history. Provide a brief history of the business and its challenges explaining why the SBA loan is needed and how it will help the business.
10. Business lease. If applicable, include a copy of your business lease, or note from your landlord, giving terms of proposed lease.

"In addition, if you were purchasing an existing business, which you are not, you would need to provide the SBA the following additional documentation":

- current balance sheet and P&L statement of business to be purchased
- previous two years federal income tax returns of the business
- proposed bill of sale including terms of sale
- asking price with schedule of inventory, machinery and equipment, furniture and fixtures

"I won't lie—I am a bit overwhelmed. It seems like this will take forever to complete," Ken responded.

"It does take some time and your franchisor may help you with this as will the attorney or CPA working with you on the business deal. The good thing about completing the SBA loan application is that it forces you to really dig deep into the business, marketing, and financial aspects of your business and will likely help you out when your business is launched," John said.

"Are there any good free resources you suggest I check out that can help me navigate the loan application process?" Ken asked.

"Again, I will defer to the SBA.gov website, but I know the SBA works closely with a large network of partners that leverage SBA resources. You may want to check out some of these resources":

- SBA district/branch offices—at least one in every state
- SCORE, previously known as Service Corps of Retired Executives is a 501(c)(3) nonprofit organization that provides free business mentoring services to entrepreneurs in the United States — (approximately three hundred chapters nationwide)
- SBDCs—Small-business development centers (approximately nine hundred locations nationwide associated with higher education institutions (colleges and universities)
- WBCs—Women's business centers (approximately one hundred educational centers nationwide)

"Thanks. That is really helpful. How long does the loan application process typically take?" Ken asked.

"It depends on the bank or institution you are working with, but usually you should expect to get some type of feedback on your loan application within two to four weeks. I suggest that all my clients in this position check in each week for a status update. A lot of times the lending institution will need additional documentation," John said.

"OK, so to put this in my own words, if I wanted to try to get a loan to help finance the purchase of the water franchise, I can go through a bank, SBA loan, micro or alternative lenders, as well as region-specific lenders. Most of the lenders will require some personal guarantee and probably at least 20 percent of the purchase price in cash. There are a number of factors that will determine if I will get a loan, including my credit history and business plan. In addition, some franchisors do offer some form of financing to help with the business acquisition. Overall, the SBA loan route may be my best bet based on the amount of funding needed and the attractive terms, but there is no guarantee that I will get the loan," Ken said.

"That is about right," John agreed. "Now that we have discussed the option of using cash or acquiring a loan to finance your business, let's look at the option of having friends and family invest in your business."

"That would be helpful. Pam and I both approached several family members and friends about investing, but did not find any takers," Ken said. "Either way, I would be interested in learning more about this option."

5. Friends and Family

"According to most of my budding entrepreneur clients, friends and family remain the best shot that many entrepreneurs have to raise outside money to launch a business. There are essentially two ways family and friends can invest in your business: (i) as an investor, and (ii) as a lender. When one invests in a business, he or she is an owner of the business and is entitled to a share of the profits, losses, distributions, or dividends from the business, whereas a lender is simply receiving a stated interest payment on the funds lent to the business, along with the return of the loan principal back at maturity. The downside of lending funds to a business is that you don't have any of the upside of ownership, but at the same time you are generating a stated return on the funds lent. In other words, a lender is providing a loan to the business, which promises to repay the loan plus interest over a specified period of time. Buying a bond is the same as being a lender. If you buy a bond, you are, in effect, a debt lender, whereas an equity investor buys an ownership stake in the company. The value of the investor's capital will rise or fall according to the company's performance in the marketplace. If you own a stock or a mutual fund that owns stock, you are an equity investor."

"What option is more popular among family and friends?" Ken asked.

"It all depends on the facts and circumstances," John said.

"I hate when you say that," Ken said with a smile.

"I know, so do I, but it is true. Some business owners seeking financing would prefer an equity investor because there would no pressure on the business to pay back the loan, whereas some business owners don't want to give up any ownership of the business, and prefer family and friends lend the funds to the business. There is no right or wrong answer—the most important thing is to do what you are comfortable with, although a lot depends on what the investor wants to do. As we all know, money talks." John said.

"OK, so are there any tips about how to best approach family and friends about investing in my business?" Ken asked.

"This is a tricky question because I am not sure there is an answer. What works for you may not work for me and vice versa. A lot depends on your relationship with the people you are soliciting, the business you are opening, your business track record, and, of course, the amount of money you are asking for. I bet you agree that asking a brother or sister for $500 is a lot easier than asking for $35,000. With that in mind, here are a few tips that have worked for some of my clients."

"Ready," Ken said.

"Choosing the right family member or friend to approach is crucial. It is important to know who you are pitching. It likely won't make sense to approach your little brother who just graduated from college or your uncle who relies on social security. It usually makes sense to approach friends and family members who have some business and investment background and who knows the risks and benefits of what they are getting into. Remember, if your business doesn't work out and you can't repay your obligations, relationships will suffer. At the very least, narrow your list down to friends or family who you think believe in you and have faith that you will succeed, who understand your plans and are clear about the risks. Of course, that person should also have the financial capacity to make the investment. Obviously, this is a tough thing to gauge because some people act like they have a lot of money and actually don't, and there are plenty of people who are very modest but have plenty of money. To this end, I have a client who looks like a hippie, rides a bike to work, lives in a modest two-bedroom apartment, but is worth close to $10 million. On the other hand, I have a number of clients who drive fancy cars and wear expensive clothes, and they can't pay my bills. You just never know. It is also helpful to think about whether you want to solicit funds from a small group of family and friends or seek smaller amounts from a larger group. I think you just have to get a feel for the number of potential family members and friends you can approach and then devise a strategy."

"Interesting," Ken said.

"Choose an investment type," John continued. "Are you going to be asking for equity investors, lenders, or a mixture? It is best to have a plan in mind and stick to it. This will help show your family and friends that you have a plan and are confident in the business model."

"Right."

"Have a business plan or presentation," John said. "Approaching potential investors with a written plan or presentation is a much more professional and organized approach for soliciting funds than trying to wing it with a five-minute speech. The presentation or plan will help your potential investors focus on what you want them to read and will make you look much more professional. I would not suggest having an overly long presentation, because the potential investor will likely not want to go through everything and, in fact, it may be a turnoff. I would keep the plan or presentation under fifteen or so pages."

"Good one."

"Be honest and be yourself," John said. "I think a great tactic for approaching family and friends about investing in your business is to be yourself and be honest about the business prospects and risk. No start-up or new business is a sure thing, and every new business comes with some degree of risk. To that end, I think it is helpful to be up-front with the family members and friends you approach for funding. Remember, you are going to see these people again whether your business succeeds or fails—it is always best practice to be honest and straightforward about the risks and potential upside because I just don't think that the investment will be worth losing a family member or friend over."

"I think that is a fair statement," Ken said. "Pam and I spoke to a few close family members and some friends, and we just didn't find any takers. We were definitely up-front and honest and tried to approach only the people we thought would be interested. One mistake we may have made is that we relied on an oral pitch and did not have a plan or presentation to show, but I am not sure that would have made a difference. I have a really close family, and in my case I think it is best to not mix family and business."

"One thing I want to add," John said, "though it does not seem to be wholly relevant to you if you are not going to pursue the friends and family option, but if you were going to pursue this option, you must be careful not to violate certain US Securities and Exchange Commission (SEC) rules pertaining to soliciting investors. I don't want to get into too much detail because the rules are complicated, but I do think it is important to have some basic knowledge of the rules."

Every offering of securities has to either (1) be registered with the Securities and Exchange Commission, or (2) qualify under one of the applicable exemptions from registration.

Typically, a friends-and-family round of financing is done by (1) issuing stock or membership interests to investors in exchange for their money, or (2) issuing a promissory note (e.g., convertible debt). Because the SEC's definition of what constitutes a security is broad, when you issue stock or an equity interest to your friends or family members in exchange for money, such a transaction is likely to be considered a securities offering regardless of how small the investment is.

The problem is that registering your investment is very expensive, so you will probably need to rely on an exemption. Regulation D contains three exemptions to the registration requirements. The exemption found under Rule 506 allows an unlimited amount of securities to be issued to an unlimited number of accredited investors and up to thirty-five sophisticated nonaccredited investors. Accredited investors include individuals who have (i) a net worth or joint net worth with his/her spouse that exceeds $1 million at the time of the purchase (not including the value of the primary residence), or (ii) income exceeding $200,000 in each of the two most recent years (or joint income with a spouse exceeding $300,000 for those years) and a reasonable expectation of such income level in the current year. If your friends-and-family investors are all accredited investors, extensive disclosure is not necessary. However, the offering must be conducted without general solicitation or advertising. If some of the investors are not accredited, you will need to provide extensive disclosure to the investors (i.e., more disclosure in the private placement memorandum (PPM), risk factors, financial statements, and so on. Also, note that all nonaccredited investors in a Rule 506 offering must be sophisticated, which means that the company must reasonably believe that nonaccredited investors (either alone or together with their investment representatives) have sufficient financial and business knowledge to allow them to evaluate the risks and merits of an investment. Additionally, you'll need to comply with your state's regulations (typically a requirement to file a copy of the Form D and pay a filing fee).

"Wow, I never even thought about this," Ken said. "The friends and family I approached would not be accredited, but I believe they would be considered sophisticated, and I approached only a few people, well under thirty-five. But what happens if the investor I approach is neither sophisticated nor accredited?"

"There is an exemption, but it could prove expensive," John said. "Rule 504 of Regulation D allows you to raise up to $1 million from nonaccredited and nonsophisticated investors. However, Rule 504 involves the preparation of disclosure statements that are relatively complex and expensive. State securities laws regulate Rule 504 offerings and the amount and type of disclosure that needs to be provided."

"Seems like the SEC is interested in protecting investors from making investments without proper information or necessary background to understand the investments," Ken said.

"Yes, that is exactly right. The mission of the US Securities and Exchange Commission is to protect investors, maintain fair, orderly, and efficient markets, and facilitate capital formation. The SEC mission is pretty straightforward: all investors, whether large institutions or private individuals, should have access to certain basic facts about an investment prior to buying it and for as long as they hold it."

"Makes sense, and it actually makes me feel good that someone is looking out for the little guy," Ken said. "What's the deal with crowdfunding—how do they get around SEC filing requirements?"

"Another great question," John responded. "Basically, in March 2015, The SEC adopted final rules to facilitate smaller companies' access to capital. The new rules update and expand Regulation A, an existing exemption from registration for smaller issuers of securities. The rules are mandated by Title IV of the Jumpstart Our Business Start-Ups (JOBS) Act. According to the SEC there are two tiers to the new regulation: Tier 1 'for offerings of securities of up to $20 million in a twelve-month period, with not more than $6 million in offers by selling security-holders that are affiliates of the issuer' and Tier 2 'for offerings of securities of up to $50 million in a twelve-month period, with not more than $15 million in offers by selling security-holders that are affiliates of the issuer.' Both have similar requirements, but Tier 2 investment requires further disclosure."

"OK. But what if I just want to raise $25,000–$100,000 using a crowdfunding platform?" Ken asked.

"Title III of the JOBS Act is what specifically addresses this question. To take advantage of Title III and be exempt from any SEC registration, these conditions must be met":

- Organizations may solicit only $1 million annually.
- Only registered broker-dealers and funding portals may intermediate purchases or investments.
- Investors can make a maximum investment of $2,000 or 5 percent of their income if their net worth and annual income are both less than $100,000.
- Investors with over $100,000 in net worth or income may invest up to 10 percent of either.
- Businesses must offer total disclosure to all investors.

"On October 30, 2015, Federal regulators finalized crowdfunding rules under the JOBS Act, giving issuers access to a much larger group of investors — but under certain conditions. Companies will be able to gather up to $1 million in crowdfunding cash per year without registering with the Securities and Exchange Commission ("SEC"). The issuer will have to provide investors details about their business, how they'll use the money, a list of officers and directors, and disclose anyone who owns at least 20 percent of the company.

Before the new rules, private companies could seek money only from "accredited investors." That's defined as individuals who own more than $1 million in assets, excluding their primary residence, or have maintained an income of more than $200,000 for at least two years.

I believe Title III will have a huge impact on helping small businesses raise capital. Estimates suggest that when enacted, potential start-up investors within the United States will increase from approximately 3 million to over 200 million."

"Thanks. That is helpful. I think Title III is a really great thing and will be a big help to start-ups and small businesses. What about all these crowdfunding websites I have heard about recently?" Ken asked.

"Crowdfunding is essentially the art of funding a project or venture by raising monetary contributions from a large number of people, typically via the Internet. Crowdfunding is a form of alternative business financing. It brings a project initiator, who proposes the idea and/or project to be funded, which is then supported financially by a group of individuals. As of 2014, there are believed to over 550 crowdfunding platforms. It is important to conduct your own due diligence on the platform or website to make sure it can work with your idea or project. The following are some of the more popular crowdfunding sites":

- Kickstarter
- Indiegogo
- GoFundMe
- Razoo
- Crowdrise

"Thanks. Can I seek business financing from all these crowdfunding sites?" Ken asked.

"It depends. For example, Kickstarter seems to be popular for films, games, and music, and art, design, and technology type projects. But the following are what my clients tell me are the more popular crowdfunding sites for start-ups":

- AngelList
- CircleUp
- CrowdFunder
- EquityNet
- Fundable
- Rocket Hub

"Each of these crowdfunding sites works a little bit differently. However, the core goal of each platform is to match a business initiator with a network of potential investors. Some of the sites help match the business initiator with angel investors or venture capitals, whereas other sites will match you with individual investors, accredited and nonaccredited. Depending on the site, the amount of investment being sought can vary from $25,000 to $1 million or more." John said.

"Crowdfunding seems like a really cool concept, but I am still interested in learning more. Do you mind providing me some of the advantages and disadvantages of using a crowdfunding platform to come up with the $75,000 or so of funds I still need for my water business?" Ken asked.

"No problem. In my opinion, the main advantages of crowdfunding for a start-up business are the following":

- Crowdfunding minimizes the difficult and stressful fundraising process (and its associated time and cost) so entrepreneurs spend more time where it counts—on the business.
- You can pitch your business idea to many more people than you know personally.

- You can target the amount of money you want to raise. If the business idea is a hit, you get every penny.
- If you are successful with your crowdfunding project, you can get a huge amount of media attention and social media hype, which can help your business.
- You may be able to get some feedback about your business idea from investors on the platform.
- Using a crowdfunding platform can be a valuable marketing strategy and help create awareness and a buzz about the business idea.

"And what about some of the disadvantages?" Ken asked.
"There are a few":

- If the target funding amount is not satisfied, potential investors get their money back and the business goes away empty-handed.
- Because you are not pitching potential investors in person, you could lose out on receiving valuable feedback or positive criticism that can help you hone your business model.
- Unsophisticated investors might invest in your business who are not well informed or do not understand the risks associated with the investment.
- You could risk reputation damage if you are not able to secure the amount of financing sought.
- There is a risk of other people seeing your business idea and copying it or pursuing it themselves.

"That is really helpful. I think if I was looking for around $10,000 to $15,000 dollars and had a unique type of product or idea I might consider using a crowdfunding platform to raise funds. However, in the case of my water franchise opportunity, I just don't think crowdfunding will be a good option," Ken said.

6. Using Retirement Funds to Buy or Finance Business—the Basics

"I kind of agree with you. That being said, I think we are ready to move on to the fun stuff and the real reason Pam wanted us to chat: the option of using retirement funds to buy a business. The first time we met I spent some time reviewing all the types of retirement accounts and some of their features. I know you and Pam have retirement funds, but before we can jump into what options are available for investing retirement funds in a business, we need to address the rules surrounding accessing your retirement funds, and what restrictions, if any, may be imposed," John said.

"I didn't even think about that. I just thought that since it is my 401(k), I can touch the funds anytime I want, the same with my IRA," Ken said.

"Well, you are right about your IRA funds—they can be accessed anytime and rolled over to another retirement account or taken as distribution—but not so with a defined contribution plan, such as a 401(k) plan, 403(b), or 457(b) plan." John said.

"I am really happy I am talking to you, I had no idea that any of these rules existed. Can you expand on this?" Ken asked.

"Of course," John said.

A. 401(k) Plan Funds

"Let's start with the rules surrounding a defined contribution plan, such as a 401(k) plan," John said.

"Great," Ken agreed.

"In general, you may not take a distribution from a 401(k) plan until a certain event occurs, often called a 'triggering event.' The actions that trigger a distribution under a 401(k) plan will change depending on the type of plan documents you have adopted. Typically, distributions of elective deferrals cannot be made until one of the following occurs":

- you reach age fifty-nine and a half
- the plan terminates and you do not establish or maintain a successor-defined contribution plan

- you have a severance of employment
- you become disabled
- you die
- you incur a financial hardship

"The 2001 Economic Growth and Tax Relief Reconciliation Act expanded the rollover opportunities between employer-sponsored retirement plans, such as 401(k) plans and IRAs. Since 2002, individuals may roll over both pretax and after-tax 401(k) plan fund assets from a 401(a), 403(a), 403(b), and governmental 457(b) plans into a traditional IRA tax free and penalty free."

"Is there a tax or penalty when I move funds from my 401(k) to an IRA or another 401(k) plan?" Ken asked.

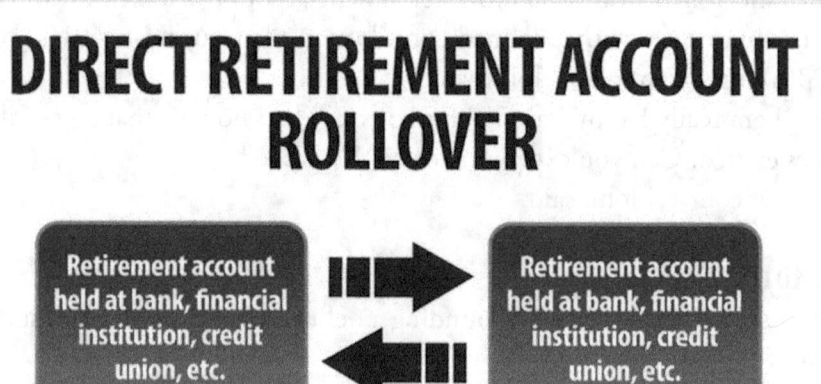

DIRECT RETIREMENT ACCOUNT ROLLOVER

Retirement account held at bank, financial institution, credit union, etc.

Retirement account held at bank, financial institution, credit union, etc.

"Generally no," John answered. "As long as the funds were moved directly from your current 401(k) plan to a new retirement account, this is referred to as a direct rollover and is tax free and penalty free. A direct rollover can be done as many times as you wish—there is no limit."

"I've heard about people taking their retirement funds and then moving them to a new retirement account within a certain time period," Ken said. "What's the deal on that?"

"That's called an indirect rollover, and I will go through all the details shortly," John answered. "Essentially, you have sixty days from the day you receive the funds to deposit them into a new retirement account or there will be tax on the distribution amount, as well a potential 10 percent early distribution penalty if you are under the age of fifty-nine and a half. An indirect rollover is not a good idea if you have a defined contribution plan, such as a 401(k), since there could be withholding on the amount. There are better options available, such as the loan feature, which we spend a considerable amount of time discussing down the road."

INDIRECT RETIREMENT ACCOUNT ROLLOVER

Retirement account held at bank, financial institution, credit union, etc.

Retirement account held at bank, financial institution, credit union, etc.

Rollover to new IRA Custodian must be complete within 60 days – only can be done one time every 12 months for all IRA accounts in the aggregate

"Terrific," Ken said.

"Let's get back to discussing the common plan-triggering events and the ways you can get access to your retirement funds," John continued. "One thing I want to make clear is that the triggering rules that will apply to your current employer 401(k) are based on the plan documents. Not all 401(k) plan documents are the same, so it's important to read the plan document or ask the plan administrator to find the answer for you. You know the saying 'In God we trust'? Well in this case, you can say 'In plan we trust' because everything you can and can't do with respect to the 401(k) is based on the plan documents. This includes whether the plan includes a profit-sharing component, the percentage of employer matching contributions, permitted investment options, whether the loan feature applies, who will be the trustee and plan administrator, and so on."

"I think I have a basic understanding of what the triggering rules are," Ken said. "Can we look at them in a bit more detail?"

"Let's start with plan termination," John said. "If the plan you are participating in as an employee is terminated, that is usually treated as a triggering event allowing you to roll your funds into another retirement plan without tax or penalty. If your employer 401(k) plan terminates, your plan documents will likely allow you to request distributions from your plan. In other words, the ability to roll over the retirement funds to an IRA or another 401(k) plan. In addition, most 401(k) plans allow a plan participant who has left his or her job with the employer who adopted the plan the ability to receive distributions of the plan's vested account balance."

Disability

"You may also begin receiving distributions from your 401(k) plan if you become disabled," John said. "It would be up to the plan participant to prove that he or she is disabled by providing supporting medical documentation to the plan administrator."

Death

"Of course, all 401(k) plans allow the beneficiaries of a plan participant to begin receiving distributions upon that participant's death," John noted. "It is common to name your spouse as your primary 401(k) plan beneficiary unless he or she consents to the naming of another beneficiary."

Hardship Distributions

"And your 401(k) plan may also provide for hardship distributions if you have an immediate and heavy financial need," John said. "This need is determined based on all relevant facts and circumstances. Indeed, your financial need may be considered immediate and heavy by the IRS even if it was reasonably foreseeable or due to your own choices and decisions. Specifically, the IRS regulations consider the following to be financial hardships":

- expenses for your medical care or the medical care of your spouse or dependents
- costs directly related to the purchase of your principal residence (but not your mortgage payments)
- tuition, related educational fees, and room and board expenses for the next twelve months of postsecondary education for you, your spouse, your children, or your dependents
- payments necessary to prevent your eviction from your principal residence or foreclosure on your mortgage on that residence
- funeral expenses
- certain expenses relating to the repair of damage to your principal residence

"How do they calculate hardship distributions?" Ken asked.

"Hardship distributions from a 401(k) plan are usually relegated to the amount of your elective deferrals and do not include any income earned on the deferred amounts," John answered. "However, a plan can permit employer matching contributions and employer discretionary contributions to be included in hardship distributions. Hardship distributions cannot be rolled over to another plan or IRA. According to the IRS, a distribution is treated as a hardship distribution only if it is made on account of the hardship to satisfy the immediate and heavy financial need of the employee."

"Got it," Ken said.

"It's also important to remember," John said, "that hardship distributions are a permanent reduction of an account balance and cannot be repaid. They can have a significant impact on a plan participant's retirement account balance."

Immediate and Heavy Financial Need
"On the other hand," John said, "you are not permitted to obtain a distribution that exceeds the amount needed to relieve your immediate and heavy financial need. In addition, you are not allowed a distribution if your financial hardship need can be fulfilled through other reasonable avenues, including

- your spouse's assets and any available assets of your children, if they are minors;
- reimbursement or compensation by insurance;
- liquidation of assets;
- cessation of elective contributions to your plan;
- receipt of distributions or nontaxable loans from your plan; or
- borrowing from commercial sources on reasonable terms in an amount sufficient to satisfy the need.

"OK," Ken said.

"After you have elected to take a hardship distribution from your 401(k) plan," John said, "you are prohibited from making contributions to your plan and other retirement plans for at least six months after receiving your hardship distribution. Hardship distributions are includible in gross income unless they consist of designated Roth contributions. They may also be subject to an additional tax on early distributions of elective contributions. Unlike loans, hardship distributions are not repaid to the plan. Thus, a hardship distribution permanently reduces your solo 401(k) account balance."

"How do you figure out if a hardship distribution is appropriate?" Ken asked.

"The IRS looks at all relevant facts and circumstances," John answered. "The place to start, of course, is your personal resources. However, your retirement assets are relevant in making an overall determination. Your resources are deemed to include the assets of your spouse and minor children when they are reasonably available to you. Thus, for example, a second home—whether owned by you or your spouse as community property, joint tenants, tenants by the entirety, or tenants in common—usually will be deemed a resource. Interestingly, the amount of an immediate and heavy financial need may include any amounts necessary to pay any federal, state, or local income taxes or penalties reasonably anticipated to result from the distribution. The IRS defines an immediate and heavy financial need is a hardship that can not be relieved by other resources reasonably available to the plan participant:

- through reimbursement or compensation by insurance or otherwise;
- by liquidation of the employee's assets;
- by cessation of elective contributions or employee contributions under the plan;
- by other distributions or nontaxable (at the time of the loan) loans from plans maintained by the employer or by any other employer; or
- by borrowing from commercial sources on reasonable commercial terms in an amount sufficient to satisfy the need.

"According to the IRS," John continued, "a distribution is deemed necessary to satisfy an immediate and heavy financial need if all of the following requirements are satisfied":

- The distribution is not in excess of the amount of your immediate and heavy financial need.
- You have obtained all distributions, other than hardship distributions, and all nontaxable (at the time of the loan) loans currently available under all your plans.
- You are prohibited, under the terms of the plan or an otherwise legally enforceable agreement, from making elective contributions and employee contributions to your plan and all

other plans for at least six months after receipt of the hardship distribution.

Other Ways to Take a Distribution

"Are there some other ways to take a distribution?" Ken asked.

"Yes," John answered. "Even if no triggering event has occurred, there may be other ways you can take money out of your 401(k) plan as a distribution. These are often referred to as in-service distributions. In general, there has to be a triggering event in order for you to get access to your retirement funds prior to the age of fifty-nine and a half. There is one major exception to this rule, and that is the in-service distribution option. An in-service distribution is when a participant, who is still employed by the plan sponsor, is allowed to take a distribution from the plan.

"In-service withdrawals from 401(k) plans carry very specific restrictions. Only employer contributions are eligible for in-service distributions and not employee deferrals. What that means is that any employee deferral contributions made by the plan participant to the plan are not eligible for in-service distributions and are subject to the triggering rules described above. Only employer profit-sharing contributions can be used for an in-service distribution. The in-service distribution gets you access to your funds prior to turning fifty-nine and a half but will still require you to pay tax and penalty, if under the age of fifty-nine and a half, on the amount of the distribution."

"How do you know if you're eligible?" Ken asked.

"In order to be eligible to take an in-service distribution of profit-sharing funds, your plan documents must allow for them. Even if the plan documents allow for in-service distributions, they will usually put restrictions on when the in-service distribution can be made. This could be the plan's normal retirement age, an early retirement age, or any age. It could also be after a fixed period of time. However, the contribution must be at least two years old or the account must be at least five years old. Remember, if you are over fifty-nine and a half or can satisfy one of the triggering events, you will not need to worry about the in-plan service distribution rules, as you will have the ability to take a distribution of vested funds from the plan."

"How do I take a distribution from my 401(k) plan?" Ken asked.

"Depending on the terms of your plan, the distributions you take may be 'nonperiodic' lump-sum distributions or 'periodic' distributions such as annuity or installment payments. Specifically, if a distribution in excess of $1,000 is made and you (or your designated beneficiary) have waived the 'qualified joint and survivor annuity' option, you may receive the funds as"

- a lump-sum payment,
- a partial payment,
- installment payments not to exceed your life expectancy or the joint and last survivor life expectancy of you and your designated beneficiary, or
- by applying the distribution to a purchase of an annuity contract. Note: most 401(k) plans do not require that plan distributions take the form of a life annuity or joint and survivor annuity as required under the Retirement Equity Act (REA) of 1984.

"Wow," Ken said. "This totally caught me off guard. Are you saying that if Pam or I want to access our retirement from our current employer 401(k) plan, we have to be over the age of fifty-nine and a half, we have to leave the job, or the company terminates the plan, assuming we don't satisfy any of the hardship distribution exceptions?"

"That is pretty much right on point," John said.

"So I guess if I decide to use my retirement funds to help fund the water franchise, I have to leave my job since I am under the age of fifty-nine and a half. And since Pam loves her job at the law firm, I don't think using her 401(k) plan funds are an option."

"Makes sense," John said.

"What about former employer retirement funds?" Ken asked.

"That works, too. You can usually access former employer 401(k) funds and use them in various structures we will discuss to buy or finance a business venture. As we will discuss shortly, pretax 401(k) funds can be rolled into an IRA or rolled into another 401(k) plan. After-tax (Roth) 401(k) funds, however, can only be rolled into a Roth and cannot be rolled into the majority of 401(k) plans.

B. IRA Funds

"What about IRA funds?" Ken asked.

"Good question. According to the Employee Benefits Research Institute, as of 2012, individual retirement accounts (IRAs) are a vital component of US retirement savings, holding more than 25 percent of all retirement assets in the nation. A substantial portion of these IRA assets originated in other tax-qualified retirement plans, such as defined benefit plans (pensions) and 401(k) plans, and were moved to IRAs through rollovers from those plans."

(i) Direct Rollover to an IRA

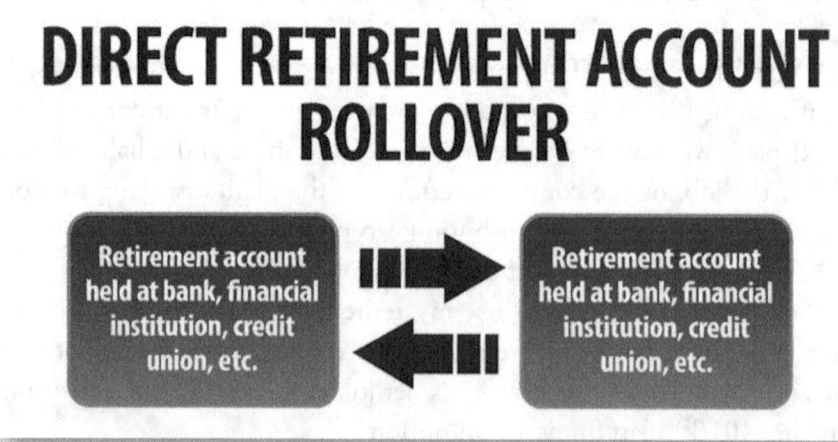

DIRECT RETIREMENT ACCOUNT ROLLOVER

Retirement account held at bank, financial institution, credit union, etc.

Retirement account held at bank, financial institution, credit union, etc.

"A direct rollover occurs when a plan participant who has access to his or her retirement funds moves the eligible qualified retirement plan funds (i.e., 401(k) plan) to an IRA custodian. In other words, a 'direct rollover' is between a qualified retirement plan and an IRA, whereas a 'transfer' is between two IRA financial institutions. In general, employer 401(k) plan providers must offer the direct rollover option if it is reasonable to anticipate that the total amount of eligible rollover distributions to a recipient for the year would be more than $200."

"I understand," Ken said.

"A direct rollover may be accomplished by any reasonable means of direct payment to an IRA. Regulations state that the reasonable means may include a wire transfer or mailing a check to the new IRA custodian."

John handed Ken an IRS chart that summarized all the IRA rollover rules (See Exhibit D). "I think the chart is really helpful to better understand the rollover options for your retirement funds. If I could summarize the chart for most people with retirement funds, including you, just remember that a 401(k) plan can be rolled into a traditional IRA tax free and penalty free, and a traditional IRA can be rolled into a 401(k) plan tax free. In both cases these rollovers are considered direct rollovers, and there is no limit on the number of times they can be done. The only thing to be aware of is that a Roth IRA cannot be rolled into a 401(k) plan. I know you mentioned that you have a small Roth IRA, so unfortunately you would not be able to roll her Roth IRA into a 401(k) plan if you ever had the option. There are some other quirky rollover rules that pertain to SIMPLE IRA, but I don't think you need to worry about them."

"What about an indirect rollover from a 401(k) plan to an IRA?" Ken asked.

"An indirect rollover occurs when the IRA assets or qualified retirement plan assets are moved first to the IRA holder or plan participant before they are ultimately sent to an IRA custodian."

(ii) Sixty-Day Indirect Rollover Rule

An individual usually has sixty (60) days from receipt of the eligible roll-over distribution to roll the funds into an IRA. The sixty-day period starts the day after the individual receives the distribution. Usually, no exceptions apply to the sixty-day time period. In cases where the sixty-day period expires on a Saturday, Sunday, or legal holiday, the individual may execute the rollover on the following business day. However, to avoid abuse of the rule, the tax code prescribes that taxpayers can complete an indirect IRA rollover only once in a twelve-month period, which the IRS in the past has interpreted to apply to IRAs on an account-by-account basis. In turn, the "separate accounts" treat-ment of the IRA rollover rule potentially allows taxpayers to chain together multiple IRA rollovers in an attempt to circumvent the one-year rule and gain "temporary" use of IRA funds for an extended period of time. Even though IRS Publication 590 seems to suggest that the sixty-day rule would apply to separate IRA accounts, many tax professionals have typically advised clients that the IRS could interpret the rule to apply to all IRAs because of the abuse of the sixty-day distribution rule that could potentially occur.

Lo and behold, a recent tax court decision clarified how the IRS would interpret the sixty-day rollover rule and whether it would apply to all IRAs or only to separate IRAs. In *Bobrow v. Commissioner*, the IRS shut down the separate IRAs rollover strategy altogether. That case arose because a taxpayer botched a version of the sequential separate accounts rollover strategy and drew the IRS's ire in the process. It ended with a finding of guilt for not only botching the rollovers but for having the tax court (re)interpret IRC Section 408(d)(3)(B) as well. In the decision, the tax court applied the one-year IRA rollover rule across all IRAs, invalidating the separate IRA rollover treatment not only for Bobrow but all taxpayers as well.

The details are interesting. A tax attorney named Alvan Bobrow took $65,000 out of his traditional IRA account, intending to replace that money within sixty days, as the tax law states, in order to have the transaction treated as an IRA rollover rather than a taxable distribution.

Right before Bobrow repaid the $65,000 to his traditional IRA account, however, he took $65,000 out of a different IRA account. Then, just before the sixty-day period for that withdrawal expired, Bobrow's wife took $65,000 out of her traditional IRA, with a $65,000 repayment to Bobrow's second IRA account taking place just days later. Eventually, the Bobrows repaid the wife's IRA withdrawal and took the position that all of the transactions were tax-free IRA rollovers. The IRS disagreed, arguing in part that the nested withdrawals and repayments didn't line up the way the Bobrows contended.

It's worth noting that Mr. Bobrow could have completed the transfer of funds without doing an indirect rollover. With an IRA transfer between institutions there's no limit on the number of IRA transfers that can be done in a year.

Being a tax attorney, Bobrow chose to represent himself in the tax court after the IRS imposed taxes on him and his wife, in light of the multiple indirect IRA rollovers he did during the year in question. Rather than simply saying that Bobrow's serial withdrawals weren't eligible for tax-free IRA rollover status because they came in quick succession and were nested within each other, the tax court suggested that in all instances taxpayers are limited to one tax-free indirect IRA rollover per twelve-month period. That broader finding conflicted with the IRS's own guidance in its publication 590 on IRAs, which contemplates situations in which completely unrelated transactions using multiple IRAs could all qualify for tax-free IRA rollover treatment.

In the aftermath of the Bobrow case, the IRS has now issued IRS Announcement 2014-15, stating that it will acquiesce to the tax court decision, update its Proposed Regulations and Publication 590, and issue new Proposed Regulations soon that will definitively apply the one-year IRA rollover rule on an IRA-aggregated basis going forward.

Now, an individual receiving an eligible rollover distribution may roll over the entire amount received or any portion of the amount received. The amount of the eligible rollover distribution that is not rolled over to an IRA is usually included in the individual's gross income and could be subject to a 10 percent early distribution penalty if the individual is under the age of fifty-nine and a half.

So what does all this mean? It is important to remember that this sixty-day rule applies only to indirect rollovers—in other words, to funds that are not being transferred directly between retirement account custodians (i.e., financial institution, bank, trust company, etc.). When funds are moved from retirement account to retirement account, that's considered a direct rollover or IRA transfer, and there is no sixty-day limit or limit on the amount of direct rollovers that can be done in a year.

John handed Ken a piece of paper that summarized the direct and indirect rollover rules:

The one-IRA-per-twelve-month (indirect rollover) limit does not apply to

- rollovers from traditional IRAs to Roth IRAs (conversions),
- trustee-to-trustee transfers from one IRA another IRA,
- IRA-to-plan rollovers,
- plan-to-IRA rollovers, or
- plan-to-plan rollovers.

"What about doing a sixty-day rollover from my 401(k) plan?" Ken asked.

"In general, when a plan participant requests a distribution from an employer qualified retirement plan, IRS rules require the employer to withhold 20 percent from the amount of the eligible rollover distribution. Just to be clear, the 20 percent withholding rule applies only to indirect rollovers and not direct rollovers. As a reminder, an indirect rollover occurs when plan funds are transferred directly to the plan participant first and not a financial institution. If an individual receives an eligible rollover distribution and then elects to roll over the assets to an IRA custodian within sixty days, the individual can make up the 20 percent withheld by the employer retirement plan provider for federal income tax purposes."

"Makes sense," Ken said.

"Employer-sponsored retirement plans are required to withhold at a rate of 20 percent on all eligible rollover distributions of taxable funds or assets, unless the participant elects to directly roll over the distribution to an IRA or another eligible retirement plan. In other words, when taking an indirect rollover from an employer-qualified retirement plan (401(k) plan), the employer is required to withhold 20 percent of the eligible rollover distribution. The 20 percent withholding requirement is not applicable for IRA-to-IRA transfers or for direct rollover distributions (between financial institutions)."

"Thanks for the information," Ken said "It makes sense that when I leave my job I'll do a direct rollover to another retirement account. What happens if I just decide to take a distribution and pay tax and penalty on the 401(k) funds? Is that an option?"

"Yes and no," John said. "Remember those pesky plan-triggering rules we discussed?"

"Yes," Ken responded.

"Well, even if you want to take a taxable distribution, if there is no plan-triggering event or hardship exception that you can satisfy, then you cannot take a taxable distribution even if you want to," John said.

"That is crazy," Ken exclaimed. "Isn't it my money? Why can't I take it when I want?"

"Hey, I feel your pain," John answered. "But the rules are the rules. It is technically your retirement savings, but until there is a 401(k) plan-triggering event, the funds must remain in the plan. Sorry, I know it is frustrating, but all we can do is comply with the law. The good news is that the funds are growing without tax, which will be a benefit for you down the road."

"So just to get this straight, the only way I can get access to my 401(k) plan funds is if there is a plan-triggering event even if I am willing to pay tax and penalty?" Ken asked.

"Yes, that is correct. You always have the option of doing a 401(k) plan loan, if the plan offers it, but we will get more into this in a little bit," John said. "However, unlike a 401(k) plan, an IRA does not have any triggering event rules. Therefore, if you have IRA funds you would be interested in accessing, then you can take an IRA distribution any time, you just have to pay tax and a 10 percent early distribution penalty since you're under the age of fifty-nine and a half."

"I guess if I left my job and the funds were rolled into an IRA, I could take a taxable distribution from an IRA?" Ken asked.

"Yes, that is correct. There are no triggering rule requirements for taking a taxable distribution from an IRA. Because the 401(k) funds you have are pretax, they would have to be rolled into a traditional IRA. An IRA owner may take distributions from his or her IRA at any time," John said. "The determination of whether the distribution is taxed depends on the type of IRA (i.e., traditional or Roth), the age of the IRA owner, and in the case of a Roth IRA, the duration of time the account has been established. The IRA owner is required to include traditional IRA distributions in his or her taxable gross income. The IRA owner who receives a distribution will report the distribution on his or her individual federal income tax return (Form 1040) and pay tax on the distribution based on the individual's federal income tax rate."

John added, "These IRA-related transactions are not treated as distributions subject to tax":

- rollovers
- transfers
- recharacterizations
- IRA revoked within seven-day period
- the portion of a distribution relating to nondeductible traditional IRA contributions

"OK, so unlike a 401(k) plan I can take a distribution from an IRA anytime I want, but I would have to pay ordinary income tax and a 10 percent penalty on the amount of the distribution since I am under the age of fifty-nine and a half. Is there any way to get around the 10 percent early distribution penalty?" Ken asked.

"In general," John said, "traditional IRAs are designed to encourage retirement saving and at the same time discourage people from taking money away from their retirement savings before reaching the age of fifty-nine and a half. The age fifty-nine and a half was selected by Congress because it was believed to be the age when one began transitioning from active employment to retirement. Remember that early distributions are subject to an additional tax. The IRS assesses a 10 percent penalty on the taxable portion of early distributions. However, the 10 percent early distribution penalty does not apply in the following situations":

Death of the IRA Owner

An IRA distribution to beneficiaries is not subject to the 10 percent early distribution penalty. In other words, upon the death of the IRA owner, the distribution of the owner's IRA to his or her beneficiaries is not subject to the 10 percent penalty.

Disability

Distributions received by a disabled IRA owner are not subject to the 10 percent early distribution penalty. Prior to making the disability distribution, the financial organization may require written evidence from the disabled IRA owner to verify disability. The IRA owner can demonstrate this by using IRS Form 1040, Schedule R, Credit for the Elderly or Disabled.

Rollovers and Conversions
Amounts rolled over to an IRA or properly converted to an IRA are not subject to the 10 percent early distribution penalty.

First-Time Homebuyer Expenses
Distributions taken for qualified first-time homebuyer expenses are not subject to the 10 percent early distribution penalty. There is a $10,000 lifetime limit with this exemption.

Return of Nondeductible Contributions
The 10 percent early distribution penalty would not apply to the portion of a distribution that represents a return of nondeductible contributions or after-tax assets received through a rollover.

Substantially Equal Periodic Payment
The 10 percent early distribution penalty shall not apply to distributions that are part of a series of substantially equal periodic payments made at least annually over the IRA owner's life expectancy or joint life expectancy of the IRA owner and his or her beneficiary. The rules that apply to this option can be found in IRC Section 72(t) and are quite complex.

Health Insurance
An IRA owner who received federal or state unemployment compensation for twelve consecutive weeks may take IRA distributions to pay for health insurance. These distributions are not subject to the 10 percent early distribution penalty. The IRA owner must take a distribution in the year he received his unemployment or in the year that follows. This exemption does not apply to distributions taken more than sixty days after the IRA owner regains employment.

Medical Expenses

Distributions used for reimbursed medical expenses that exceed 7.5 percent of the IRA owner's adjusted gross income are not subject to the 10 percent early distribution penalty.

Higher Education Expenses

IRA distributions used for qualified education expenses of the IRA owner, his or her spouse, spouse's child, or grandchild are not subject to the 10 percent early distribution penalty.

IRS Levy

Distributions taken because of IRS tax levies imposed on the IRA owner are not subject to the 10 percent early distribution penalty.

Qualified Reservist Distributions

Qualified reservists (including National Guard personnel) called to active duty after September 11, 2001, for a period of at least 180 days or for an indefinite amount of time are permitted to take penalty-free distributions from their IRA. This applies to distributions taken between the date of the order or call to duty and the end of the active duty period. Note that the distribution taken will still be subject to federal income tax.

"Thanks, but I don't think I will be able to satisfy any of the exemptions to the early distribution penalty, so I would be looking at ordinary income tax plus a 10 percent penalty, which would be pretty steep. What about my Roth IRA? Do you mind going over the IRA distribution rules in a bit more detail so I can better explain them to Pam?" Ken asked.

C. Roth IRA Funds

"Yes, no problem. Distributions from a Roth IRA that are not qualified may be subject to income tax and an additional 10 percent early distribution penalty. A qualified distribution is a distribution from a Roth IRA that meets both of the following two categories of requirements":

1. It occurs at least five years after the Roth IRA was established and funded his or her first Roth IRA.
2. It is distributed under one of the following circumstances:
   - The Roth IRA holder is at least age fifty-nine and a half when the distribution occurs.
   - The Roth IRA holder becomes disabled before the distribution.
   - The beneficiary of the Roth IRA holder receives the assets after his or her death.

"It's also important to remember that the IRS uses special rules when determining the source of the Roth IRA assets being distributed and the potential tax implications, including funds converted to a Roth IRA," John continued. "Based on the IRS ordering rules, Roth IRA assets are distributed in the following order, keeping in mind that once assets from one source run out, the assets from the next source are distributed":

1. regular Roth IRA participant contributions
2. taxable conversion and rollover amounts
3. nontaxable conversion and rollover amounts
4. earnings on all Roth IRA assets

"In determining what portion of the distribution is considered to come from contributions as opposed to earnings, you must follow the ordering rules outlined above. For example, Jim made a $5,000 contribution to his Roth IRA in 2010. In 2011, at age forty-five, Jim's Roth IRA was worth $6,000, and he needed all $6,000 to pay a personal expense. Based on the Roth IRA ordering rules, Jim would be able to take his $5,000 Roth contribution back without tax or penalty, but would be required to pay tax and a 10 percent early distribution penalty on the $1,000 of income generated since he was under the age of fifty-nine and a half. This is in contrast to a Roth 401(k) plan that follows a pro rata basis formula for determining the taxation of Roth 401(k) distributions, which is less taxpayer friendly than the Roth IRA distribution ordering rules discussed above. Also, it is important to remember that the Roth IRA distribution ordering rules to all your IRAs in the aggregate."

"Right," Ken said.

"The taxation rules for taking a pretax IRA distribution are much more straightforward than a Roth IRA. You can take distributions from your IRA at any time. There is no need to show a hardship to take a distribution. However, your distribution will be includible in your taxable income, and it may be subject to a 10 percent additional tax if you're under age fifty-nine and a half." John said.

"So the amount of the taxable distribution gets added to the income I earned during the year?" Ken asked.

"Bingo, exactly. For example, if you earned $100,000 as a W-2 employer from your sales job and you took at $10,000 IRA distribution, you would owe income tax on $110,000 plus a 10 percent early distribution penalty on the amount of the IRA distribution. Taking a taxable distribution can certainly bump you up into a higher tax bracket, so that is something you must be cautious about," John said.

7. Taking a Taxable Distribution of Retirement Funds

"Does taking a taxable distribution make sense for me?" Ken asked.

"It very well may. Again, it all comes down to the facts and circumstances. If the tax and penalty hit will be minimal, and the distribution amount will be a huge help to launch your business or keep it going, then you may think it makes sense. Unfortunately, there is no right or wrong answer, it is really what the situation calls for. Of course, the disadvantage is that you will lose the power of tax deferral as once you take distribution the funds are no longer considered tax-deferred retirement funds and are now treated as taxable personal funds. Bottom line, if you need the money to make the business happen or keep it from going out of business, then I think it is probably worth taking a taxable distribution, especially considering the IRA funds are quite minimal in your case. However, hopefully we will be able to find you a better option that will help you keep your IRA funds benefiting from the power of tax deferral, or tax-free growth in the case of the Roth IRA." John said.

"OK, makes sense, I guess this would be a last resort," Ken said.

"I agree," John said.

"I hope I didn't make your head spin or scare you out of starting a business. The next time we meet I want to introduce you to the concept of using retirement funds to make investments and the rules surrounding what types of investments are not permitted. These rules are known as the prohibited-transaction rules. I think this is a good starting point for under-standing what potential options are available for using retirement funds to buy a business. Once we have reviewed the IRS prohibited-transaction rules we can get into details on the various options available to you if you elect to use retirement funds to finance your water franchise." John said.

"OK, that sounds great," Ken responded.

3

The Prohibited-Transaction Rules

The next time the two men met, Ken bought the coffee and scones and took a seat at their regular table. Ken mentioned how much he appreciated all the time John had taken to help him get a better idea of the financing options available to buy the water franchise.

"No problem, it is my pleasure," John said. "I am a bit cramped for time today, so let's get started discussing the IRS prohibited-transaction rules involving the use of retirement funds to make an investment. You may think it is strange that I start with the rules about what you can't use retirement funds for before discussing what type of investments can be made with them, but I actually think it is easier this way. Once you have a clear idea on the type of transactions the IRS views as prohibited with respect to your retirement funds, it will make understanding what retirement funds are allowed to invest in much clearer."

John pulled out some notes and dug in.

THE BASICS OF PROHIBITED TRANSACTIONS

"Even though it sounds daunting," John said, "it's really not. But it is a little fuzzy. The IRC doesn't describe what a self-directed IRA can invest in, only what it cannot invest in. Specifically, IRC Sections 408 and 4975 prohibit disqualified persons from engaging in certain type of transactions. The purpose of these rules is to encourage the use of IRAs for the accumulation of retirement savings and to prohibit those in control of IRAs from taking advantage of the tax benefits for their personal account."

"I guess that makes sense—much easier to list what you can't do than everything you can do." Ken said.

"Exactly," John responded. "Imagine how long the tax code provision would be if it had to list every possible investment that could be made with retirement funds. Certainly much simpler to just list the categories or types of investments that are not permitted to be made using retirement funds. The IRS prohibited-transaction rules are based on the premise that investments involving IRAs and related parties should be handled in a way that benefits the retirement account and not the IRA owner personally."

"So if no harm would be coming to anyone except me, by my own hand, why should the IRA be so concerned about investments involving my IRA and my family members?" Ken asked.

"Basically," John answered, "that's the only way the IRS can protect its very important revenue-generating distribution rules. They need to make sure that if people want to use their IRA funds for personal purposes they pay tax and a penalty if they are under the age of fifty-nine and a half. In other words, it's the IRS's position that if you want to use retirement funds for personal purposes that's OK so long as you pay the appropriate tax and penalty."

"Fair enough, I guess," Ken said. "I'd want to protect my revenue too."

"Exactly," John said. "So in developing the disqualified person rules, the IRS is basically saying that they believe an IRA holder and his or her lineal descendants are one and the same, and if IRA funds are being transferred directly or indirectly to a disqualified person it is the same as though the IRA holder him or herself were personally benefiting. This is an important point for using retirement funds to invest in your own business, and we will soon learn why there are really only two ways it can be done without triggering the prohibited-transaction rules."

"That position makes sense," Ken said.

John nodded. "Yes. If you think about it, by giving money to your parents or children you are clearly benefiting to some degree because of the close family relationship. For example, using your IRA to pay your children's tuition or your parents' mortgage is either directly or indirectly benefiting you because if your parents or kids benefit, you are benefiting to some degree. The IRS's position is that if you were able to transact with a disqualified person and use IRA funds, you could simply transfer the IRA funds to a child or parent, and that would be just like them taking the money personally, which would eliminate the need to take a taxable distribution. This is something the IRS would definitely not appreciate."

"I think I get it," Ken said. "So if I could take some of my IRA funds and give them to my wife and kids, it would be pretty much the same as if I got to use the money personally."

"Right," John said. "The IRS was concerned that if they allowed this, people would be able to circumvent the distribution rules and avoid paying tax on their IRS accounts while simultaneously receiving some degree of benefit from the funds because they were used to help a close family member, such as a parent, child, or spouse."

"Ah, because I wouldn't have paid tax on that money otherwise, and I would still get to use it for my personal benefit."

"Remember, in the case of a traditional pretax IRA, you were granted a tax deduction for the IRA contribution on the expectation that you would eventually pay tax on the accumulated IRA account value," John said. "If you were able to take the IRA funds and give them to a parent, spouse, or child, it would be like you were gaining use of the IRA funds without having to pay any tax or the 10 percent penalty, if applicable."

"And if that was possible, everyone would do it to avoid paying some taxes on that money," Ken said.

"Sure," John said. "And the IRS would be left with very little tax revenue from the IRA account, and it would also lose tax revenue because of the use of the IRS deduction in the year of contribution—a double whammy."

"So prohibited-transaction rules are actually very important for the IRS," Ken said.

"The bottom line," John said, "is that most Americans' largest asset by the time they retire is their IRA. The self-directed IRA structure has become popular over the last several years because the 2008 financial crisis hit those retirement assets hard and showed people how important it is to diversify their retirement investments. The IRS has actually granted retirement investors with a wide array of investment options when using retirement funds, but there are a number of important rules the IRS has codified that govern how IRA retirement funds are to be used."

"I never thought of the IRA as being the most important tool in America for retirement," Ken said.

"It really is," John said. "According to the Investment Company Institute November 2013 Publication, IRAs represent more than one-quarter of US total retirement market assets, compared with 17 percent two decades ago, with $5.7 trillion in assets at the end of the second quarter of 2013. And they've only risen in importance on household balance sheets. In June 2013, IRA assets were 9 percent of all household financial assets, up from 4 percent of assets two decades ago. In May 2013, 46.1 million, or 38 percent of US households reported they owned IRAs. IRAs are such an important asset for retirees that it makes navigating the IRS prohibited-transaction rules even more crucial."

"But like you said," Ken said, "the tricky part is that the IRS doesn't tell you what you can invest in or how you should use your IRA assets, they only tell you what you can't invest in or how you can't use those assets."

"Exactly," John said. "So prohibited transactions are important to follow if you want to gain maximum advantage from the work you are doing to create and grow your IRA retirement assets."

"Are the penalties for violating prohibited-transaction rules harsh enough to be worth worrying about?" Ken asked.

"Yes," John said, "they're steep. And if your IRA is your most valuable asset, as it is for most Americans, it will trigger a hefty tax and penalty with significant financial ramifications to your retirement."

"Are the prohibited-transaction rules the same for traditional and Roth IRAs?" Ken asked.

John nodded. "The same rules apply to all retirement accounts, including IRAs, Roth IRAs, SEP-IRAs, SIMPLE IRAs, and 401(k) qualified retirement plans. The one main difference between the application of the prohibited-transaction rules for IRAs and 401(k) plans is that an IRA cannot purchase life insurance but a 401(k) plan can. I'll expand on the rules shortly."

"I wonder why I never heard of prohibited-transaction rules before we started talking?"

"You're not alone," John said. "Most Americans have never heard of the prohibited-transaction rules for good reason. After all, most retirement investors use their retirement funds to buy traditional financial assets, such as stocks, mutual funds, and ETFs. With those investments, the chance of engaging in a prohibited transaction is slim to none. For people who are looking to use their retirement funds to make alternative-asset investments, such as real estate or investing in a private business, the prohibited-transaction rules become very important. The good news is that the harsh penalties are easily avoidable. As long as you stay away from breaking the rules, you have no reason to fear the IRS when making investments with your retirement funds."

"OK," Ken said. "Since I am thinking of using retirement funds to invest in my own business, I guess it is important that I pay attention to what you are about to discuss."

"Yes, for sure. Let's look at prohibited transactions that are restricted because they pertain to 'disqualified persons,' 'conflicts of interest,' and 'self-dealing.' And we should also look at exceptions and exemptions to the restrictions, as well as certain categories of transactions that are not allowed with a retirement account, such as the purchase of collectibles or life insurance, in the case of an IRA. Though there are many different scenarios stipulated in IRC Section 4975, and extensive case law clarifying those scenarios, the restrictions themselves are not complicated, and I can simplify them as much as possible to make them easier to follow. Even so, it can be helpful to get advice from a tax professional just to make sure you're on the straight and narrow path."

John then explained everything Ken needed to know about disqualified persons.

DISQUALIFIED PERSONS

If a self-directed IRA transaction is restricted, it is likely because they pertain to a disqualified person. Who does the IRS consider a disqualified person?

Generally, this is referring to you (the IRA holder) and most of your immediate family, including your direct lineal ancestors or descendants, as well as any business entities that hold a controlling equity or management interest in your self-directed IRA.

Specifically, a disqualified person is one of the following:

A. **You**, as the IRA holder, plan participant, or any person with authority for making a retirement account investments

B. **A Trustee or Custodian**, or any person providing services to the retirement account

C. **The Owner** or business that adopted the qualified retirement plan (401(k))

D. **An Employee Organization**

E. **A 50 Percent Owner** of C or D

F. **A Family Member** of A, B, C, or D, which includes your spouse, parents and grandparents, children and grandchildren, and their spouses, but not brothers, sisters, aunts, uncles, cousins, stepsiblings, or friends

G. **A Partnership, Corporation, Trust, or Estate** that is more than 50 percent owned or controlled by A, B, C, D, or E

H. **A 10 Percent Owner, Officer, Director, or Highly Compensated Employee** of C, D, E, or G

I. **A 10 Percent or More Partner or Joint Venturer** of C, D, E, or G

In order to determine whether a proposed transaction is prohibited and violates IRC Section 4975, it is important to examine all the parties engaged in the proposed transaction rather than just the IRA owner.

According to IRC Section 4975, a retirement account is prohibited from engaging in certain types of transactions. The types of prohibited transactions can be best understood by dividing them into three categories: (1) direct or indirect prohibited transactions, (2) self-dealing prohibited transactions, and (3) conflict-of-interest prohibited transactions.

DIRECT OR INDIRECT PROHIBITED TRANSACTIONS

What is a direct or indirect prohibited transaction? Essentially, it is a transaction between the retirement account and a disqualified person, which either directly or indirectly benefits that disqualified person. It is important to remember that the IRS prohibited-transaction rules are primarily in place to ensure that the use of retirement funds is in no way directly or indirectly benefiting the plan participant or any of his or her lineal descendants. The reason is clear. The IRS holds that if you wish to make personal use of your retirement funds to help yourself or a close family member, doing so is essentially like helping yourself. Accordingly, you must take a distribution and pay the tax and penalty if you are under fifty-nine and a half years old. Those prohibited-transaction rules are the way the IRS polices and protects their distribution rules—a significant revenue source for the IRS and Treasury. In addition, when it comes to accumulating 401(k) and IRA funds, most of the funds are in pretax form, meaning the IRS provided the 401(k) plan participant or IRA holder with a tax deduction with the anticipation that the benefit provided to the taxpayer would be paid back in the form of taxation on the appreciated assets of the retirement account at a later time. It makes sense, then, that the IRS is so concerned with making sure that retirement funds are not used for any personal purpose that would allow someone to circumvent the distribution rules and taxation on the funds used. The IRS and Department of Labor need to protect their distribution rules because that is how they ensure that the IRS and Treasury receive the taxes they believe they deserve from retirement distributions.

Direct and indirect prohibited transactions are different. A direct prohibited transaction is the simplest type of prohibited transaction to uncover because it deals with scenarios involving a disqualified person and the retirement account directly. In contrast, an indirect prohibited transaction concerns transactions that do not appear to directly benefit a disqualified person but could do so indirectly based on certain facts and circumstances. For example, using your retirement account to pay your personal credit-card bill would be a clear direct prohibited transaction. However, using your self-directed IRA to invest in a company of which you own 15 percent might be considered an indirect prohibited transaction based on certain facts and circumstances.

For example, you cannot use your retirement account to do the following with a disqualified person:

- sell, exchange, or lease property
- lend money or extend credit
- furnish goods, services, or facilities
- transfer income or assets

IRC SECTION 4975—PROHIBITED-TRANSACTION RULES

John handed Ken a copy of IRC Section 4975(c) and (d) for his review (see Exhibit E). "Here are some scenarios pertaining to IRC Section 4975(c)(1)(A) that illustrate prohibited transactions to do with directly or indirectly selling, exchanging, or leasing property to a disqualified person. Bear in mind that the examples may not seem relevant to your situation since you are looking to use retirement funds to buy a business, but I think it is helpful to get a handle on the application of all the prohibited-transaction rules before we examine in detail the available options for using retirement funds to finance your own business."

IRC Section 4975(c)(1)(A): The Direct or Indirect Sale, Exchange, or Leasing of Property between a Retirement Account and a Disqualified Person

- Joe sells an interest in a piece of property owned by his retirement account to his son—PROHIBITED
- Beth leases real estate owned by her retirement account to her daughter—PROHIBITED

- Mark uses his retirement account funds to purchase an LLC interest owned by his mother—PROHIBITED
- Victor leases an interest in a piece of property owned by his retirement account to his son—PROHIBITED
- Tracy sells real estate owned by her retirement account to her father—PROHIBITED
- Ben sells real estate he owns personally to his retirement account—PROHIBITED
- Jason transfers property he owns personally to his retirement account—PROHIBITED
- Katy purchases real estate with her retirement account funds and leases it to her son—PROHIBITED
- David uses his retirement account funds to purchase an interest in an entity owned by his father—PROHIBITED
- Ted transfers property he owns personally subject to a mortgage to his retirement account—PROHIBITED
- Sally uses personal funds to pay expenses related to her retirement account real-estate investment—PROHIBITED
- Jane uses personal funds to pay taxes and expenses related to her retirement account real-estate investment—PROHIBITED

"Here are other scenarios pertaining to IRC Section 4975(c)(1)(B) that illustrate prohibited transactions to do with directly or indirectly lending money or extending credit to a disqualified person" John said:

IRC Section 4975(c)(1)(B): The Direct or Indirect Lending of Money or Other Extension of Credit between a Retirement Account and a Disqualified Person

- Ted lends his wife $70,000 from his retirement account—PROHIBITED
- Mary personally guarantees a bank loan to her retirement account to purchase real estate—PROHIBITED

- Dan uses his retirement account funds to lend $18,000 to an entity owned and controlled by his father—PROHIBITED
- Ken lends his son $4,000 from his retirement account—PROHIBITED
- Rick uses the assets of his retirement account as security for a loan—PROHIBITED
- Brandon uses his personal assets as security for a retirement account investment—PROHIBITED
- Chuck uses retirement account funds to lend $45,000 to an entity owned and controlled by his Mother—PROHIBITED
- Eric acquires a credit card for his retirement account bank account—PROHIBITED

Real-Life Examples

Peek v. Commissioner, 140 TC 12 (2013)

In *Peek*, the tax court held that a personal guarantee by an IRA owner of a loan to the owner's IRA is a prohibited transaction since it is a loan of money or extension of credit between a plan and a disqualified person under IRC Section 4975(c)(1)(B).

However, what if the loan was not made directly to the IRA but was made to an entity owned by the IRA? Is a personal guarantee by the IRA owner of such a loan a prohibited transaction? That was the subject of the Peek case. *Peek* involved two IRA owners (Mr. Fleck and Mr. Peek) who jointly invested in a corporation (FP) formed by them to acquire the assets of another company (AFS). The IRAs were the only shareholders of FP.

FP acquired the assets of AFS in exchange for a combination of cash and notes, including a promissory note from FP to the sellers secured by personal guarantees from both IRA owners. Fleck and Peek were fiduciaries of their respective IRAs due to retaining authority and control over such IRAs and thus were disqualified persons under IRC Section 4975(c)(1)(A), and each IRA constitutes a "plan" under IRC Section 4975(e)(1).

Nevertheless, they argued that because their personal guarantees did not involve the plan itself—i.e., since the guarantees were between disqualified persons (Fleck and Peek) and an entity (FP) other than the IRAs themselves—the guarantees were not prohibited.

This argument was flatly rejected by the tax court, which noted that IRC Section 4975(c)(1)(B) also prohibits indirect loans and/or extensions of credit between a plan and a disqualified person and that the "obvious and intended meaning" of (c)(1)(B) "prohibited Mr. Fleck and Mr. Peek from making loans or loan guarantees either directly to their IRAs or indirectly to their IRAs by way of the entity owned by the IRAs."

It is also prohibited, according to IRC Section 4975(c)(1)(C), to use your retirement account to directly or indirectly furnish goods, services, or facilities to a disqualified person.

IRC Section 4975(c)(1)(C): The Direct or Indirect Furnishing of Goods, Services, or Facilities between a Retirement Account and a Disqualified Person

- Andrew buys a piece of property with his retirement account funds and hires his father to work on the property—PROHIBITED
- Rachel buys a condo with her retirement account funds and personally fixes it up—PROHIBITED
- Betty owns an apartment building with her retirement account and hires her mother to manage the property—PROHIBITED
- Bill purchases a condo with his retirement account funds and paints the walls without receiving a fee—PROHIBITED
- Henry buys a piece of property with his retirement account funds and hires his son to work on the property—PROHIBITED
- Mary buys a home with her retirement account and her son makes repairs for free—PROHIBITED
- Beth owns an office building with her retirement account and hires her son to manage the property for a fee—PROHIBITED
- Jackie owns an apartment building with her retirement account funds and has her father manage the property for free—PROHIBITED

- Doug receives compensation from his retirement account for investment advice—PROHIBITED
- Matt acts as the real-estate agent for his retirement account—PROHIBITED

Indirect Prohibited Transactions

Indirect prohibited transactions inspire a lot of debate because the determination of whether a prohibited transaction occurred is largely based on the facts and circumstances.

Indirect prohibited transactions are transactions that may not violate any of the direct prohibited-transaction rules on their face, but still may be considered a prohibited transaction by the IRS. For example, when an individual uses a retirement to invest in a company in which he owns a 15 percent share, this would not seem to be a prohibited transaction because the individual IRA holder owns less than 50 percent of the entity, and the entity does not seem to be a disqualified person under IRC Section 4975. However, if the facts turned out that the company needed the funds to avoid bankruptcy, or the investment was made to secure a job within the company, the IRS could argue that the investment directly or indirectly helped the IRA holder personally.

Many tax professionals fail to focus on the indirect prohibited-transaction rules outlined in IRC Section 4975 and just focus on the direct prohibited-transaction rules. The IRS seems to be using the indirect prohibited-transaction rules as a tool for scrutinizing IRA transactions that seem to benefit the IRA holder but don't violate the direct prohibited-transaction rules under IRC Section 4975.

Subject to the exemptions under IRC Section 4975(d), an indirect prohibited transaction usually involves one of the following:

IRC Section 4975(c)(1)(D): The Direct or Indirect Transfer to a Disqualified Person of Income or Assets of a Retirement Account

- Ken is in a financial jam and takes $32,000 from his retirement account to pay a personal debt—PROHIBITED

- John uses his retirement account to purchase a rental property and hires his friend to manage the property. The friend then enters into a contract with John and transfers those funds back to John—PROHIBITED
- Melissa invests her retirement account funds in a real-estate fund and receives a salary for managing the fund—PROHIBITED
- Jim uses a house owned by his retirement account for personal use—PROHIBITED
- Seth deposits retirement account funds into his personal bank account—PROHIBITED
- Spencer buys precious metals using his retirement account funds and uses them for personal gain—PROHIBITED
- Bryan purchases a vacation home with his retirement account funds and stays in the home on occasion—PROHIBITED
- Elliot buys a cottage on the lake with her retirement account funds and rents it out to her daughter and son-in-law—PROHIBITED
- Allison purchases a condo on the beach using her retirement account and lets her son use it for free—PROHIBITED
- Kelly invests her retirement account funds in an investment fund and then receives a salary for managing the fund—PROHIBITED
- Larry uses his retirement account funds to purchase real estate and earns a commission as the real-estate agent on the sale—PROHIBITED
- Steve uses his retirement account funds to lend money to a company he owns and controls—PROHIBITED
- Gordon invests his retirement account funds into a business he owns 75 percent of and manages—PROHIBITED

Self-Dealing Prohibited Transactions

"Self-dealing" is a term for a situation that arises when someone benefits on both sides of a deal. According to IRC Section 4975(c)(1)(E), self-dealing, which is a form of indirect prohibited transaction, occurs when you directly or indirectly use the income or assets of your retirement account to further your own interests or benefit your own accounts.

IRC Section 4975(c)(1)(E): The Direct or Indirect Act by a Disqualified Person Who is a Fiduciary Whereby He/She Deals with Income or Assets of the Retirement Account in His/Her Own Interest or for His/Her Own Account

- Debra, who is a real-estate agent, uses her retirement account funds to buy a piece of property and earns a commission from the sale—PROHIBITED
- Ben wants to buy a piece of property for $120,000 and would like to own the property personally but does not have sufficient funds. As a result, Ben uses $110,000 from his retirement account and $10,000 personally to make the investment—PROHIBITED
- Nancy uses her retirement account to invest in a real-estate fund managed by her son, and Heidi's father receives a bonus for securing Nancy's investment—PROHIBITED
- Karen uses her retirement account to invest in a company she controls, which will benefit her personally—PROHIBITED
- Brett uses his retirement account funds to invest in a partnership in which he and his family will own greater than 50 percent of the partnership—PROHIBITED
- Pam uses her retirement account funds to invest in a business she and her husband own and operate, and she and her husband earn compensation from the business—PROHIBITED
- Rick uses his retirement account funds to lend money to a business he controls and manages—PROHIBITED
- Lance invests his retirement account funds in a trust from which he and his wife would gain personal benefit—PROHIBITED
- Helen uses her retirement account funds to invest in a real-estate fund managed by her son, who receives a bonus for securing her investment—PROHIBITED
- Stanley invests his retirement account funds into a real-estate project involving his development company in order to secure the contract—PROHIBITED

- Warren uses his retirement account funds to invest in his son's business, which is in financial trouble—PROHIBITED
- Alex uses his retirement account funds to buy a note on a piece of property for which he is the debtor—PROHIBITED

Real-Life Examples

One real-life example of a self-dealing prohibited transaction is *Rollins v. Commissioner, T.C. Memo 2004-60.* This is an important case in the self-directed IRA LLC context because it illustrates how one can engage in a prohibited transaction with an entity even if the entity is not a disqualified entity per se. The Rollins case also is important for examining whether a potential transaction could be considered an indirect prohibited transaction under IRC Section 4975.

The facts in *Rollins* are as follows: Mr. Rollins owned his own CPA firm. He was sole trustee of its 401(k) plan. Mr. Rollins caused his plan to lend funds to three companies in which he was the largest, but not the controlling, stockholder (9 percent to 33 percent). The companies had twenty-eight, seventy, and eighty other stockholders respectively. Mr. Rollins made the decision for the companies to borrow from his 401(k) plan. The loans were demand loans secured by each company's assets. The interest rate was market rate or higher. Mr. Rollins signed loan checks for his plan and signed notes for borrowers. All loans were repaid in full.

Mr. Rollins acknowledged that he is a disqualified person with regard to the plan because he owns Rollins, the CPA firm, but he contends that (1) none of the corporations that were the borrowers was a disqualified person, (2) none of the loans was a transaction between him and the plan, and (3) he "did not benefit from these loans, either in income or in his own account."

The tax court held that an IRC Section 4975(c)(1)(D) indirect prohibition did not require an actual transfer of money or property between the plan and the disqualified person. The fact that a disqualified person could have benefited as a result of the use of plan assets was sufficient. The tax court held that the transactions were used by Rollins, or for his benefit, and were assets of the plan. These assets of the plan were not transferred to Rollins. For each of those transactions, however, Rollins sat on both sides of the table: he made the decisions to lend the plan's funds, and he signed the promissory notes on behalf of the borrowers.

One of the more interesting parts of the Rollins case was the tax court's emphasis that as the taxpayer, the burden of proof as to whether an indirect prohibited transaction had occurred is the responsibility of the taxpayer. In other words, at its core, the Rollins case is a burden-of-proof case that illustrates the breadth of the application of IRC Section 4975(c)(1)(D) as well as the difficulty of meeting that burden of proof. Mr. Rollins was not a majority owner of any of the borrowers, but he was the largest shareholder for each company, and he signed the notes for each borrower.

Would the same decision have been made if Mr. Rollins was not the largest shareholder or had not, as the court put it, "sat on both sides of the table" (e.g., by not signing the notes on behalf of the borrowers)? It's not entirely clear if that would have influenced the court since it was still Mr. Rollins's burden (as the disqualified person) to prove that the transaction did not enhance or was not intended to enhance the value of his investments in the borrowers. That seems to be a very tough burden to meet. Moreover, as the court noted, the fact that a transaction is a good investment for the plan has nothing to do with the problem.

The lesson is that caution should be exercised whenever a disqualified person is sitting "on both sides of the table."

ERISA Advisory Opinion Letter 93-33A

In this advisory opinion, an IRA owner proposed to use his IRA to buy land and a building at a high school founded by his daughter and son-in-law and lease the property back to the school at either fair market rent or lower rent depending on the school's ability to pay. Presumably, this school was a nonprofit organization without stockholders.

The IRA owner, having discretion to invest the IRA's assets, was a fiduciary and a disqualified person. The IRA owner's daughter and son-in-law were the sole directors and officers of the school. As such, by virtue of IRC Section 4975(e)(2)(F), they also were disqualified persons. Consequently, the Department of Labor concluded that the proposed sale-and-leaseback transaction would constitute the use of IRA assets for the benefit of disqualified persons (i.e., the IRA owner's daughter and son-in-law) in violation of IRC Section 4975(c)(1)(D). It seemed that the major factor here was the arrangement to lease the property at a rent dependent on the school's ability to pay. In fact, the Department of Labor took the broad view that either IRC Section 4975(c)(1)(D) or (E) would be violated if a transaction were part of an agreement, arrangement, or understanding in which the fiduciary caused plan assets to be used in a manner designed to benefit any person in whom such fiduciary had an interest that would affect the exercise of his or her best judgment as a fiduciary.

Conflict-of-Interest Prohibited Transactions

According to IRC Section 4975(c)(i)(F), a prohibited transaction also occurs when a disqualified person is connected to a transaction involving the income or assets of the retirement account. This is called a conflict-of-interest prohibited transaction.

IRC Section 4975(c)(i)(F): Receipt of Any Consideration by a Disqualified Person Who is a Fiduciary for His/Her Own Account from Any Party Dealing with the retirement account in Connection with a Transaction Involving Income or Assets of the retirement account

- Jason uses his retirement account funds to loan money to a company that he manages and controls and also owns a small interest in—PROHIBITED
- Cathy uses her retirement account to lend money to a business that she works for in order to secure a promotion—PROHIBITED
- Eric uses his retirement account funds to invest in a fund that he manages, where his management fee is based on the total value of the fund's assets—PROHIBITED

"And here's a real-life example":

Technical Advice Memorandum 9118001
In this technical advice memorandum, the IRS concluded that loans made by a law firm's pension and profit-sharing plans to its clients to provide those clients with financial support while they awaited settlement on their lawsuits were prohibited transactions under IRC Sections 4975(c)(1)(D) and 4975(c)(1)(E) of the IRC.

The law firm's partners, who were fiduciaries with authority over plan assets, directed a bank, as the plan trustee, to lend clients money pending the outcome of their suits. The district office contended that this was a transaction prohibited by IRC Section 4975(c)(1)(D) since the partners of the law firm were acting as a lending institution and the law firm was indirectly using and benefiting from plan assets. The taxpayer disagreed and argued that the loans were made to clients from the plan assets solely to benefit plan participants, and that it is a common business practice in personal-injury law firms to advance funds to clients awaiting settlement.

The IRS determined that the loans were prohibited under IRC Section 4975(c)(1)(D) because the employer, who is a disqualified person under IRC Section 4975(e)(2)(C), benefited from the use of plan assets. As the IRS stated, the parties benefiting from the loans (i.e., the party whose business object is being served) were the partners in the law firm. It did not matter that the clients could have received loans elsewhere or that the loans were good investments, nor did it matter that it was common practice for law firms to advance funds to clients pending conclusion of their lawsuits. So long as a benefit is derived by a disqualified person through the use of a plan asset, a transaction is prohibited under IRC Section 4975(c)(1)(D).

In addition, the IRS found that the loans were also prohibited under IRC Section 4975(c)(1)(E). The partners of the law firm were fiduciaries since they exercised their authority with respect to the management of plan assets by directing the trustee (the bank) to enter into loans with their clients in conjunction with their legal representation. As such, the partners, in their capacity as plan administrators, dealt with the assets of the plan in their own interest.

STATUTORY EXEMPTIONS TO THE PROHIBITED-TRANSACTION RULES

Ken was doing a good job taking in all the information that John was giving him.

"There are a lot of situations to consider," Ken said.

"Yes," John said. "Like I said, the IRS doesn't tell you what you can do—only what you can't—and that understanding develops like any tax law."

"But the good thing is I don't need to be an expert and know everything since I am focused on just one category of transaction: using my retirement funds to buy a business," Ken said.

"Exactly. And here comes the good part and something that you will definitely find interesting. Congress has created several ways to grant exemptions from the very broad prohibited-transaction rules. This allows some wiggle room when it comes to navigating prohibited-transaction rules for certain specific circumstances."

"Oh," Ken said. "Tell me more."

"The most popular way for satisfying a prohibited-transaction exemption is the statutory exemption, because anyone who complies with the terms of the statute will be able to benefit from the exemption."

John continued to explain.

"In IRC Section 4975(d), Congress created certain statutory exemptions from the prohibited transactions outlined in IRC Section 4975(c). These exemptions were made because Congress believed there is a legitimate reason to permit them, as long as certain specified requirements are satisfied. In such situations, Congress has decided to issue blanket prohibited-transaction exemptions permitting certain type of transactions, as long as certain requirements prescribed in the statute are met.

"The most common prohibited-transaction exemption involves participant loans from a 401(k) plan, which unfortunately do not apply to IRAs. IRC Section 4975(d)(1) describes conditions under which loans are allowable. The other common statutory exemption can be found under IRC Section 4975(d)(13), and it covers the purchase of 'qualifying employer securities' with a 401(k) plan. We will spend a considerable amount of time on this topic because it is the basis for the most popular option for using retirement funds to buy a business—the rollover business start-up solution, or ROBS."

"OK, great," Ken said. "Now we are cooking."

"Yes," John agreed. "I don't want to get into the ROBS solution now, because I think there are several items we should cover first, but don't worry—we will be spending the majority of our future meetings on the ROBS solution."

PLAN ASSET RULES

"The first item should be the plan asset rules." John said.

"What are those?" Ken asked.

"The plan asset rules," John answered, "are a group of rules that work to extend the prohibited-transaction rules and certain ERISA fiduciary standards to certain types of investments. The plan asset rules are usually designed to apply 'look-through' rules to interests held by a retirement account in an investment fund, such as a hedge fund."

"Such as?"

"Let's assume that you have looked at all the prohibited-transaction rules under IRC Sections 4975 and 408. You feel pretty comfortable that your transaction would not be prohibited, but you are told there is another set of rules—the plan asset rules—that you may need to look at before being totally comfortable that the transaction would not violate the prohibited-transaction rules."

"Great," Ken said sarcastically.

"Better to know than be surprised," John said.

"Absolutely," Ken agreed.

"In late 1986," John continued, "the Department of Labor issued regulations relating to the definition of plan assets. The plan asset rules were developed in order to examine situations when a 401(k) plan or IRA was invested in a pass-through entity, such as an LLC or partnership. They were put in place to determine the assets of the plan for the purpose of applying the prohibited transaction and ERISA rules."

"How do they work?" Ken asked.

"The plan asset regulation describes circumstances in which there is a 'look-through,' which, if applicable, treats not only the interests in an investment fund owned by retirement accounts as 'plan assets' but also the assets of the investment fund. If the look-through applies, the retirement account fiduciary and prohibited transaction sections apply to parties dealing with the assets of the investment fund, such as the investment fund's investment manager."

"OK," Ken said.

"Under the plan asset rules, if the aggregate retirement account ownership of an entity is 25 percent or more of all the assets of the entity, then the equity interests and assets of the 'investment entity' are viewed as assets of the investing retirement account for the purposes of the prohibited transactions rules, unless an exception applies."

"Got it," Ken said.

"Also, if a retirement account or group of related qualified plans owns 100 percent of an 'operating company,' the operating company exception will not apply and the company's assets will still be treated as plan assets."

"I see," Ken said.

"So in summary," John continued, "the plan asset rules can be triggered if

- 100 percent of an operating company is owned by one or more retirement account and disqualified persons, in which case all the assets of the operating company are deemed plan assets (assets of the retirement account); or
- if 25 percent or more of an investment company is owned by IRAs/401(k) plans and disqualified persons, in which case all the assets of the investment company are deemed plan assets (assets of the IRA/401(k)).

"In determining whether the 25 percent threshold is met," John continued, "all IRA and 401(k) owners are considered, even if they are owned by unrelated individuals."

"So why do we care about the plan asset rules?" Ken asked. "What's the big deal if I want to use retirement funds to buy a business?"

"The big deal is that if we structured an investment where the operating business was owned 100 percent by retirement accounts, the plan asset rules could technically trigger a prohibited transaction even if the transaction satisfied the rules under IRC Section 4975. This is an important rule that can trip up many people looking to use an entity owned 100 percent by a retirement account, especially if the entity is an LLC. We will soon discuss a case that deals with the situation where an individual used an entity wholly owned by an IRA to purchase a business and the tax court held that he engaged in a prohibited transaction. We will also learn that using retirement funds to invest in a business in which a disqualified person will be actively involved will need to satisfy the prohibited-transaction exemption under IRC Section 4975(d)(13). Without an exemption, using an IRA or an LLC in such a transaction will likely trigger the prohibited transaction, as well as potentially triggering plan asset rules."

"OK, I'm eager to learn more about this. I'm happy you went through the difference between an IRA and 401(k) plan and an LLC and corporation. It will definitely make understanding the difference between a self-directed IRA and ROBS much easier."

EXCEPTIONS TO THE PLAN ASSET REGULATIONS

"Are there exceptions?" Ken asked.

"Yes," John said. "One very important one in your case, since you will be starting an operating business. The plan asset look-through rules do not apply if the entity is an operating company or the partnership interests or membership interests are publicly offered or registered under the Investment Company Act of 1940 (e.g., Real estate investment trust). They also do not apply if the entity is an operating company, which refers to a partnership or LLC that is primarily engaged in real-estate development, venture capital, or companies making or providing goods and services, such as a gas station, unless the operating company is owned 100 percent by a plan."

"Can you explain that a little more?" Ken said.

"In other words, if an IRA or 401(k) plan owns less than 100 percent of an entity that is engaged in an active trade or business, such as a restaurant or manufacturing plant, the plan asset rules would not apply. However, the IRA or 401(k) plan investment may still be treated as a prohibited transaction under IRC Section 4975."

"I see," Ken said.

"In addition," John continued, "the unrelated business taxable income (UBTI) rules, which we will go through in detail shortly, may apply to the IRA or 401(k) plan investing in an LLC or other pass-through entity engaged in an active trade or business, subjecting it to tax on the income or gains generated from the operating business."

"How can the plan asset rules impact my business investments?" Ken asked.

"The plan asset rules are typically triggered only if your IRA/401(k) plan assets will own 100 percent of an operating company, such as a franchise."

Consequences of a Transaction Falling under the Plan Asset Rules

"So what happens if a transaction falls under the plan asset rules?" Ken asked.

"The plan asset rules typically impact investment funds," John said, "such as hedge funds, private equity funds, real-estate funds, or private equity funds. The impact of the plan asset rules are not as significant for individual retirement account investors because the prohibited-transaction rules under IRC Section 4975 will likely catch any transaction that would be subject to the plan asset rules. However, in the case of a hedge fund, if the fund invested in an entity whose assets are considered plan assets, the manager of the entity would be a plan fiduciary to the extent it exercises any authority or control respecting management or disposition of the entity's assets or provides investment advice for a fee. Any manager that is considered a plan fiduciary would be required to comply with ERISA's pro-hibited transaction provisions and could run afoul of those rules, creating an unintended prohibited transaction. Parties to a prohibited transaction can be subject to penalties under ERISA and excise taxes under the IRC."

"OK," Ken said. "What then?"

"Then all assets of the entity," John continued, "are deemed owned by the retirement account, and all transactions between the investment entity or its assets and a disqualified person may be prohibited. It is important to remember that the fact that a transaction does not trigger the plan asset rules does not mean that the transaction may not be deemed a prohibited transaction under IRC Section 4975. In other words, a transaction that does not fall under the plan asset rules can still be treated as a prohibited transaction."

"How about another example to show me the scope of the plan asset rules?" Ken asked.

"Sure, no problem. Let's assume Jane's IRA owns 65 percent of ABC, LLC, which is an investment fund company. ABC, LLC makes a loan to Jane. The loan is subject to the plan asset rules and will be considered a prohibited transaction pursuant to IRC Section 4975. Note that any income generated by ABC, LLC that is allocated to the IRA would also likely be subject to the unrelated business income tax."

"So," Ken said, "failing the plan asset rules could create potentially trig-ger some unexpected prohibited-transaction rule exposure and could cause some unexpected tax implications."

"Absolutely," John agreed. "But remember, since you will be buying a franchise, which is categorized as an operating company, as long as retire-ment funds do not own 100 percent of the entity you will not have to worry about the plan asset rules. That being said, the prohibited-transac-tion rules under IRC Section 4975 would still apply unless an exception applies under IRC Section 4975(d). We will soon learn more about one very important exception for people looking to use retirement funds to buy a business: the IRC Section 4975(d)(13) exception for purchasing 'qualify-ing employer securities' or ROBS. Now that you have some understanding of how the plan asset rules work and how they can potentially trigger the

IRS prohibited-transaction rules, let's briefly look at some other disqualified transactions using retirement funds."

"Sounds good," Ken said.

OTHER PROHIBITED ASSETS

"There are a number of other investments," John continued, "that are not permitted. These investments do not fall under the prohibited-transaction rules under IRC Section 4975, but are outlined under IRC Section 408. I talked about those in detail already. But just to review, a retirement account cannot purchase collectibles such as

- any work of art,
- any metal or gem,
- any alcoholic beverage,
- any rug or antique,
- any stamp, and
- most coins.

"In addition, an IRA is not permitted to purchase life insurance contracts, but a 401(k) plan is permitted." John said.

"Right," Ken said, "I remember being surprised by that."

"Well," John explained, "the basic reason these types of assets are prohibited from being purchased with retirement funds is that they are usually hard to value and difficult to sell."

"Makes sense," Ken said.

S AND C CORPORATION INVESTMENTS

"In addition to the IRS prohibited-transaction rules outlined in IRC Section 4975," John continued, "a retirement account is not permitted to own stock in an S corporation."

"Why is that again?" Ken asked.

"Because of the shareholder restrictions imposed on S corporations," John answered. "S corporations are C corporations that elect to pass corporate income, losses, deductions, and credits through to their share-holders for federal tax purposes. To qualify for S corporation status, the corporation must meet the following requirements":

- It must be a domestic corporation.
- It may have only allowable shareholders, including individuals, certain trusts, and estates.
- It may not include partnerships, corporations, or nonresident alien shareholders.
- It may have no more than one hundred shareholders.
- It may have only one class of stock.

"Because a retirement account is considered a trust for federal income tax purposes," John said, "which is not treated as a permitted shareholder for an S corporation, allowing a self-directed IRA or 401(k) plan to become a shareholder would violate the S corporation rules and cause the S election to be invalid, making the entity a C corporation again for tax purposes."

"But a retirement account can own stock in a C corporation, right?" Ken asked.

"That's right. Millions of retirement accounts own Apple and IBM stock, which are C corporations. In addition, we will soon see that using a C corporation is one of the requirements of the ROBS solution."

"OK," Ken said, "I understand I can't engage in four categories of transactions with my retirement account":

1. collectibles, with a special carve-out for precious metals and IRS-approved coins,
2. life insurance contracts if I am using an IRA,
3. S corporation stock, and
4. any transaction that directly or indirectly benefits me or any other disqualified person—the IRC Section 4975 prohibited transactions.

"You got it," John said.

"I was just wondering something," Ken said. "Who determines whether I've engaged in a prohibited transaction?"

"That's actually a good question," John said. "Through an arrangement between the IRS and the Department of Labor (DOL), it's the DOL's responsibility to determine whether a specific transaction is a prohibited transaction and to issue prohibited-transaction exemptions. When the IRS discovers what appears to be a prohibited transaction in an individual's IRA, it turns the matter over to the DOL to make the determination. The DOL reviews the situation and responds to the IRS, which in turn responds to the taxpayer. If the IRA grantor wants to apply for a prohibited-transaction exemption, he or she must apply to the DOL."

"So does the DOL issue the exemptions?" Ken asked.

"It does have that authority," John said. "What's known as 'prohibitive transaction class exemptions,' or PTCEs, are available for anyone, while another class of exemptions, called 'individual prohibited-transaction exemptions,' or PTEs, are issued only to the applicant."

PENALTIES FOR ENGAGING IN A PROHIBITED TRANSACTION

"This makes sense to me," Ken said, "but I was wondering what the penalties are if someone does engage in an IRS prohibited transaction?"

"As you can imagine," John said, "the penalties are quite steep. The IRS needs to make them painful in order to protect the distribution taxation rules, which are a big revenue source for the government."

"I get it," Ken said.

"In general," John continued, "the penalty under IRC Section 4975 starts at 15 percent for most type of retirement plans."

"Wow," Ken said, "that is harsh."

"Actually," John said, "it's even harsher for IRAs. If the IRA holder/owner or IRA beneficiary engaged in a transaction that violated the prohibited-transaction rules set forth under IRC Section 4975, the individual's IRA would lose its tax exempt status, and the entire fair market value of the IRA would be treated as taxable distribution, subject to ordinary income tax. In addition, the IRA holder or beneficiary would be subject to a minimum penalty of 15 percent as well as a 10 percent early distribution penalty if the IRA holder or beneficiary is under the age of fifty-nine and a half."

"Holy smokes," Ken said.

"Yeah," John said. "Although the penalty for engaging in a prohibited transaction generally starts out at 15 percent for most types of retirement plans, the penalty is more severe for IRAs. The initial tax on a prohibited transaction is 15 percent of the amount involved for each year (or part of a year) in the taxable period. If the transaction is not corrected within the taxable period, an additional tax of 100 percent of the amount involved is imposed. Both taxes are payable by any disqualified person who participated in the transaction, other than a fiduciary acting only as such. If more than one person takes part in the transaction, each person can be jointly and severally liable for the entire tax. According to IRC Section 408(e), when an IRA is involved in a transaction that is prohibited under IRC Section 4975, the IRA loses its tax-exempt status, and the IRA holder is treated as receiving a distribution on the first day of the tax year in which the prohibited transaction occurred. The distribution amount that the IRA holder is deemed to have received is equal to the fair market value of the IRA as of the first day of such tax year. In other words, the entire IRA is blown up and no longer treated as an IRA as of the first day of the taxable year in which the prohibited transaction occurred."

"I want to avoid that," Ken said. "Can you give me some examples?"

"Sure," John said. "Let's say Jim, who is fifty-two, decides to borrow $25,000 from his traditional IRA for personal use on May 15 of year X. Jim's IRA account has a value of $100,000 on January 1 of year X. The Department of Labor reviews the transaction and holds that Jim engaged in a prohibited transaction. Jim's IRA would be deemed immediately disqualified as of January 1 of the year in which the prohibited transaction occurred (year X), resulting in current income tax treatment (ordinary income tax) and an excise tax penalty of 10 percent for a premature withdrawal from an IRA based on the fair market value of Jim's IRA on January 1 of year X—$100,000."

"Poor Jim," Ken said.

"X was not a good year for him," John agreed. "So let's say Jim used his IRA to invest in collectibles or life insurance, a prohibited transaction under IRC Section 408, not IRC Section 4975. In that case, only the assets used to purchase the investment would be considered distributed for purposes of imposing ordinary income tax or an excise tax penalty, not the entire IRA as it would have been in the case of a prohibited transaction under IRC Section 4975. Therefore, assuming the same facts as the first example, if Jim purchased antiques for $25,000 instead of making a loan with his IRA, Jim's IRA would be deemed immediately disqualified as of January 1 of the year in which the prohibited transaction occurred (year X), resulting in current income tax treatment (ordinary income tax) and an excise tax penalty of 10 percent for a premature withdrawal from an IRA in the amount of $25,000—the cost of the antiques."

"Still hurts," Ken said.

"Yes, and the pain is spread around," John said. "For the disqualified person involved in the transaction, the initial tax on a prohibited transaction is 15 percent of the amount involved for every year, or portion thereof, in the 'taxable period,' which is the period beginning when the transaction occurred and ending on the date of the earliest of either (1) the mailing of a notice of deficiency for the tax, (2) assessment of the tax, or (3) correction of the transaction. The 15 percent excise tax is followed by an additional tax of 100 percent if the disqualified person is recalcitrant."

"Ouch," Ken said.

"One more thing, if you engage in a prohibited transaction with an IRA, the entire IRA account is blown up, for lack of a better word, and the entire IRA is treated as being distributed as of January 1 of the year the prohibited transaction occurred, whereas, for a 401(k) plan, only the particular prohibited transaction is subject to tax and penalty, not the entire plans assets. Also, the plan is not terminated." John said.

"The good thing when it comes to prohibited transaction penalties," John added, "is that they are easily avoidable."

"Basically," Ken said, "just don't engage in a prohibited transaction and you have nothing to worry about."

"Exactly," John said. "For most retirement investors who will be investing in stocks and other traditional financial products, there is really not much to worry about when it comes to a prohibited transaction. The likelihood of engaging in a prohibited transaction in such circumstance is almost impossible, especially if you are buying stocks, mutual funds, and ETFs from a major financial institution. But for an investor looking to use retirement funds to make nontraditional investments, such as real estate or a private business investment, you really need to make yourself aware of the prohibited-transaction rules because of the harsh penalties."

"I get it," Ken said. "Investor beware."

"It's critical to understand what you can't do when it comes to the IRS," John said. "We need this information in advance of making important decisions about how we will invest or allocate our retirement assets. But I think it's time we start talking about the options available for using retirement funds to buy or finance a personal business or franchise."

"I can't wait," Ken said.

Available Options for Using Retirement Funds to Buy or Finance a Business

Ken was excited about meeting John again because they were finally going to discuss options for using retirement funds to buy a business. Ken appreciated the time John had spent with him up to now, but he was ready to focus on the possibility of using his retirement funds to invest in the water franchise.

Ken arrived early and, as always, ordered two cappuccinos and two scones and sat down at their usual table. John arrived a few minutes later and sat down. They spent a few minutes catching up and then were ready to get started.

"Ken, I know you have been eagerly awaiting today's chat, so let's get right to it." John said.

"We previously went over the different ways one can personally finance a business venture—using personal cash, getting a loan, partnering up with friends and family, or taking a taxable distribution." John said.

"Now let's spend some time going through the three primary ways for using retirement funds to fund a business." John said. "We briefly touched on the three options earlier on, but here they are again."

1. the self-directed IRA
2. the 401(k) plan loan feature
3. ROBS

"Let's start with the self-directed IRA because even though I included it as a business-funding option, it is usually not available for someone wishing to invest in their own business," John said.

1. SELF-DIRECTED IRA

As you know," John said, "a self-directed IRA is an IRA structure that allows the IRA holder—you—to have more control over your retirement funds. A self-directed IRA is not a new type of IRA. It is simply the vehicle that allows you to make traditional as well as alternative-asset investments with your IRA funds."

"Right," Ken said. "But there are different kinds."

"Yes," John said. "But before we get into the different types of self-directed IRA, let's talk about what it is.

"A self-directed IRA offers the ability to use retirement funds to make almost any type of investment on one's own without the consent of any IRA custodian or person. The IRS only describes the type of investments that are prohibited, which we spoke about last time, and which are very few.

"The following are some examples of investments that can be made with your self-directed IRA":

- residential or commercial real estate
- domestic or foreign real estate
- raw land
- foreclosure property
- mortgages
- mortgage pools
- deeds
- private loans
- tax liens
- private businesses
- limited liability companies
- limited liability partnerships
- private placements

- precious metals and certain coins
- stocks, bonds, mutual funds
- foreign currencies

"Using a self-directed IRA LLC to make investments offers the investor the ability to make traditional as well as nontraditional investments, such as real estate, in a tax-efficient manner."

"OK, so if you want to make alternative-asset investments, such as real estate and precious metals, you would use a self-directed IRA?" Ken asked.

"Yes, that is correct. Some 401(k) plans also offer alternative-asset investment options, but the self-directed IRA is definitely the most popular way of making alternative-asset investments with retirement funds, since not everyone owns a business, which is needed to adopt a 401(k) plan." John said.

"I remember we spent a lot of time discussing the advantages of tax deferral and investment diversification, but is that the main reasons most people establish self-directed IRAs?" Ken asked.

"Yes. Clearly, tax deferral is the main reason people would use a self-directed IRA to make investments. We spent a good amount of time on this, so I don't think we need to review again, but there are a number of other reasons using a self-directed IRA to make retirement investments has become so popular."

1. Diversification

   Most Americans have an enormous amount of exposure to the financial markets. Whether it is through retirement investments, such as IRAs or 401(k) plans, or personal savings, many of us have most of our savings connected in some way to the stock market. In fact, over 90 percent of retirement assets are invested in the financial markets. With close to $20 trillion in retirement assets as of 2013, you can see the scope of that exposure. Investing in nontraditional assets such as real estate offers a form of investment diversification from the equity markets. In general, the belief is that the more diversified your retirement investment portfolio is, the greater chance that your asset movements will be subject to a lower correlation, meaning they are less likely to move in the same direction. However, diversification does not ensure profit, protect against loss, or guarantee success. However, history still suggests that stocks are a solid investment over the long term. For example, according to historical records, the average annual return for the S&P 500 from its inception in 1928 through 2014 is approximately 10 percent. However, that number can be very misleading. Accurate calculations of average returns—taking all significant factors into account—can be challenging. For example, according to the S&P/Case-Shiller Twenty-City Composite Home Price Index—which measures the value of residential real estate in twenty major US metropolitan areas—as of 2015, the ten-year average return was 0.8 percent, but was 7.06 percent over the last three years. Overall, the belief is that the use of nontraditional asset classes can help protect your portfolio when the market is down and help protect you from losing more than the market.

2. Invest in Something You Understand

Many Americans became frustrated with the equity markets after the 2008 financial crisis. Thankfully, we have seen financial markets rebound since then and have even seem some years of over 20 percent growth in the equity markets. Nevertheless, many Americans are still somewhat shell-shocked from the market swings and not 100 percent sure what exactly goes on in Wall Street. Real estate, for comparison, is often a more comfortable investment for the lower and middle classes because they grew up exposed to it, whereas the upper classes often learned about Wall Street and other securities during their younger years and college days. Everyone has heard someone talk about the importance of owning a home or the amount of money that can be made by owning real estate. From Donald Trump to reality TV, real estate is fast becoming mainstream and one of the most trusted asset classes for Americans. It is, of course, not without risk, but many retirement investors feel more comfortable understanding the real-estate market and buying and selling real estate than they do stocks.

3. Inflation Protection
Rising food and energy prices, coupled with high federal-debt levels and low interest rates, have recently fueled new inflationary fears. As a result, some investors may be looking for ways to protect their portfolios from the ravages of inflation. It is a matter of guesswork to estimate whether these inflation risks are real, but for some retirement investors, protecting retirement assets from inflation is a big concern. Inflation can have a nasty impact on a retirement portfolio because it means that a dollar today may not be worth a dollar tomorrow. Inflation also increases the cost of things that are necessary for humans to live and enjoy life, such as food, gas, shelter, clothing, medical services, and so on, decreasing the value of money so that goods and services cost more. For example, if someone had an IRA worth $250,000 at a time of high inflation, that $250,000 will be worth significantly less or have significantly less buying power. This can mean the difference between retiring and working the rest of your life. Buying hard assets is seen as one way of protecting your assets against inflation. Many investors have long recognized that investing in commercial real estate or precious metals can provide a natural protection against inflation, as rents tend to increase when prices do, acting as a hedge against inflation.

4. Hard Assets
Many nontraditional assets, such as real estate and precious metals, are tangible hard assets that you can see and touch. With real estate, for example, you can drive by with your family, point out the window, and say, "I own that." For some, that's important psychologically, especially in times of financial instability, inflation, or political or global upheaval.

"Thanks so much. That is really helpful," Ken said.

"OK, so now that we have reviewed what a self-directed IRA is and why one would use it to make retirement account investments, let's talk about the three different types of self-directed IRAs one can establish," John said.

"There are essentially three types of self-directed IRAs. There is no right answer as to which type of self-directed IRA you should establish. Even though the self-directed IRA may not prove to be a good option for investing in your business, it is worth understanding because it may be an option for other types of retirement account investments down the road, such as real estate, precious metals, or investing in a friend's business. Just bear with me for a little bit, and I think you will be happy you did."

1. Financial Institution-Offered Self-Directed IRA

"The most popular self-directed IRA account offered is the financial institution self-directed IRA," John said.

"Let me guess why it's popular," Ken said. "The banks are pushing it."

"Correct," John said with a smile. "It's typically offered by the major financial institutions, such as Bank of America, Wells Fargo, Fidelity, Vanguard, and so on. With this type of self-directed IRA, the IRA holder is usually only able to make IRA investments offered by the financial institution, such as stock, mutual funds, and ETFs. Even though these types of IRA accounts are called "self-directed IRA" accounts, they are limited in their investment scope and don't allow IRA investors to make any nontraditional investments, such as real estate."

"How do the financial institutions get away with limiting the investment options available?" Ken asked.

"A financial institution that offers IRA accounts is not required to offer its IRA investors the opportunity to make all allowable types of IRA investments. For example, even though real estate is an IRS-approved investment, an IRA custodian is not required or obligated to offer that investment option. That's why most financial institutions offering IRA accounts will restrict the IRA investment option to financial products they already offer. They don't earn anything when they allow their clients to pull money out of the IRA account to buy real estate from a third party."

"Got it," Ken said.

2. Custodian-Controlled Self-Directed IRA

"On the other hand," John said, "a custodian-controlled self-directed IRA offers an IRA investor more investment options than a financial institution self-directed IRA."

"Hold on a second, John," Ken said. "Can you explain this concept of IRA custodian in greater detail?"

"Sure," John said. "With a custodian-controlled self-directed IRA, a special nonbank trust company will serve as the custodian of the IRA. In most cases, these special nonbank custodians are established in South Dakota because of the more lenient capital requirements."

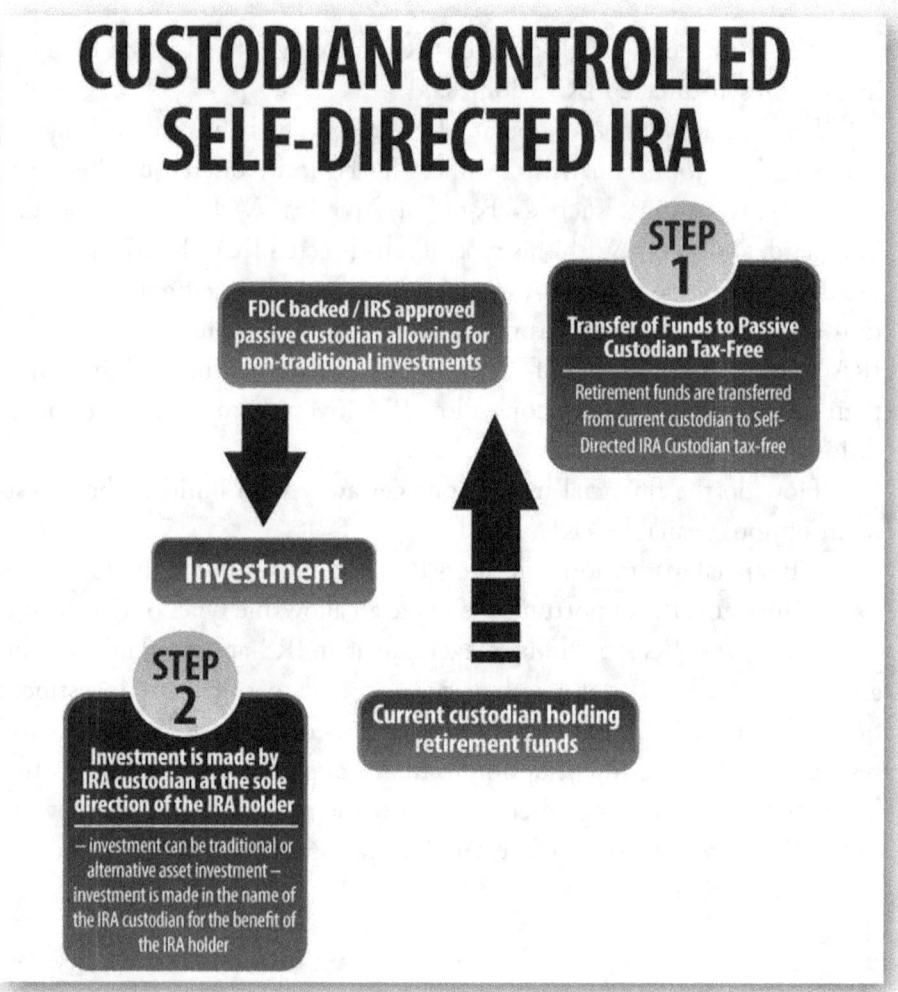

CUSTODIAN CONTROLLED SELF-DIRECTED IRA

STEP 1

FDIC backed / IRS approved passive custodian allowing for non-traditional investments

Transfer of Funds to Passive Custodian Tax-Free

Retirement funds are transferred from current custodian to Self-Directed IRA Custodian tax-free

Investment

STEP 2

Investment is made by IRA custodian at the sole direction of the IRA holder

— investment can be traditional or alternative asset investment — investment is made in the name of the IRA custodian for the benefit of the IRA holder

Current custodian holding retirement funds

"In South Dakota? Sounds like the wild west."

"Not at all. It's very controlled and regulated. In fact, these IRA custodians are governed by the South Dakota trust laws and are permitted to establish IRA accounts per the IRC. Since the majority of IRA custodians are nonbank custodians, the IRA account funds are deposited in an omnibus custodial account at an FDIC-insured bank or financial institution that the trust company administers."

"You mean the funds are not held by the custodian directly?"

"That's right. The majority of IRA trust companies do not actually touch the IRA funds; they simply provide all required IRA administration. The IRA funds are deposited in an FDIC-insured bank or financial institution that the IRA custodian controls and will then invest at the client's sole direction."

"Do they do anything else for you other than administration?"

"Unlike a traditional financial institution like Vanguard or Schwab," John said, "the majority of custodians that offer self-directed IRAs for alternative-asset investments don't provide investment advice or sell or market financial products. They make their money by opening and administering self-directed IRA accounts. Usually, they charge annual and transaction account fees. In some cases, fees are based on your account value as well."

"Here's my worry. I've never heard of the majority of these custodians. How can I be sure that they won't just steal my IRA funds?"

"Great question," John said. "The whole idea around the self-directed IRA is that the custodian will only make investments at the direction of the IRA holder. The IRA custodian is not considered a fiduciary to the self-directed IRA since it does not offer any investment advice or have control over the investment decisions you make for the account. The IRA custodian can move the IRA assets only at the behest of the IRA holder. And remember, IRA funds deposited in an FDIC-insured account are protected and guaranteed by the government up to $250,000 until you withdraw them. On top of everything else, almost all IRA custodians carry two types of insurance policies to cover any theft or fraud: an errors and omission insurance policy and a crime insurance policy."

Ken grinned.

"The errors and omission insurance policy is kept in the event of errors that may occur with processing any given transaction where funds are lost and are not able to be recovered. The errors and omission policy provides coverage of up to $1 million. The crime insurance policy is kept in the event of a malicious or deliberate removal of funds from our investors' account(s). This policy also provides coverage of up to $1 million."

"OK," Ken said, "I feel much better about using a special IRS custodian to make self-directed IRA investments when I know my money is so protected. The big question I have then is do I want to use a custodian-controlled self-directed IRA or a checkbook control self-directed IRA LLC?"

John nodded. "That's a very important decision that depends on several factors."

He took out his pen and drew a few lines on the notepad.

"The first question you need to answer," John continued, "is what type of investment will you be making? You might make a different decision about the type of self-directed IRA structure you should develop depending on whether you invest in real estate or do a one-off private equity investment. Also, the amount of retirement funds you'll be using matters since IRA-custodian fees are an important consideration. And there's also the frequency and number of investments you'll be doing with your self-directed IRA account."

"Well, in my case," Ken said, "If I don't use my retirement funds to buy a business and can get access to my retirement funds, I could see myself using about $105,000 of my $135,000 retirement fund to buy real estate and possibly make some hard-money loans. So maybe I'll buy one home and do one to two hard-money loans. I'd like the loans to be short term—under eighteen months—and I'd like to continue making more loans as each comes due. For the real estate, I envision holding the home for about a year while renting it out, then selling it and looking to buy one or two more homes with that money. I really hope to buy the home straight out in cash, without any leverage."

"Great," John said. "So you'll be doing multiple transactions from your self-directed IRA. Let me ask you a question though. How important is limited liability protection to you?"

Ken sat back. "I know we spent a lot of time discussing LLCs so I am pretty comfortable with this concept. I would guess an LLC would be really helpful for buying real estate, but if my IRA was buying an interest in an LLC or corporation or doing a long-term investment, I am not sure I would need to use an LLC."

"I think that makes a lot of sense, and assuming the fees were reasonable, I would agree that a custodian-controlled self-directed IRA would make a lot of sense for a one-time investment into a business entity or long-term hold investment." John said.

3. The Self-Directed IRA LLC

"OK, before we get into fees, let me give you a little background on the self-directed IRA LLC, also known as the checkbook control IRA or checkbook IRA."

In the 1996 case of *Swanson v. Commissioner*, 106 T. C. 76 (1996), the tax court gave its blessing to a new type of self-directed IRA structure—the self-directed IRA with checkbook control, or simply "checkbook IRA"— that is much simpler than investing through a regular custodian-controlled self-directed IRA account.

With a checkbook control self-directed IRA, you (the IRA holder) will have total control over your IRA funds, and you will no longer have to get each investment approved by the custodian of your account like in a custodian-controlled self-directed IRA. Instead, all IRA LLC decisions are truly yours. When you find an investment that you want to make with your IRA funds, as manager of the LLC you simply write a check or wire the funds straight from your self-directed IRA LLC bank account to make the investment.

Under the checkbook IRA format, the IRA is set up with a passive IRA custodian. The self-directed IRA account is then typically funded either by retirement funds rolled over or transferred from a current retirement account or via direct contribution. Then, an LLC is created in which your new IRA, care of the IRA custodian, purchases all the membership units/ interests. Now the IRA funds are in an account in the name of the LLC at a local bank or credit union. When you find an investment that you want to make with your IRA funds, as manager of the LLC you simply write a check or wire the funds straight from your self-directed IRA LLC bank account to make the investment. The self-directed IRA allows you to eliminate the delays associated with an IRA custodian, enabling you to act quickly when the right investment opportunity presents itself.

"Ken, I have put together the following diagram that I think will help you better understand how the checkbook control self-directed IRA LLC works."

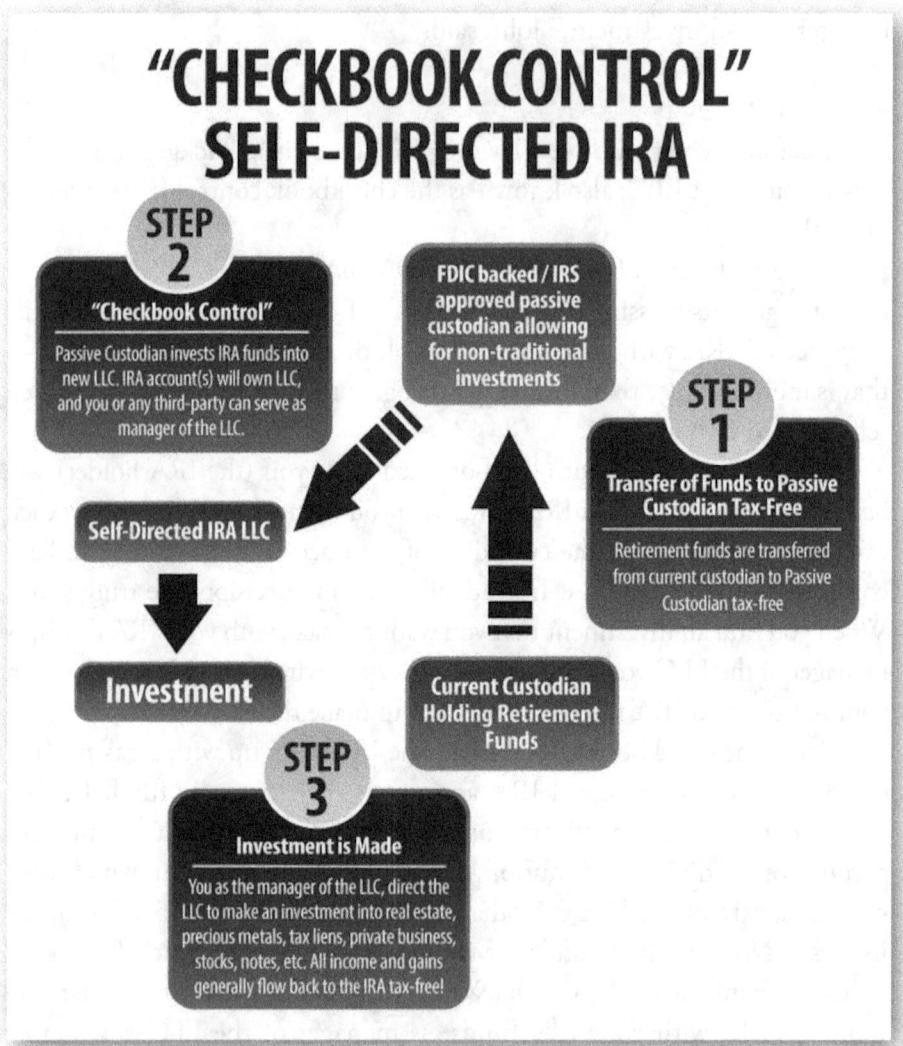

John handed Ken a document that highlighted some of the main differences between the checkbook control self-directed IRA LLC and the custodian-controlled self-directed IRA.

MAIN DIFFERENCES BETWEEN CUSTODIAN-CONTROLLED IRA AND CHECKBOOK CONTROL IRA LLC

Checkbook Control

With a self-directed IRA LLC, you have even more advantages than using a custodian-controlled IRA, including what's called "checkbook control." As manager of the self-directed IRA LLC you will have the ability to make IRA investments without seeking the consent of a custodian. Instead, all decisions are truly yours.

Access

With a self-directed IRA LLC, you will have direct access to your IRA funds, allowing you to make an investment quickly and efficiently. There is no need to obtain approvals from your IRA custodian or deal with time delays in waiting for the custodian to execute all investment documentation. Your IRA funds will be held at a local bank instead of at a custodian you have never worked with before.

Speed

With a self-directed IRA LLC and as manager of the LLC, when you find an investment that you want to make with your IRA funds, simply write a check or wire the funds straight from your self-directed IRA LLC bank account to make the investment. The self-directed IRA LLC allows you to eliminate the delays associated with a custodian-controlled self-directed IRA account, enabling you to act quickly when the right investment opportunity presents itself.

Lower Fees

Another advantage to a self-directed IRA LLC account is that over the long term you will save money on IRA-custodian fees compared to fees for a custodian-controlled IRA. With the checkbook control self-directed IRA LLC structure, you will not be required to seek IRA-custodian consent when making IRA investments, allowing you to eliminate IRA custodian-related transaction fees and account-valuation fees associated with a custodian-controlled self-directed IRA. With a self-directed IRA LLC with checkbook control, in general, you no longer have to pay either transaction fees or custodian fees based on IRA account value.

"Can I just stop you for one minute?" Ken asked John. "Can you elaborate on the fees in a bit more detail?"

"No problem," John said. "In general, if you will be investing between $100,000 and $199,000 of IRA funds initially, the average full-service IRA custodian fee will be between $400 and $699 depending on the custodian. These fees might be higher if you are doing multiple investments. If your self-directed IRA account gained in value and went above $200,000, then the average full-service self-directed IRA custodian fee would be between $500 and $850 a year. Again, these fees would probably increase depending on the custodian you choose and whether you do multiple investments. All fees are taken from your IRA account."

"Why am I paying so much if the account is self-directed?" Ken asked. "After all, I'm the one directing the custodian to make the investment, and the custodian doesn't provide any investment advice or even serve as fiduciary of my IRA account."

"Right," John said. "But the fees your IRA pays allow the IRA custodian to properly establish your account, maintain it, direct your investments, and administer the account. For example, if you directed the IRA custodian to make a real-estate investment on behalf of your IRA, the IRA custodian needs to review and sign all real-estate transaction documents. The custodian will then need to process your investment direction and send the funds to the appropriate place to purchase the real estate. On an annual basis, the IRA custodian will then be required to complete and file the IRS Form 5498—IRA Contribution Information—which provides the IRS with updated valuation information on your IRA. In addition, the IRA custodian will be required to report to the IRS all IRA contributions, distributions, and any Roth IRA conversions made during the year. That's why, even if you will be the one selecting investments and directing the custodian to make them, the IRA custodian will be somewhat involved in the establishment of the self-directed IRA account, the self-directed IRA transaction process, and the annual administration of the account. So in reality, if you have $200,000 in your self-directed IRA and elect to use the custodian to make the self-directed IRA investment, you would be paying approximately 0.5 percent of your account value each year in fees. That may or may not seem fair to you, but that is usually what the cost will be to make self-directed IRA investments through a custodian."

"OK. What about the checkbook control self-directed IRA LLC structure?" Ken asked.

"Right," John said. "As you may recall, with a checkbook control self-directed IRA LLC structure, the IRA investment activity is happening at the LLC level and not at the IRA-custodian level. For example, once your IRA funds have been transferred to the IRA custodian, that IRA custodian would then invest the funds into an LLC in return for a 100 percent interest in the LLC. Procedurally the funds are then sent from the custodian to the LLC bank account where the manager of the IRA LLC has control over the LLC assets. From the local LLC bank account, the IRA manager—typically the IRA holder—can make the investment by check or wire transfer. Because all the investment activity is happening at the LLC level and not the IRA-custodian level, overall, the fee for using an IRA custodian for a checkbook control self-directed IRA LLC is typically less expensive than for a custodian-controlled self-directed IRA. The reason is quite simple: the checkbook control IRA custodian does less work. Once the IRA funds have been invested in the LLC in return for ownership in the LLC, all investment activity happens at the LLC level. In other words, the IRA holder does not need to go through the IRA custodian to complete the IRA LLC investment. As manager of the LLC, the IRA holder can simply make the investment by check or wire straight from the IRA LLC bank account. The IRA custodian is not required to approve the investment and is not involved in any facet of the transaction, including the preparation and execution of any of the investment documentation or the funding of the transaction. The majority of IRA custodians in the market that work with checkbook control self-directed IRA LLC accounts charge a flat fee that is not based on account value of transactions. The average IRA-custodian fee for the first year for establishing a checkbook control self-directed IRA LLC is usually between $199 and $250, and after year one the fee typically drops to an average of between $135 and $199. The initial fee is typically a little higher because of the need to establish the self-directed IRA account, which is a one-time event."

"That sounds a lot more 'self-directed,'" Ken said.

"Yes," John agreed.

"What kind of costs can I expect with a checkbook control self-directed IRA?" Ken asked.

"Depending on the state where the LLC is formed and the IRA custodian you choose, the cost can vary between $1,000 and $1,500, with annual fees anywhere from $150 to $250," John said. "The checkbook control self-directed IRA has a higher up-front establishment fee than a custodian-directed self-directed IRA, but because checkbook IRA LLC annual IRA-custodian fees are usually lower than with a custodian-directed self-directed IRA, the checkbook control self-directed IRA LLC ends up being a little less costly over the years," John said. "The fees are important, but for real-estate investors the checkbook control usually offers a number of attractive features that make it appealing, such as the ability to make investments quickly and easily without needing to involve the IRA custodian."

"OK, thanks. Sorry for the interruption," Ken said.

"No problem, let's move on to the next advantage of using a self-directed IRA LLC," John said.

Limited Liability Protection

By using a self-directed IRA LLC with checkbook control, your IRA will benefit from the limited liability protection afforded by using an LLC. By using an LLC, all your IRA assets held outside the LLC will be shielded from attack. This is especially important in the case of IRA real-estate investments where many state statutes impose an extended statute of limitation for claims arising from defects in the design or construction of improvements to real estate.

Asset and Creditor Protection

By using a self-directed IRA LLC with checkbook control, the IRA holder's IRA will usually be protected for up to $1 million in the case of personal bankruptcy under the 2005 Federal Bankruptcy Act. In addition, most states will shield a self-directed IRA from creditors' attack against the IRA holder outside of bankruptcy. Therefore, by using a self-directed IRA LLC, the IRA will usually be protected against creditor attack against the IRA holder.

Privacy Protection

With a self-directed IRA LLC, the investment will be made in the name of the LLC, whereas with a custodian-controlled self-directed IRA the name of the IRA owner will be in the name of the investment, allowing the public to easily locate the asset's owner. For example, if an IRA LLC is established in Nevada or Delaware, which offer strong privacy protection, identifying the owner of the LLC would be extremely difficult.

John handed Ken a chart that summarized the differences between all three types of self-directed IRA structures.

	Financial Institution Offered Self-Directed IRA	Custodian Controlled Self-Directed IRA	"Checkbook Control" Self-Directed IRA
Ability to take control of your retirement funds	Yes	Yes	Yes
Ability to make annual IRA contributions	Yes	Yes	Yes
Ability to accept rollover or transfer of retirement funds	Yes	Yes	Yes
Ability to make traditional investments, such as stocks	Yes	Yes	Yes
Ability to make alternative asset investments, such as real estate	No	Yes	Yes
Limited Liability Protection	No	No	Yes
Ability to hold IRA funds at local bank	No	No	Yes
Ability to use LLC managed by IRA holder to make investments	No	No	Yes
$1,000,000 of personal bankruptcy protection	Yes	Yes	Yes

"OK, do you mind if I summarize the differences between the three self-directed IRAs you mentioned so I can make sure I understand?" Ken asked.

"Of course, go for it," John said.

"So, the traditional financial institutions, such as Fidelity and Chase, claim they offer self-directed IRA structures, but in reality all you are able to purchase is equity-related investments that they offer, such as stocks and mutual funds. The custodian-directed self-directed IRA allows you to make traditional as well as alternative-asset investments, such as real estate, but all investments must go through the custodian. And finally, the checkbook control self-directed IRA LLC allows one to make traditional as well as alternative-asset investments using a special purpose LLC vehicle that is owned 100 percent by the LLC and managed by me or any person, allowing the manager to make investments by simply writing a check from the local LLC bank account. The self-directed IRA LLC is great for real-estate investors or anyone looking to make multiple investments with retirements funds and have the capacity to write checks or make investments quickly, whereas the custodian-directed self-directed IRA is great for one-off investments, such as private business investments, precious metals, or hedge-fund type investments." Ken said.

"That is 100 percent accurate—nice job. Looks like the cappuccino is working, and you are staying awake and listening to what I am saying," John said with a laugh.

"I am actually really interested in this topic, but one thing I am not so clear on is why I can't use my self-directed IRA to invest in my business." Ken said.

"I am happy you brought up this point, because I am about to get to it right now," John said. "As I just discussed, the self-directed IRA allows one to make traditional as well as alternative investments with retirement funds. Irrespective of which of the three self-directed IRA structures you use, the IRS prohibited-transaction rules we spoke about last time we met will still apply."

"Right, I forgot about those rules," Ken said.

"I understand. That is why it is so important to work with a tax professional who understands the IRS prohibited-transaction rules when looking to make alternative-asset investments with retirement funds," John said.

"Got it," Ken said.

"And remember, the IRC does not describe what a self-directed IRA can invest in, only what it cannot invest in. IRC Code Sections 408 and 4975 prohibit disqualified persons from engaging in certain type of transactions. The IRS has restricted certain transactions between the IRA and a disqualified person. The rationale behind these rules was a congressional assumption that certain transactions between certain parties are inherently suspicious and should be disallowed. The definition of a disqualified person (IRC Code Section 4975(e)(2)) extends to a variety of related party scenarios, but generally includes the IRA holder, any ancestors or lineal descendants of the IRA holder, and entities in which the IRA holder holds a controlling equity or management interest. Do you remember the examples I gave for IRC Section 4975(c)(1)(A), which discussed transactions involving the direct or indirect sale, exchange, or leasing of property between an IRA and a disqualified person?" John asked.

"I actually do," Ken responded.

"Good. So you can see where the issues start to arise about using retirement funds to invest in your own business," John said.

"I do. But can you explain further?" Ken asked.

"Of course. Let's start by dissecting IRC Section 4975(c)(1)(A). The section is basically saying that IRA funds cannot be used in any sale or exchange transaction with a disqualified person. So if you used your IRA funds to invest in a business that you are personally involved in, and you are a disqualified person because it is your IRA, the transaction would violate the rules under IRC Section 4975(c)(1)(A)," John said.

"OK, I may be confused, but how can I buy Apple or IBM stock with my IRA?" Ken asked.

"Good question. This is confusing stuff, so don't feel bad. You are correct. You are a disqualified person because it is your IRA, but remember you don't own more than 50 percent of Apple or IBM, so the company is not a disqualified person and hence the investment would not be a prohibited transaction," John said.

"But what about the example you gave where someone owned less than 50 percent and the investment into the entity by their retirement account triggered a prohibited transaction?" Ken said.

"You are right—the good old Rollins case. As a reminder, Mr. Rollins owned less than 50 percent of the entity and was not even an employee of the business, but his use of 401(k) funds as a loan to the company triggered a prohibited transaction," John stated.

"So what is the deal? Mr. Rollins owned less than 50 percent of the entity and was not even an employee, and the IRS still argues that the loan of 401(k) funds to the business was a prohibited transaction?" Ken asked.

"Yes. I know it's confusing because your first thought is that since a disqualified person owns less than 50 percent of an entity, the entity should not be considered a disqualified person, but IRC Section 4975(c)(1)(E) addresses this issue. IRC Section 4975(c)(1)(E) is known as the 'self-dealing' prohibited transaction provision, as it reads, 'The direct or indirect act by a Disqualified Person who is a fiduciary whereby he/she deals with income or assets of the IRA in his/her own interest or for his/her own account.' Essentially the IRS has used IRC Section 4975(c)(1)(E) in *Rollins* and in other instances as a sword to attack transactions where the investment may not satisfy any of the other provisions of IRC Section 4975(c), but, based on the facts and circumstances, should be prohibited."

"Like a catch-all weapon?" Ken asked.

"Yes, kind of. The Rollins case teaches us that the burden of proof of whether a prohibited transaction occurred rests at the feet of the IRA holder, and it is up to the IRA holder to prove that no direct or indirect personal benefit was generated from the IRA investment. It is based on the facts and circumstances, but as I tell all my clients, if the IRS knocks on your door and asks you about an IRA transaction, and you cannot prove that the IRA investment did not directly or indirectly benefit you, then the transaction is likely prohibited and you should not do it. So clearly, buying Apple stock with your IRA where you will own 0.00001 percent of the company would not be considered prohibited even if you are an employee of Apple because, due to the size of Apple, the IRA purchase of company stock would have no personal bearing on you. In contrast, investing your IRA funds in a closely held business that you will work at and earn a salary from, and that will benefit from the IRA stock purchase transaction, could trigger a prohibited transaction under IRC Section 4975. For example, using your IRA funds to buy 50 percent or 100 percent of a new business that you will be working at full time would likely trigger a prohibited transaction, and that fact would be hard to refute, versus owning 2 percent of a large business where the investment will have no bearing on your job or the financial standing of the company," John said.

"All this is so confusing," Ken said. "I can use my IRA to buy Apple or Google stock but not to buy shares in a business or franchise where the IRA will own more than 50 percent, and I will be personally involved in the business, but I can potentially invest IRA funds in a business that my IRA will own less than 10 percent of that won't directly or indirectly benefit me?"

"Pretty much. I know it's confusing, but a lot is based on facts and circumstances. The rule I usually tell all my clients to follow is don't invest IRA funds in any nonpublic company that you work at or have a personal ownership in. I think that will keep you away from the prohibited-transaction rules," John stated.

"Other than the Rollins case, do you have an example of someone using a self-directed IRA to buy a nonpublic company business they worked at?" Ken asked.

"Actually I do, and it is right on point to the question of whether you can use a self-directed IRA to invest in your new water business," John said.

T. L. Ellis, TC Memo. 2013-245

On October 29, 2013, the tax court in T. L. Ellis, TC Memo. 2013-245,(October 29, 2013) held that establishing a special purpose LLC to make an investment did not trigger a prohibited transaction, as a newly established LLC cannot be deemed a disqualified person pursuant to IRC Section 4975.

In T. L. Ellis, TC Memo. 2013-245, Mr. Ellis retired with about $300,000 in his 401(k) plan, which he subsequently rolled over into a newly created self-directed IRA.

The taxpayer then created an LLC taxed as a corporation and had his IRA transfer the $300,000 into the LLC. The LLC was formed to engage in the business of used-car sales. The taxpayer managed the used-car business through the IRA LLC and received a modest salary.

The IRS argued that the formation of the LLC was a prohibited transaction under IRC Section 4975, which prohibits self-dealing. The tax court disagreed, holding that even though the taxpayer acted as a fiduciary to the IRA (and was therefore a disqualified person under IRC Section 4975), the LLC itself was not a disqualified person at the time of the transfer. As a side note, this is the primary reason establishing a self-directed IRA is not a prohibited transaction. After the transfer, the LLC was a disqualified person because it was owned by Mr. Ellis's IRA, a disqualified person. Additionally, the IRS claimed that the taxpayer had engaged in a prohibited transaction by receiving a salary from the LLC. The court agreed with the IRS. Although the LLC (and not the IRA) was officially paying the taxpayer's salary, the tax court concluded that since the IRA was the sole owner of the LLC, and the LLC was the IRA's only investment, the taxpayer (a disqualified person) was essentially being paid by his IRA.

The tax court ruled that a prohibited transaction had occurred because Mr. Ellis received a salary from the LLC, which was wholly owned by his IRA.

"That's interesting," Ken said. "Mr. Ellis would have done exactly what I would have thought would be legal if I hadn't spoken with you. I'm really glad I am talking to you about this, because who knows what I would have done if I just did some searches online," Ken said.

"Thanks. The Ellis case is important because it offers clear guidance to anyone looking to use a self-directed IRA to invest in an active business that will be operated by a disqualified person. The case puts up a definitive barrier to anyone trying to use a self-directed IRA to invest in an LLC or corporation that will be actively managed by a disqualified person," John said.

"Just so I understand, it wasn't the establishment of the LLC owned by the IRA and managed by the IRA holder—Mr. Ellis—that created the prohibited transaction, but it was the use of the IRA funds to buy an active business from which Mr. Ellis earned a salary?" Ken asked.

"Exactly. If Mr. Ellis had used the funds to buy a business run by a third-party nondisqualified person, he would not have any prohibited transaction issues. However, we will soon talk about a potential tax that could be triggered in this type of situation."

"That was a really good example. One question: I assume I can use a self-directed IRA to invest in a business owned by a nondisqualified person?" Ken asked.

"Yes, absolutely. Just like you can buy Apple or IBM stock, you can invest in any business not involving you personally or any disqualified person—a friend, sibling, aunt, uncle, cousin, colleague, or any non-disqualified person are all good. One thing to remember is that your IRA can invest in any business not involving a disqualified person that is not established as an S corporation. You probably don't remember much about our conversation about S corporations, but an they usually can only have individuals as shareholders, and an IRA is a trust. Thus, if your IRA purchases stock in an S corporation, the transaction would not be considered prohibited per IRC Section 4975, but the S corporation election would no longer be valid, and the S corporation would revert back to a C corporation, which would probably not make the other shareholders very happy because of its double taxation regime," John said.

"OK. So I can invest in any business entity other than an S corporation, such as an LLC, partnership, C corporation, and so on, and the entity cannot be owned by me or any disqualified person?" Ken asked.

"Yes, that is pretty much correct. I think it is good practice never to invest retirement funds in any business in which you or any disqualified person have any personal interest. The Rollins case is all the proof you need that the IRS can be very aggressive in these situations. If no retirement funds are mixed with your or any disqualified person's personal funds, there would be no risk of a prohibited transaction," John said.

"OK, so I could use a self-directed IRA to invest in a friend's or sibling's business, but not my own or a business associated with any disqualified person?" Ken asked.

"Yes, that is correct. One more thing to add that is quite important and not widely known to many investors: there could be a tax imposed on using retirement funds to invest in an active trade or business held through a pass-through entity, such as an LLC."

"Wait. Are you telling me I owe tax if my IRA buys Apple or Google stock?" Ken asked.

"No, that would be a shock to you and millions of Americans," John said with a chuckle. "Remember, almost all public companies are C corporations, and a C corporation is not treated as a pass-through entity for tax purposes. It is recognized as an entity separate from its shareholders, which actually blocks any of the income generated by the C corporation from flowing through to the shareholders and keeps it in the C corporation for taxation. Only once the earnings have been taxed can any retained earnings be distributed to shareholders in the form of a dividend. In contrast, an LLC, S corporation, or partnership is treated as a pass-through entity for taxation—kind of like a funnel—and all the income of the pass-through entity flows to the members/partners without any partnership level taxation," John said.

"OK, I think I understand. Apple, Google, and almost all public companies that sell shares in the public markets are C corporations and not pass-through entities, and as a result all the business income gets trapped or blocked at the corporate level," Ken said.

"Correct," John said.

"This may be a dumb question, but why do I care about this?" Ken asked.

"It's a very good question. In the case of your current water business transaction the rules I am about to discuss are not relevant—you will not be using a self-directed IRA to buy your business because of the prohibited-transaction rules. However, if, down the road, a nondisqualified person wants to use their retirement funds to invest in your water business, which I believe will be established as an LLC, then what I am about to talk about will be very relevant to that retirement account investor and something you will want to know," John said.

"OK, that makes sense," Ken said.

"Let me start at the beginning. In general, if you make passive investments with your self-directed IRA, such as stocks, mutual funds, precious metals, foreign currency, rental real estate, and so on, the income generated by the investment will not be subject to any tax. Only if your self-directed IRA makes investments into an active business, such as a retail store, restaurant, real-estate development business, software company, and the like using a pass-through entity such as an LLC or partnership, will your self-directed IRA likely be subject to a tax known as the unrelated business taxable income tax, also known as UBTI or UBIT, which I will explain in detail shortly."

"Can you give me another example?" Ken asked.

"Let's say a self-directed IRA invests in an LLC that operates an active business such as a restaurant or water franchise. The income or gains generated from the investment will generally be subject to the UBTI tax. However, if the self-directed IRA invested in an active business through a C corporation, such as Apple or Google, there would be no UBTI since the C corporation blocks the income from flowing through to the self-directed IRA shareholder. This is why most Americans have never heard of the UBTI rules and why you can invest your IRA into a public company such as Apple without triggering the UBTI tax. Remember that if an IRA makes a passive investment, such as rental income, dividends, and royalties, such income would not be subject to the UBTI rules pursuant to IRC Section 512.

"Now you are probably asking what UBTI is," John said.

"How did you know?" Ken said with a laugh.

"OK, here we go," John said. "One of the advantages of using retirement funds through your self-directed IRA to make investments is that in most cases all income and gains from the investments flow back to your IRA LLC tax free. This is because an IRA is exempt from tax, pursuant to IRC Section 408. Pursuant to IRC Section 512, most of the popular forms of income generated by a retirement income will be exempt from tax. This is why most American investors look at you funny when you start telling them about the unrelated business taxable income rules, also known as UBTI or UBIT."

"I know, I never hear about it," Ken said.

"The good thing about the UBTI rules is that they won't apply to over 90 percent of American retirement investors because most types of income and gains generated by a retirement account are exempt from the UBTI rules. The IRC exempts dividends, interest, capital gains, royalties, and rental income from UBTI rules. Even so, the UBTI rules are new and somewhat intimidating to most people when learning about them for the first time. For example, buying public stocks and mutual funds with a self-directed IRA will not trigger the UBTI; neither would receiving a dividend from a public stock, or interest from a bond, or even rental income from an investment property. In the case of a self-directed IRA, the UBTI tax is triggered in three main types of investments:

1. investing in an active trade or business via a pass-through entity, such as an LLC
2. using margin when buying stock
3. using a nonrecourse loan to buy real estate

"Before I go through the three ways the UBTI tax can be triggered when using a self-directed IRA, I think it is helpful to examine why the UBTI tax came into law," John said.

"What's the back story on that?" Ken asked.

"It's pretty interesting," John said. "Back in the 1950s, Congress was concerned that for-profit companies would set up a charity and run their business through it, escaping taxation forever and thus gaining an unfair advantage because of their tax-exempt status. With that in mind, they created the UBTI rules under IRC 512. These rules can be found under IRC Sections 511–514 and have become known as the unrelated business taxable income rules, or UBTI or UBIT. If the UBTI rules are triggered, the income generated from those activities will usually be subject to a tax of approximately 35 percent. Of note, a self-directed IRA investing in an active trade or business using a C corporation, which consists of almost all public stock companies and mutual funds, will not trigger the UBTI tax. The reason is that a C corporation is not a pass-through entity, so the

C corporation essentially blocks the income from traveling to the shareholders, thus blocking the active trade or business income from flowing to the IRA. You can think of a C corporation as a box and an LLC or partnership as a funnel, which I think helps to understand why the UBTI tax would not apply to a retirement account owning shares in a C corporation."

WHAT IS UNRELATED BUSINESS TAXABLE INCOME?

"So what is unrelated business taxable income?" Ken asked.

"UBTI is defined as 'gross income derived by any organization from any unrelated trade or business regularly carried on by it; reduced by deductions directly connected with the business.' The UBTI rules apply only to exempt organizations such as charities, IRAs, and 401(k) plans. With the enactment of ERISA in 1974, IRAs and 401(k) plans, which are considered tax-exempt parties pursuant to IRC Sections 408 and 401 respectively, became subject to the UBTI rules. As a result, if an IRA or 401(k) plan invests in an active business through an LLC or partnership, the income generated by the IRA or 401(k) from the active business investment will be subject to the UBTI rules."

"OK," Ken said.

"In the case of a self-directed IRA, a transaction would not trigger the UBTI or UBIT rules if the transaction is not considered a trade or business that is regularly carried on. This typically involves passive types of activities that generate capital gains, interest, rental income, royalties, and dividends, the categories of exempt income according to IRC Section 512. However, if the tax-exempt organization, such as your self-directed IRA, engages in an active trade or business that is regularly carried on, like a restaurant, store, or manufacturing business, the IRS will tax the income."

"What's the UBTI tax rate?" Ken asked.

"IRC 511 taxes unrelated business taxable income at the rates applicable to corporations or trusts, depending on the organization's legal characteristics. In general, a self-directed IRA subject to UBTI is taxed at the trust tax rate because an IRA is considered a trust. For 2015, a self-directed

IRA subject to UBTI could be subject to close to 40% in tax if the income generated is over just $15,000 or so":

Ken looked shocked. "Pretty steep."

"Yes. In fact, they're higher than most individuals' income tax rate or the corporate income tax rate. This is one of the main reasons the UBTI tax rules are so important to understand and avoid if possible. In essence, the UBTI tax is imposed on the self-directed IRA investment and actually creates a double tax regime since the UBTI tax will apply in the year the income or gain is realized and also when the plan participant takes a distribution or is required to take a distribution after the age of seventy and a half (in the case of a pretax IRA). This is just another reason it is important to be aware of the UBTI tax rules and their potential application to self-directed IRA investments."

"So the question is, what level of business activity must you cross before triggering the UBTI or UBIT tax? Unfortunately, there is no clear test as to how much business activity one must engage in in a given year to trigger the UBTI or UBIT tax. In general, the IRS examines a number of factors to determine whether one has engaged in a high enough volume of transactions to trigger the UBTI tax. First, the IRS will examine the frequency of the transactions—how many business transactions are done in a year. Second, the IRS will examine the intent of the person—was the person intending to engage in an active trade or business. Third, the IRS will look at the scope of other activities of the retirement account to determine whether the activity is part of a business activity or an investment. Fourth, the IRS will look at the personal business activities of the IRA investor to help determine whether the IRA investment is part of an overall business model. So for example, several real-estate flips by Donald Trump's self-directed IRA could look more like a business than if they were made by a teacher or accountant."

"So the determination of whether an activity is an active trade or business and will thus trigger the UBTI or UBIT tax, which is taxed at a rate of approximately 35 percent, depends on the facts and circumstances," Ken said.

"Yes," John agreed. "Clearly if you have a store or restaurant or manufacturing plant you are in business. But for some start-ups or real-estate transactions, there can be a question as to whether the activity is a simple investment or hobby or if the activity rises to the level of a trade or business. Thankfully, the IRS has issued some guidance as to whether an activity is a hobby or investment."

John opened the Internet browser on his smartphone and pulled up the IRS page. He started reading to Ken:

In order to make this determination of whether an activity is a business or hobby, taxpayers should consider the following factors:

- Does the time and effort put into the activity indicate an intention to make a profit?
- Does the taxpayer depend on income from the activity?
- If there are losses, are they due to circumstances beyond the taxpayer's control or did they occur in the start-up phase of the business?
- Has the taxpayer changed methods of operation to improve profitability?
- Does the taxpayer or his/her advisors have the knowledge needed to carry on the activity as a successful business?
- Has the taxpayer made a profit in similar activities in the past?
- Does the activity make a profit in some years?
- Can the taxpayer expect to make a profit in the future from the appreciation of assets used in the activity?

"OK, this is really helpful," Ken said. "I guess in my case it won't be an issue because I will clearly be in business, but for a set of real-estate transactions I can see where this can be an issue."

"Yes, you are 100 percent right. The determination of whether a set of real-estate activities are treated as an investment or a business, and thus subject to the UBTI taxing regime, could be somewhat tricky Pretty important stuff considering that retirement accounts don't pay tax on investments, but investing in an active business through a pass-through entity would be subject to the UBTI tax," said John.

"OK, I think I am starting to understand the UBTI rules and its potential impact on self-directed IRA investments. As long as a self-directed IRA did not use margin, a nonrecourse loan, or invest in an active trade or business through a pass-through entity, such as an LLC, the UBTI rules would not apply," Ken said.

"Exactly," John said.

"I don't think it will be an issue for me because the self-directed IRA business-funding option does not seem like it will work for my water business since I will be actively involved in running the business. The Rollins and Ellis cases clearly demonstrate that using an IRA to fund my business won't be an option," Ken said.

"Yes, you are 100 percent correct."

"One last question. Can I take a loan from a self-directed IRA?" Ken asked.

"Unfortunately," John said, "you cannot borrow any funds from an IRA without triggering an IRS prohibited transaction. However, if you are a participant in an employer 401(k) plan or are self-employed and can adopt a solo 401(k) plan, you are able to borrow the lesser of $50,000 or 50 percent of the 401(k) plan account value and use the loan for any purpose."

"Oh, I didn't know that," Ken said.

THE 401(K) PLAN LOAN OPTION

"Yes," John said. "This loan feature is unique to a 401(k) plan, but the plan adoption agreement must include the option in the plan in order for the loan to be available to an eligible plan participant. The majority of employer 401(k) plans do include the loan feature, but an employer is not required to offer it."

"OK," Ken said.

"I know we discussed the 401(k) plan when we met earlier, but I wanted to take some time to talk about the 401(k) plan adopted by a business with employees, and the solo 401(k) plan adopted by a sole proprietor or small business with no full-time employees," John said. "I think it makes sense to talk about some of the benefits of adopting a 401(k) plan for your business because this may be something you and David may ultimately want to do for your business, even if you don't elect to use the 401(k) plan loan option."

"OK, sounds great," Ken responded.

"A 401(k) is known as an employer-sponsored employee benefit arrangement that is established for the purpose of providing retirement income for those who are eligible. 401(k) participants—eligible employees of the adopting employer—can elect to have a portion of their salary paid as a contribution toward the retirement account. Also, in the case of a pretax contribution, the amount deferred is not taxed until distributed to the employee at a later time," John said.

"What does the term 'qualified plan' mean?" Ken asked.

"The term 'qualified plan' usually means that the written arrangement and the operation of the plan meet specific qualification requirements, outlined in IRC Section 401(a)."

"What are some of the benefits as an employer to having a 401(k) plan?" Ken asked.

"Some of the key benefits as an employer include tax savings, employee appreciation, and employee attraction and retention. Also, there are tax and nontax benefits. As part of tax benefits, 401(k) plans can be less costly to fund compared to other retirement plans. As part of nontax benefits, employees view an employer-sponsored retirement plan as part of an overall benefits package, thus attracting high quality employees," John said.

"What are some of the benefits for the employees?" Ken asked.

"As with employer benefits, employees receive tax and nontax benefits. One tax benefit is that contributions and earnings are usually tax deferred until distributed from the plan. Employee elective deferrals may be made on a pretax basis. In simpler terms, this gives an immediate tax savings to participants. Also, if the employer offers a qualified Roth contribution, employees who make designated Roth contributions may be eligible to distribute those assets tax free and penalty free. Some of the nontax benefits for employees include the opportunity to participate in a 401(k) plan, which will help the employees prepare for financial security in retirement."

"OK, that is helpful. So I assume any business can adopt a 401(k) plan?" Ken asked.

"Yes," John said. "The following business types can establish a 401(k) plan":

- **Sole proprietor**. An individual is considered a sole proprietor if he/she has earned income from personal services rendered and reports the income to the IRS on Schedule C.
- **Partnership**. The plan must be established by the partnership as a business entity, not by each partner individually. Partnerships wishing to adopt a qualified retirement plan must consult either the partnership agreement or, in the absence of as partnership agreement, state law to determine the identity of the person(s) with authority to adopt the plan on behalf of the partnership. In addition, a preliminary inquiry regarding the ownership interest of any partners in other business entities must be made.
- **Corporation**. Typically, a corporation must adopt a resolution to authorize the adoption of a qualified retirement plan. The corporation also must appoint persons or entities to oversee administrative and fiduciary responsibilities with respect to the plan. Special rules come into play if the corporation is a member of a controlled group or an affiliated service group.
- **Limited liability company**. An LLC combines the benefits of a partnership and a corporation to create a separate business type. Because LLC members usually can choose to be treated as a partnership or a corporation for tax purposes, an LLC must presumably follow the respective entity's tax rules when adopting a qualified retirement plan. In the case of the LLC, the operating agreement will usually dictate what type of consent is needed to adopt the plan. If the LLC is treated as a corporation for tax purposes, a corporate resolution would need to be adopted to approve the establishment of the plan.

"OK, thanks. I am happy an LLC is able to adopt a 401(k) plan. What type of plan makes sense for my water business to adopt?" Ken asked.

"That is a great question. I think this may be a bit premature, but I will go through some of the most popular options. In your case, I would recommend either a profit-sharing plan or 401(k) plan."

Profit-Sharing Plan

Profit-sharing plan contributions are discretionary and usually are made out of profits generated by the business as a percentage of each employee's salary. Consequently, the contribution that an employer makes to a profit-sharing plan may vary from year to year, depending on a number of factors. Usually, if an employer elects to make a contribution, the same contribution percentage must be made for all eligible employees unless the employer has elected to use an allocation method, referred to as permitted disparity.

The maximum deductible contribution that can be made to a profit-sharing plan is 25 percent of eligible compensation (20 percent in the case of a sole proprietorship or single-member LLC). Eligible compensation is all of the compensation paid to the eligible plan participants during the employer's tax year. The deduction is taken by the employer on the business tax return. Employer contributions are not considered taxable income to employees for the year in which the contributions are made.

401(k) Qualified Retirement Plan

A 401(k) plan is a type of profit-sharing plan under which employees may be allowed to defer a portion of their compensation into the plan on a pretax basis. A 401(k) plan, sometimes called a cash or deferred arrangement (CODA), allows employees to receive taxable compensation in a current year or defer taxation by electing to have the employer contribute compensation into a qualified retirement plan. For 2006 and later plan years, if the plan provides, participants may make designated Roth (after-tax) contributions in amounts up to plan deferral limits. In addition to allowing employee deferrals of up to $18,000 or $24,000, if over the age of fifty, for 2015, a 401(k) plan may allow for employer matching contributions, employee after-tax contributions, and employer profit-sharing contributions. Earnings on employer contributions also are tax deferred. As with other profit-sharing plans, the overall deductible contribution limit under a 401(k) plan is 25 percent (20 percent in the case of a sole proprietorship or single-member LLC) of the aggregate unreduced compensation paid to plan participants during the employer's tax year. For 2015, the maximum amount one can contribute to a 401(k) plan is $53,000 or $59,000 if over the age of fifty.

Traditional 401(k) Plans

A traditional 401(k) plan allows eligible employees (i.e., employees eligible to participate in the plan) to make pretax elective deferrals through payroll deductions or Roth, if the plan documents permit. In addition, in a traditional 401(k) plan, employers have the option of making contributions on behalf of all participants, making matching contributions based on employees' elective deferrals, or both. These employer contributions can be subject to a vesting schedule, which provides that an employee's right to employer contributions becomes nonforfeitable only after a period of time, or can be immediately vested. Rules relating to traditional 401(k) plans require that contributions made under the plan meet specific nondiscrimination requirements. In order to ensure that the plan satisfies these requirements, the employer must perform annual tests—known as the actual deferral percentage (ADP) and actual contribution percentage (ACP) tests—to verify that deferred wages and employer matching contributions do not discriminate in favor of highly compensated employees.

Safe Harbor 401(k) Plan

A safe harbor 401(k) plan is similar to a traditional 401(k) plan, but, among other things, it must provide for employer contributions that are fully vested when made. These contributions may be employer matching contributions limited to employees who defer, or employer contributions made on behalf of all eligible employees, regardless of whether they make elective deferrals. The safe harbor 401(k) plan is not subject to the complex annual nondiscrimination tests (ADP or ACP) that apply to traditional 401(k) plans.

"Wow, this is some confusing stuff," Ken said.

"It is. Which is why it makes sense to discuss your options with a tax attorney or CPA, but for most small businesses looking at a 401(k) plan, the option is usually between a safe harbor 401(k) plan and a solo 401(k) plan, if there are no full-time employees in the business other than the owners and their spouses," John said.

"Let me explain further. If you want to avoid stress trying to navigate the very complex 401(k) plan's testing requirements each year and dealing with potential testing failures, the safe harbor 401(k) plan makes the most sense and is what most small businesses do. In 1999 a new twist on the traditional 401(k) plan became available for plan sponsors—the 'safe harbor 401(k) plan.' This twist on the traditional 401(k) plan has made it much simpler to administer. If an employer adopted this type of 401(k) plan there would be no need to worry about the ADP/ACP testing at the end of each year, and in some cases, no need to make top-heavy contributions (contributions to its key employees)—since 2002, safe harbor plans satisfy top-heavy requirements. All this in exchange for a commitment to make a minimum level of contributions that many sponsors make anyway—typically 3 percent of the employee's salary. I am not going to go through these details, but just know that if you have employees, the safe harbor 401(k) plan is a really good option when contemplating adopting a 401(k) plan," John said.

"What if I have no employees other than myself and David, the two owners?" Ken asked.

"As the name implies and as we have previously discussed, the solo 401(k) plan is an IRS-approved qualified 401(k) plan designed for a self-employed individual or the sole owner-employee of a corporation. The solo 401(k) plan, also known as a one-participant 401(k) plan, individual 401(k) plan, or self-employed 401(k) plan, is not a new type of plan. It's a traditional 401(k) plan covering a business owner with no employees, or that person and his or her spouse. These plans have the same rules and requirements as any other 401(k) plan. The solo 401(k) plan may be used by any individual who is already a business owner or one who will be establishing a business and does not have, or plan to have, full-time employees.

In addition, the solo 401(k) plan is perfect for independent contractors, such as consultants, home-business owners, and real-estate agents. The owner's spouse may also contribute to the plan as long as he or she is an employee of the business," John said.

"The solo 401(k) plan may end up being an option for us because we do not expect to have any full-time employees in the first couple of years," Ken said. "I assume if we get full-time employees, we can just move the solo 401(k) plan?"

"Yes, the plan documents would just need to be amended, so it is really not a big deal at all. The only key is to make sure that if you elect to adopt a safe harbor 401(k) plan, your new employees are offered plan benefits in line with the plan's options outlined in the plan documents," John said.

"Would my new employees be eligible right away to participate?" Ken asked.

"That depends on the plan documents," John said. "Most plans allow the employer to defer participation for up to twelve months, but most businesses reduce that restriction to between thirty and ninety days of full-time employment."

"OK, that works. I know the self-directed IRA allows one to make traditional as well as alternative-asset investments, such as real estate and private business investments. Do I have the same option with a 401(k) plan?" Ken asked.

"Yes, but it all comes down to the plan documents. The plan documents dictate what features are available to the participants. Most people believe that all solo 401(k) plans, whether attained for free at a financial institution or provided by a specialized plan provider, are the same. But the nuances that differentiate the various plan options are important to understand. In general, there are three ways to establish and use a 401(k) plan for retirement and investment purposes."

1. Financial Institution-Sponsored 401(k) Plan
"This is the most common way to establish a 401(k) plan. Most of the major financial institutions and US banks—such as Vanguard, Charles

Schwab, E*Trade, Bank of America, and CIT—provide basic solo 401(k) plan documents and investment opportunities, typically for no fee. The catch is that the 401(k) plan documents you adopt are very basic and usually limit your options to making pretax employee deferrals and pretax profit-sharing contributions while also limiting your 401(k) plan investment options to the products sold by that financial institution. In essence, the plan will let you make basic pretax employee deferral and profit-sharing contributions but will usually restrict your investment options to stocks, mutual funds, ETFs, and other traditional financial products sold by the financial institution. This type of 401(k) may permit a loan feature, as well as the ability to make Roth (after-tax) contributions, but will not allow the option to make alternative-asset investments, such as real estate and precious metals. The advantage of adopting a 401(k) plan from a major financial institution or bank can be found in the price and simplicity of such a transaction. For most small business with employees, this option is quite popular and works very well," John said.

2. Custodian-Directed Self-Directed 401(k) Plan

"This option usually offers 401(k) plan participants the ability to make traditional investments, including stock, as well as IRS-approved nontraditional or alternate investments such as real estate, precious metals, private lending, and private business investments through a trust company. The custodian-directed self-directed 401(k) plan option is usually attractive to retirement investors looking to make nontraditional investments with their 401(k) plan while having a third party administer the plan. This option is typically not used for 401(k) plans with employees, but is more common for a sole proprietorship or small business with no full-time employees other than the owners looking to adopt a solo 401(k) plan.

"These custodians or trust companies do not offer investment advice and are essentially in business to allow you to make IRS-approved nontraditional investments. Unlike a traditional financial institution such as Bank of America or Vanguard, which make money by selling financial products, these passive custodians and trust companies make their money by opening self-directed accounts and charging an annual fee. In some cases, the fees are based on account value and/or the number of transactions done in the account in a given year. Most of the institutions that allow 401(k) plans to make nontraditional investments are established as trust companies and simply let you use their plan documents and accounts to make the investments. Your solo 401(k) plan assets are usually held at an FDIC institution associated with the trust company and all investments must go through the custodian, which is why it is referred to as a custodian-directed plan. In practice, this means that you need to go through the custodian and have the custodian send the funds. In most cases, that custodian must also sign the necessary transaction documents to enable you to make a 401(k) plan investment, including real estate. In some situations, you are permitted as trustee of the plan to sign the transaction documents, including the purchase agreement, but the issuing of check payments or wires for the purchase or for ongoing expenses, such as taxes or repairs, need to go through the custodian because the custodian controls the funds. The custodian-directed self-directed solo 401(k) plan option has many attractive features, such as the ability to make nontraditional investments, but it also has some limitations, including annual fees and potential time delays that can result from having to go through the trust company to make transactions."

"One question. Why don't traditional 401(k) plans offer alternative-asset investment options? I know my employer plan does not, and I don't believe Pam's plan does either," Ken said.

"Great question. It all comes down to risk. A plan must have at least one fiduciary—a person or entity—named in the written plan, or through a process described in the plan, as having control over the plan's operation. A plan's fiduciaries will ordinarily include the trustee of the plan. The key to determining whether an individual or an entity is a fiduciary is whether they are exercising discretion or control over the plan. Fiduciaries have important responsibilities and are subject to standards of conduct because they act on behalf of participants in a retirement plan and their beneficiaries. These responsibilities include"

- acting solely in the interest of plan participants and their beneficiaries and with the exclusive purpose of providing benefits to them;
- carrying out their duties prudently;
- following the plan documents (unless inconsistent with ERISA);
- diversifying plan investments; and
- paying only reasonable plan expenses.

"The duty to act prudently is one of a fiduciary's central responsibilities under ERISA. Since a solo 401(k) plan has no full-time employees other than the owner or spouse of the owner, the ERISA rules do not apply. Thus there is no risk of breaching one's fiduciary duty since the only person in the plan is the business owner. However, in the case of a 401(k) plan with employees, the ERISA rules apply, and the trustee is deemed a fiduciary of the plan and has various responsibilities to the plan's participants. The most common way to reduce possible liability is to give participants control over the investments in their accounts and limit a fiduciary's liability for the investment decisions made by the participants. For participants to have control, they must be given the opportunity to choose from a broad range of investment alternatives. Under Department of Labor regulations, there must be at least three different investment options so that employees can diversify investments within an investment category, such as through a mutual fund, and diversify among the investment alternatives offered. In addition, participants must be given sufficient information to make informed decisions about the options offered under the plan. Participants also must be allowed to give investment instructions at least once a quarter, and perhaps more often if the investment option is volatile," John said.

"That makes sense. Now I understand why my current employer 401(k) plan restricts me to buying mutual funds that I select from a number of choices," Ken said.

"OK, let's touch on the third type of 401(k) plan."

3. Open-Architecture Self-Directed 401(k) Plan

"Like the custodian-directed 401(k) plan option, this option is typically used only for solo 401(k) plans because of investment options the plan allows for and the potential fiduciary risks it presents to the trustee(s) of the plan. The open-architecture 401(k) plan is quickly becoming the most popular self-directed option for the self-employed. The beauty of the open-architecture solo 401(k) plan is that it can usually be opened at most local banks, and it allows the business owner to serve as trustee of the plan with total control over the investments made. Self-directed 401(k) plans are provided by specialized plan-provider companies, which are able to customize the plan based on the individual's retirement and investment goals. Most of the companies that offer self-directed open-architecture 401(k) plan documents are not typical financial institutions that sell financial products or house the solo 401(k) plan account. These plan-document provider companies essentially make money by selling the plan documents and offering advisory services regarding the features of the plan. The open-architecture self-directed 401(k) plan has started to overtake the custodian-directed 401(k) plan as the most popular self-directed 401(k) plan option for the self-employed for a number of reasons":

- The plan can be opened at most local banks, which gives the plan participant more control and comfort than having the funds sit with a trustee in another state or at an unfamiliar bank.
- Once the documents have been purchased, there are typically very small annual compliance fees, since a 401(k) plan has very little administrative requirements and usually none if the plan's assets are under $250,000.
- You will have checkbook control, like the checkbook control self-directed IRA we discussed, which means that as the trustee, you can make traditional as well as alternative-asset investments from your 401(k) account by simply writing a check or executing a wire.
- You can customize the plan documents to include all options allowed by the IRS.

"OK, that is really helpful. I would definitely do the self-directed solo 401(k) plan if I was self-employed and will talk to David about establishing a solo 401(k) plan for our water business if we end up not hiring a full-time employee," Ken said.

"I think that makes sense. One more thing I want to talk about is why the solo 401(k) plan would be the best retirement plan for your business if you have no full-time employees."

SOLO 401(K) VERSUS SEP-IRA

"As I explained earlier, before the EGTRRA became effective in 2002, there was no compelling reason for an owner-only business to establish a solo 401(k) plan because the business owner could usually receive the same benefits by adopting a profit-sharing plan or a SEP-IRA. After 2002, EGTRRA paved the way for an owner-only business to put more money aside for retirement and operate a more cost-effective retirement plan than a SEP-IRA or 401(k) plan. The SEP is a pure profit-sharing employer-sponsored retirement plan that allows for a tax-deductible contribution equal to the smaller of $53,000 or 25 percent of compensation for 2015. The solo 401(k) has the following advantages":

- **Higher maximum contribution.** As I've already mentioned, a solo 401(k) plan allows you to make an employee salary deferral contribution and an employee profit-sharing deferral contribution. A SEP-IRA, on the other hand, allows only for a profit-sharing contribution equal to the lesser of $53,000 or 25 percent (20 percent in the case of a sole proprietorship or single-member LLC) of the earned income or compensation earned via the business, and it does not have an employee salary deferral contribution. So if you are sixty years old and have an S corporation from which you earn $100,000 in self-employment wages according to your W-2 form, then you can put $24,000 plus $25,000 (which is 25 percent of $100,000), or approximately $49,000, into your solo 401(k). Whereas if you established a SEP-IRA, you can defer only 25 percent of $100,000, or $25,000.

- **Catch-up contributions**. With a solo 401(k), you can contribute an extra $6,000 if you are over fifty years of age. The SEP-IRA does not allow a catch-up contribution.
- **Roth feature**. A solo 401(k) plan can be made in either pretax or after-tax (Roth) formats. A SEP-IRA permits only pretax contributions.
- **Tax-free loan option**. A solo 401(k) permits you to borrow up to $50,000 or 50 percent of your account value, whichever is less. This loan can be used for any purpose. A SEP-IRA does not allow you to borrow any money from your account without triggering a prohibited transaction. I will get into this option in greater detail shortly, as it could prove to be a very attractive business-funding option for you.
- **Ability to invest in real estate and use leverage with no additional tax**. With a 401(k), you can make a real-estate investment using nonrecourse funds without triggering the unrelated debt financed income rules and the UBTI tax. This is a really exciting feature to many real-estate investors, but will likely not be relevant to your water business venture. However, using SEP-IRA funds to purchase real estate using a nonrecourse loan would trigger the unrelated business taxable income tax.

SOLO 401(K) VERSUS SIMPLE IRA

"A SIMPLE IRA plan can be established by an employer with fewer than a hundred employees who received at least $5,000 in compensation from the employer in the preceding calendar year. A SIMPLE IRA plan is similar to a solo 401(k) plan, as both are funded by employee deferrals and additional employer contributions. However, a SIMPLE IRA has a lower deferral limit and uses an IRA-type trust to hold contributions for each employee, rather than a single plan.

"The SIMPLE IRA has all of the same disadvantages as the SEP-IRA relative to the solo 401(k) with one big exception: the SIMPLE IRA has an even lower deferral limit of $12,500 (for 2015) and a catch-up contribution that is just $2,500. In addition, the employer must provide either":

- a dollar-for-dollar match of up to 3 percent of compensation to all who defer, or
- a 2 percent nonelective contribution to all employees who are eligible to participate in the plan.

"Well, that just solidifies my choice for establishing a solo 401(k) plan," Ken said.

"I know you mentioned the loan feature as one of the more popular features of the solo 401(k) plan, but can you explain this option in detail, because it seems from what you have described so far that it may be an option for me for funding my water business."

"Agreed," John said.

CAN YOU TAKE A LOAN FROM YOUR SOLO 401(K) PLAN?

"Another really great feature of a 401(k) plan is the ability to use it as a source of tax- and penalty-free cash when it would be to your advantage to tap in to your retirement savings. The loan feature is unique to a 401(k) plan, but the plan adoption agreement must include the option in the plan in order for the loan to be available to an eligible plan participant. The plan documents will determine whether the loan feature will be available for your particular 401(k) plan. With a 401(k) plan loan, you can access your retirement funds without tax or penalty by taking out a loan using the accumulated balance of your solo 401(k) plan as collateral. Such a loan is permitted at any time, and you can borrow up to either $50,000 or 50 percent of your account value, whichever is less. This feature makes the 401(k) plan unique among retirement savings plans. There is no loan feature available with any type of IRA, including a SEP-IRA or SIMPLE IRA. The 401(k) loan feature is really the only way you can use retirement funds for any personal use without triggering a tax or penalty. The loan feature is truly helpful because it allows you to use the retirement funds and do a prohibited transaction, such as investing in your own business, paying off a personal debt, buying a car, or going on vacation and not pay a tax or penalty. Plan loans from the 401(k) are legal because of a limited statutory exception to the prohibited-transaction rules as stated in IRC Section 4975(d)(1). Specifically, IRC Section 72(p) allows you to borrow money from your 401(k) plan tax free and without penalty. As long as the plan documents allow for it and the proper loan documents are prepared and executed, you can take such a loan for any reason. If the loan payments are made on time, there are no penalties or taxes due. There are thousands of ways to use a 401(k) plan loan. In fact, you can use it for practically anything as long as that activity is not illegal. There is no need to worry about IRS-prohibited transactions because the 401(k) loan is exempt from the reach of the prohibited-transaction rules pursuant to IRC Section 4975(d)(1)."

"What could I possibly do with such a loan?" Ken said.

"Here are some ideas and popular ways to use 401(k) loan proceeds":

- obtain immediate funds for your business
- help pay personal expenses
- lend to a third party at a higher interest rate
- invest in a real-estate project that offers a higher rate of return than prime plus 1 percent
- consolidate your debt and help pay it off
- pay for college expenses
- pay for unexpected emergencies
- avoid distribution penalties while using up to $50,000 immediately without restrictions
- invest in a new franchise or business
- make an investment (such as a tax lien, private placement, or mortgage pool) that will generate a higher rate of return than prime plus 1 percent
- invest in some transaction that would otherwise be prohibited under IRC Section 4975

"In short, you can have quick, easy, and inexpensive access to $50,000 for any reason. In addition, you are not limited to taking or making only one loan, but those loans together must not exceed $50,000 or 50 percent of your account value, whichever is less, with some stipulations. Specifically, the total amount you can borrow can't, when added to the balance of all other outstanding loans, exceed the lesser of":

- $50,000 that is reduced by the highest outstanding balance of any other 401(k) plan loans during the plan
- more than half of your vested current plan outstanding balance (amount of plan funds that you have a legal right to), or $10,000

"Here are some examples to explain how those restrictions apply":

Joe
Joe is an employee of Company X, which has a 401(k) plan. Joe's 401(k) plan account has a value of $40,000. Joe is in need of funds to help pay off debt related to a health issue he had some years ago. Joe heard about the loan option and asked the plan administrator whether the option was available in the company plan. As luck would have it, the company 401(k) plan does contain a loan feature. The maximum Joe could borrow from his solo 401(k) plan would be $20,000—50 percent of his account value since he had less than $100,000 in his plan. Joe would be able to use the loan for any purpose.

Amy
Amy is a doctor and operates her business as an S corporation. She also provides consulting services. Amy adopted a solo 401(k) plan and rolled in $200,000 from a former employer's retirement plan. Amy's parents have run into some medical problems recently and have accumulated excessive medical bills that are forcing them to consider bankruptcy. Amy spoke to her CPA because she was looking for a way to help her parents out and pay off some of those bills.

The CPA mentioned that the solo 401(k) plan Amy adopted included a loan option that would allow her to borrow up to $50,000. Amy then asked about the interest rate and was told that the lowest interest rate allowed by law is the prime interest rate per the Wall Street Journal, which as of March 2015 was 3.25 percent. The CPA also mentioned that the loan would have to be paid back at least quarterly over a five-year period. Amy did the math and figured if she borrowed the full $50,000, she would be paying back about $904 to her plan each month, or about $2,712 if she elected to make quarterly loan payments. Amy felt this was doable, plus she liked the fact that she would be increasing the value of her plan at the same time.

"OK, I think I understand that I can borrow the lesser of $50,000 or 50 percent of my account value, whatever is less," Ken said.

"That is correct," John said.

"So what are the repayment terms?" Ken asked.

"Good question. Your 401(k) loan is a loan and not a gift, so like all loans it does need to be paid back. In fact, you must repay the loan over an amortization schedule of five years or less on at least a quarterly payment basis. You must pay interest on the loan, set at a reasonable rate, usually interpreted as the prime interest rate per the Wall Street Journal. Some plan administrators will set the minimum loan amount as the prime interest rate plus 1 percent. For example, as I write this passage, the prime interest rate is 3.25 percent and has been the same rate for over the past five years. Of course, there's nothing preventing you from charging more in interest."

"Huh. Why would you ever want to charge yourself a higher interest rate for your 401(k) plan loan?" Ken asked.

"Actually, when you think about it, there's an amazing logic to the idea. Take the example of Jeff, a successful dentist with a practice that has no full-time employees other than himself and his wife. Jeff and his wife are able to max out their employee deferral and employer profit-sharing contributions each year. However, they would still like to add more money to his plan if possible. Jeff discussed this dilemma with his CPA, who mentioned that if he and his wife took out a 401(k) loan and charged themselves a high interest rate, making sure it stayed under the usury or loan-shark interest rate rules in their state, they could actually put an amount of money into their plan that exceeds their annual limitation amount. Jeff mentioned that he doesn't need the money, but his CPA told him he could use those funds as he sees fit, but it would allow him to defer additional funds into his plan. His CPA gave him an example. Assuming Jeff and his wife each borrowed $50,000 from the 401(k) plan, instead of using an interest rate of 3.25 percent, they could select a 10 percent interest rate. This would allow them each to defer an extra $14,000 or so in the plan over a five-year period."

"Not bad!"

"Your loan payments must include both principal and interest. In general, it is not permitted to make balloon payments to repay your loan. However, most loan documents do allow for loan prepayment without penalty," John said.

"I think I may have some after-tax (Roth) 401(k) funds. Are those funds available for the loan?" Ken asked.

"A 401(k) includes pretax and after-tax (Roth) funds. It is possible to take a loan from the Roth portion of a solo 401(k) plan as long as the plan documents permit it. Using Roth 401(k) funds for a loan does trigger some potential tax ramifications if you default. In such a case, the determination of what portion of the Roth funds are distributed tax free and what portion is subject to tax, and potentially subject to a 10 percent early distribution penalty, is looked at on a pro rata basis. Determining the tax implication on a defaulted Roth solo 401(k) plan loan is quite complex, and it is one of the reasons some 401(k) plan administrators only allow for pretax funds to be used for a loan."

"How would I apply for a 401(k) plan loan?" Ken asked.

"In order to take out a 401(k) loan, the first step is to make sure your plan documents allow for it. If you are in a company plan, you can ask the plan administrator or human resources, and they will likely be able to tell you since the plan administrator is responsible for administering the plan loan. In the case of a solo 401(k) plan, the plan administrator is usually the same as the business owner, so approval of the loan will not be an issue. Once you have determined that your 401(k) plan loan documents allow for a loan to be taken, the next step is to determine how much you can borrow. To calculate the amount, you must determine the fair market value of your plan assets with the understanding that, in general, the maximum loan amount you can take is $50,000 or 50 percent or your account value, whichever is less. In determining the fair market value of your plan assets, if your plan is all in cash, then that is clearly not an issue, as the fair market value of the plan assets would equal the cash in the plan. However, if the plan's assets consist of nontraditional asset types such as real estate, notes, or private business investments, then you need an independent third party to provide an opinion on the value of those assets so you can determine your maximum loan amount. This would not be an issue when it is clear that the plan assets are over $100,000, since you would be entitled to borrow up to the maximum $50,000 amount. Once you know the 401(k) plan includes a loan feature and you have figured out how much you can borrow, the next step is completing the loan paperwork. It usually includes a loan agreement as well as a truth and lending disclosure statement that will provide an overview of all the terms of the loan. This will include the amount, the payment schedule, the applicable percentage of interest, and other details. In general, your spouse will also be required to sign the loan agreement, but most loan documents do not require the signature of a notary."

"Got it," Ken said.

"Having said all that, your loan application will be governed by your plan documents, so it is possible that your application process may have some unusual details or requirements. Please read them thoroughly."

"When are my loan payments due?" Ken asked.

"The 401(k) plan loan must be paid back at least quarterly over a five-year period (fifteen years if you will be using the loan proceeds to purchase a primary residence), but can be paid back quicker (i.e., weekly, biweekly, monthly) and at an interest rate of at least prime per the Wall Street Journal. As of September 1, 2015, the prime interest rate is 3.25 percent," John said. "Some plans require that the minimum interest rate be used be prime plus 1 percent, so you will need to check with the plan administrator. Of course, as I mentioned, you can always select a higher interest rate so long as it does not violate the usury (loan shark) rules."

"Can I do balloon payments on the 401(k) plan loan?" Ken asked.

"Unfortunately not. All loan payments consist of interest and principal and are constant throughout the five years. Kind of like a standard loan," John said.

"Gotcha," Ken said. "So to recap, if my plan allows a loan, I can borrow the lesser of $50,000 or 50 percent of my account value and use the loan for any purpose. The loan can be paid back over a five-year period, at least quarterly, at an interest rate of at least prime per the Wall Street Journal, which as of September 1, 2015 is 3.25 percent."

"You got it. You are getting real good at this," John said.

"Do I file the plan loan documents with the IRS?" Ken asked.

"Good question. Your 401(k) plan loan is a private loan between you, the plan participant, and the plan. The loan documents are not filed with the IRS or any government agency. Accordingly, administration of the loan is the responsibility of the plan administrator. In general, there is not much work involved in administering a 401(k) plan loan. The plan administrator must make sure that all loan payments are being paid in full and in a timely manner. That's pretty much it. In the case where a plan participant wishes to take one or more additional loans, the plan administrator should be certain that the plan allows for multiple loans and that the plan participant has not exceeded the permitted loan threshold."

"What happens if you miss a loan payment?" Ken asked.

"Loan payments must be made in a timely manner or they will be considered delinquent. A delinquent loan is not the same as a defaulted loan. A 'defaulted loan' is an IRS-defined term, and a 401(k) plan loan is deemed to be in default when it no longer meets the requirements found in Treasury Regulation 1.72(p)-1.

"A 401(k) plan would be considered in default only under the following circumstances":

- the 401(k) plan loan is not paid within the least permissible term of the loan (usually five years)

- the 401(k) plan loan is not paid according to the amortization schedule, with loan payments made at least quarterly and including interest and penalty
- the 401(k) plan loan exceeds the maximum allowable amount
- an event designated by the 401(k) plan occurs

"If there is a default, you can try to cure the default if the plan documents allow for a cure period. In such a case, the plan documents may allow for a certain period of time for you to make up the missed payments. This cure period cannot extend beyond the end of the calendar quarter in which the loan payment was missed.

If you do default on a plan loan, you will trigger a deemed taxable distribution. This is not a real distribution, but it is treated as such for tax purposes. This means that the entire loan balance or the loan amount above the allowable limit—if the maximum loan amount is exceeded—is considered a taxable distribution in the taxable year that the amount is deemed distributed. The deemed distribution is considered a taxable event and is subject to a 10 percent early distribution penalty if you are under the age of fifty-nine and a half in the year of default. Even if your plan loan is in default and those funds are deemed distributed, you must still repay your loan. The loan repayment amount is actually treated as an after-tax contribution to your plan. You cannot roll over the deemed distribution from your 401(k) plan loan default into another retirement account. Once the distribution occurs, those funds become personal assets and are no longer considered retirement assets. However, the amount of the defaulted loan, even if it goes unpaid, is still considered an outstanding loan when calculating the amount available to you for future loans.

It is possible, however, to roll over your outstanding 401(k) loan to a new qualified plan so you are not in default. Most plan documents will not allow a plan participant with an outstanding loan to roll the outstanding loan to another 401(k) plan. In fact, some plans will not allow you to roll funds out of the plan until the loan has been paid off or the participant takes the loan as a distribution. That being said, there are plan documents that allow for an outstanding loan to be rolled into another 401(k) plan that offers a loan program. It all depends on the plan documents that govern your new plan."

"Right," Ken said. "Anything more?"

"Yes, for example, you can never roll over an outstanding loan into a new IRA, because IRAs do not permit loans. The key is whether your new employer's plan allows for the rollover of outstanding loans and similar loan provisions. When a loan cannot be rolled over into a new retirement plan, you must either pay off the remaining loan (including principal and interest) or treat the outstanding loan balance as a taxable distribution."

"OK, so let's talk about how the 401(k) plan loan feature can work for me," Ken said.

"Sure. Let's start with taking a 401(k) plan loan from your current employer plan. You mentioned that your current plan allows for a loan. Is that correct?" John asked.

"Yes," replied Ken.

"OK, so you can take a loan from the 401(k) plan and borrow up to $50,000, but the issue is that if you start your water business, you expect to leave your job, so in that case the loan would come due and you would owe tax and a 10 percent penalty on the amount of the outstanding loan, which is not very attractive. So taking a loan from your current employer 401(k) plan is not a viable option based on your facts and circumstances," John said.

"What about Pam's 401(k) account?" Ken asked.

"Now that is a really great option," John responded. "The law firm 401(k) plan does offer a loan feature and since Pam does have over $100,000 in her plan, she would be able to borrow up to $50,000. The funds can be used for any purpose, including investing in your business. The more I am talking about this, the more I am really starting to like this option for you. I assume Pam is not leaving her job, so there is not a huge risk of being forced to pay back the loan prematurely. In addition, Pam is a partner in the firm and does quite well, so I doubt coming up with a monthly payment of approximately $904 will be a major issue."

"I like this option as well," Ken said. "This could work out well for us. We will get tax-free and penalty-free use of up to $50,000, which is all I really need to buy into the water business; and the funds Pam pays back to the plan will actually increase the value of her 401(k) account. It really seems like a win-win situation for the both of us. Of course, I have to run it by Pam, but I am loving this option."

"Me too," John said. "Now that we have discussed the self-directed IRA option for funding your business, which is not really viable, and the 401(k) plan loan option, which may turn out to be the answer, let's turn to the final option and the most controversial of the three business-funding options: the rollover business start-up solution or ROBS."

"OK, I have been eagerly awaiting this discussion because I came across the ROBS solution quite frequently when I was researching business-funding options online," Ken said.

"What I propose is that I provide an overview of the ROBS solution and then when we meet next time I will get into all the details, such as history, step-by-step overview, risks, and IRS position. We have covered a lot today so I don't want to overload you," John said.

"That makes sense," Ken said.

ROLLOVER BUSINESS START-UP SOLUTION (ROBS)

"When it comes to using retirement funds to buy or finance a business that you or another 'disqualified person' will be involved in personally, there is only one legal way to do it, and that is through the business acquisition solution, also known as a rollover business start-up solution (ROBS). The ROBS solution takes advantage of an exception in the tax code under IRC Section 4975(d)(13) that allows one to use 401(k) plan funds to buy stock in a C corporation, which is known as 'qualifying employer securities.' The exception to the IRS prohibited-transaction rules found in IRC Section 4975(d)(13) permits a 401(k) plan to buy qualifying employer securities, which is defined as stock of a C corporation. This is the reason one cannot use a self-directed IRA LLC to invest in a business that the IRA holder or a disqualified person will be personally involved in, or why a 401(k) plan cannot invest in a business operated via an LLC in which the plan participant or disqualified person will be involved without triggering the prohibited-transaction rules. Hence, in order to use retirement funds to invest in a business in which a disqualified person (you) will be personally involved, one needs a C corporation to operate a business that adopts a 401(k) plan."

"OK, I remember the Ellis case you reviewed when discussing the self-directed IRA as a business-funding option. What makes the ROBS so different than a self-directed IRA?" Ken asked.

"In a lot of respects, using a self-directed IRA LLC or a 401(k) plan to purchase stock in a corporation would seem to be subject to the same rules. However, as I just mentioned, using a self-directed IRA to purchase a business that would entail the personal involvement of a disqualified person would trigger the prohibited-transaction rules under IRC Section 4975. However, the ROBS solution, as I will explain in detail the next time we meet, takes advantage of an exception to the prohibited-transaction rules under IRC Section 4975(d)(13) that allows a 401(k) plan (not an IRA) to buy stock in a C corporation (not an LLC), which is referred to as 'qualifying employer securities.' That is why using a self-directed IRA to buy your business would not be a viable option, and why the ROBS solution could be an option."

"So how does the ROBS arrangement work?" Ken asked.

"The ROBS arrangement typically involves rolling over a prior IRA or 401(k) plan account into a newly established 401(k) plan, which either an already existing or newly established C corporation has sponsored, and then investing the rollover 401(k) plan funds in the stock of the C corporation. The funds are then deposited in the C corporation bank account and are available for use for business purposes," John said.

"So the three key components seem to be having retirement funds that are available for rollover, having a C corporation, and establishing a 401(k) plan?" Ken said.

"That is pretty much right on point," John responded.

"The ROBS solution sounds like a no brainer. Am I missing something?" Ken asked.

"I think you will understand the ROBS solution better after I go through its background and some of the controversy surrounding it involving the IRS and DOL," John said. "I think this is a good time to pause for today and pick up next week when we meet again. We covered a lot of ground today, and I think it will be beneficial to get into the ROBS in detail when we are both fresh."

"That works for me," Ken said. "How about next Tuesday at noon—same place?"

"Perfect. See you next week," John said.

5

The Rollover Business Start-Up Solution (ROBS)

K en arrived early for the Tuesday meeting with John. He waited in line, bought two cappuccinos and two scones, took a seat at their regular table, and waited for John. John arrived a few minutes later with a stack of papers. Ken was ready to go, and John jumped right into discussing the ROBS solution.

"I have been looking forward to today all week," Ken said.

"OK, I hope I don't let you down," John joked.

"I know last week I briefly explained how the ROBS worked," John continued, "but I think it will be helpful to take a step back and get into some of the background of the ROBS and the legal foundation behind it."

"OK, that sounds great," Ken said.

"Before I really jump into discussing the ROBS solution, I want to briefly offer you my personal thoughts on the structure. Even though the ROBS solution is 100 percent legal per the IRS, it is probably my least favorite self-directed retirement solution for a number of reasons. Overall, I think the idea of using a majority of your hard-earned retirement funds to invest in a business is a risky and potentially self-defeating proposition. The SBA statistic on small-business start-up failures pretty much sums it up—close to 50 percent of all new businesses fail within the first five years. That is a really high number. It is one thing to use a percentage of your savings to launch a new business, but the majority of people doing the ROBS solution are investing all or close to all of their retirement funds into the business. I always say that if Warren Buffet or any wealthy person came to me and asked about using the ROBS solution to buy a business, I would never suggest it as an option. The ROBS solution should be looked at as a last resort when there are no other options available. There are a number of reasons for this, including the requirement to use a C corporation, costs, and potential IRS scrutiny. I actually started working with the ROBS solution in 2010 only after the IRS offered follow-up guidance to the initial memorandum they released on the ROBS solution in October 2008," John said.

IRS POSITION

"OK, but why does the IRS care so much about my retirement funds?" Ken asked.

"This is a question that I get all the time," John responded.

"Remember the RMD rules we discussed sometime back? Those rules require anyone with a pretax IRA or 401(k) plan (Roth IRA funds are not subject to the RMD rules) to start taking a certain percentage of their retirement account as a taxable distribution each year. As we discussed, the purpose of the RMD rules is certify that people don't just accumulate retirement accounts, defer taxation, and leave these retirement funds as an inheritance. Therefore, the IRS cares very much about the value of your pretax retirement funds and wants your account to grow in value so that the Treasury can benefit from the RMD tax payments. So think about this—if someone invests all their retirement funds in the stock market, the retirement account may go up and down and may even drop close to 40 percent, like it did in 2008, but the chance that it would go to zero is quite small. That being said, people certainly lost a huge percentage of their stock investments if they owned Enron or Lehman Brothers, but the chance of having all your retirement funds in the stock of a company that goes to zero is really minimal. But if you take all your pretax retirement funds and invest in an ice cream store in Alaska or some other business that ends up going bankrupt, and the entire retirement account investment has been lost, the IRS is now left with no RMD or a much reduced amount, which makes them unhappy and will negatively impact the Treasury. For the IRS it all comes down to tax revenues, and since the odds of building a successful and profitable business are much smaller than generating positive returns in the stock market, the IRS is much happier when retirement funds are invested in public markets versus start-ups," John said.

"I understand the position of the IRS, but is that fair? Why should the IRS be able to tell me how to invest my retirement funds? So long as the investment is legal the IRS shouldn't care." Ken said.

"I understand your position. I get this a lot from clients and I agree that it doesn't sound fair. We will see in a minute that the IRS is not saying the ROBS solution is illegal, or a prohibited transaction, or even a tax shelter. What they are saying is that there is a high degree of abuse in its implementation, and a number of these business are failing. As we will see, the tax code does allow for the purchase of qualifying employer securities by a 401(k) plan of C corporation stock, which is the foundation for the ROBS solution, but that is not to say the IRS has to love it or won't carefully look at and examine these transactions in greater detail to confirm compliance," John said.

"OK, you said you don't like the ROBS structure, but if it is legal why do you still have an issue with it?" Ken asked.

"I will get into this point in detail shortly, but it comes down tax inefficiency, cost, and potential IRS scrutiny—things a start-up or small business would want to do without. Prior to 2010 I had serious reservations about this structure based on the information presented by the IRS, and even thought the IRS could potentially try to argue that it was a prohibited transaction, so I stayed away from them until I heard more from the IRS, which I did in 2010. But before I get into the IRS's position on ROBS, let's briefly discuss the legal foundation for the ROBS solution."

"OK, that works," Ken said.

"Navigating the tax rules and tax code may get a bit complex, so I will try to break it down as clearly as I can," John said.

Legal Foundation of the ROBS Solution

"The IRC and ERISA have firmly codified the ability to use retirement funds to invest in the stock of a sponsoring company as long as certain IRS and ERISA rules are followed. IRC Section 4975(c) includes a list of transactions that the IRS deems prohibited. However, IRC Section 4975(d) lists a number of exemptions to the prohibited-transaction rules. Specifically, IRC Section 4975(d)(13) lists an exemption to the prohibited-transaction rules for any transaction that is exempt from Section 406 of ERISA by reason of Section 408(e) of such act, which essentially covers the purchase of qualifying employer securities by a corporation," John said.

"So how long have people been doing the ROBS?" Ken asked.

"It's really hard to tell. What is clear is that when IRC Section 4975(d)(13) was enacted in 1974, the exemption was likely intended to apply to large corporations, such as publically traded corporations, since at that time all publically traded companies were C corporations. It appears that the IRS was OK if shareholders in large corporations used their 401(k) plan funds to purchase stock in the company they worked for. The idea was that it would offer incentive to the employee and help the company retain the employee. Because prior to the mid-1980s almost all new businesses were formed as corporations, it is certainly plausible that the IRS understood that this exemption under IRC Section 4975(d)(13) could be used by smaller corporations and even start-ups. In fact, the definition for 'adequate consideration' for the purchase of 'qualifying employer securities' has a provision for nonpublicly traded securities." Although, I am not sure the IRS and DOL ever expected that the exemption would become so popular among new businesses and start-ups as a business-funding mechanism," John said.

"What is clear is that business owners have been using retirement funds to help acquire or invest in a business for a number of years," John said.

"To start, as we previously reviewed, IRC Section 4975(c)(1)(A) prohibits the direct or indirect sale, exchange, or leasing of property between a plan and a disqualified person. Thus, the sale of securities between an employer and a plan or the leasing of property to the employer by the plan is prohibited. However, IRC Section 4975(d)(13) provides a statutory exemption for the acquisition, sale, or lease by plans of certain employer securities or real property."

John handed Ken a copy of IRC Section 4975 and asked him to look at (d)(13) (See Exhibit E)

"IRC Section 4975(d)(13) states: any transaction that is exempt from Section 406 of such Act by reason of Section 408(e) of such Act (or which would be so exempt if such Section 406 applied to such transaction) or which is exempt from Section 406 of such Act by reason of Section 408(b)(12) of such Act."

"Wow, that is confusing," Ken joked.

"I know. Let me try to break it down for you. Section 408(e) of ERISA provides that Section 406 of ERISA—the prohibited-transaction rules—shall not apply to the acquisition or sale by a plan of qualifying employer securities, as defined in ERISA Section 407(d)(5), provided that (1) the acquisition or sale is for adequate consideration; (2) no commission is charged with respect to the acquisition or sale; and (3) the plan is an eligible individual account plan as defined in ERISA Section 407(d)(3). ERISA Section 407(d)(5) essentially defines a qualifying employer security as stock. Although the term 'stock' is not defined in Title I of ERISA, it is generally believed to mean stock in a corporation and not an LLC interest. Pursuant to ERISA Section 406, the acquisition or sale of qualifying employer securities must be for 'adequate consideration.' Except in the case of a 'marketable obligation,' adequate consideration for this purpose means a price not less favorable than the price determined under ERISA Section 3(18), subject to a requirement that the acquisition or sale must be for 'adequate consideration.' An exchange of company stock between the plan and its employer-sponsor would be a prohibited transaction, unless the requirements of ERISA Section 408(e), which I just mentioned, are met. In order to take advantage of the prohibited-transaction exemptions under IRC Section 4975(d), the rules under IRC Section 4975(f)(6) must not apply. Section 4975(f)(6)(A) states that the exemption of IRC Section 4975(d) shall not apply in the case of a trust described in IRC Section 401(a), which is part of a plan providing contributions or benefits for employees some or all of whom are owner-employees shall not apply to a transaction in which the plan directly or indirectly (i) lends any part of the corpus or income of the plan to, (ii) pays any compensation for personal services rendered to the plan to, or (iii) acquires for the plan any property from or sells any property to any such owner-employee, a member of the family of any such owner-employee, or any corporation in which any such owner-employee owns, directly or indirectly, 50 percent or more of the total combined voting power of all classes of stock entitled to vote or 50 percent or more of the total value of shares of all classes of stock of the corporation. Therefore, since the 401(k) plan will be purchasing qualified employer securities directly from the newly formed corporation and not from an owner-employee or family member, the purchase of corporate stock will not be treated as a prohibited transaction pursuant to IRC Section 4975. ERISA Section 407(b)(1) usually places limitations on the acquisition and holding of qualifying employer securities—normally 10 percent of plan assets. However, the section includes an exception to the 10 percent ownership rule for eligible individual account plans (ERISA 407(b)(1)). As set forth in ERISA Section 407(d)(3), a qualified 401(k) profit-sharing plan is included in the definition of eligible individual account plans. In addition, pursuant to ERISA Section 404(a)(2), these plans do not violate ERISA's diversification and, to the extent it requires diversification, prudence requirements."

"You are right; the tax code is really complicated. I know now why I didn't go to law school," Ken said.

John handed Ken a piece of paper. "It does get complex, but for the ROBS solution all you need to remember is on this list."

- IRC Section 4975(c) outlines all the prohibited-transaction rules.
- IRC Section 4975(d) outlines the exemptions to the prohibited-transaction rules outlined in IRC Section 4975(c).
- IRC Section 4975(d)(13) refers to ERISA Section 408 (exemptions from prohibited transactions), which states that the prohibited-transaction rules outlined in ERISA Section 406(e) will not apply to purchase of qualifying employer securities as defined in ERISA Section 406.

- o Qualifying employer securities are defined as stock and widely understood to mean stock in a corporation and not an interest in an LLC or partnership. Since an S corporation can have only individuals as shareholders, S corporation stock would not meet the definition of qualifying employer securities.
- ERISA Section 407(a) prohibits the acquisition or holding of employer securities or employer real property. ERISA Section 407(a) does permit plans to acquire or hold a total of no more than 10 percent of its assets in the form of qualifying employer securities or qualifying employer real property or any combination of these types of property. Generally, an eligible individual account plan, which includes a 401(k) plan, is exempted from this limitation. To meet the requirements of ERISA 408(e), four requirements must be met:
  - o The plan must be an eligible individual account plan, which is defined as (i) a profit-sharing, stock bonus, thrift, or savings plan, (ii) an employee stock ownership plan, or (iii) a money purchase plan that was in existence on the date of enactment of ERISA and that on such date invested primarily in qualifying employer securities. Such term excludes an IRA or annuity described in section 408 of the IRC.
  - o Securities or real property must be qualifying.
  - o Acquisition must be for adequate consideration.
  - o No commission may be charged with respect to the acquisition.

"OK, this is really helpful, and your breakdown of the rules helped me understand the legal foundation for the ROBS solution," Ken said.

"But I do have a couple of questions," Ken added.

"Of course, go ahead," John responded.

"Can you just briefly summarize why an IRA and LLC cannot be used in the ROBS solution? You probably mentioned it, but I just want to be clear," Ken said.

"No problem. In order to get around the prohibited-transaction rules found in IRC Section 4975(c), we must find an exception under IRC

Section 4975(d). IRC Section 4975(d)(13) has a specific exemption to the prohibited-transaction rules, which cover the purchase of qualifying employer securities. As I just mentioned, a qualifying employer security is defined as stock in a corporation. Unfortunately, an investment in an LLC would not meet the definition of stock under the ERISA rules. Even though the LLC looks like a corporation for corporate limited liability purposes, it is treated as a partnership or flow-through entity for tax purposes. And as a result an LLC interest is generally not considered stock. In addition, there is not much guidance on this, especially if an LLC is treated as a corporation for tax purposes (check the box election) would satisfy the definition of stock as required pursuant to IRC Section 4975(d)(13). I think it best practice to use a C corporation if one is looking to purchase qualifying employer securities and take advantage of the prohibited-transaction exemption under IRC Section 4975(d)(13). With respect to using an IRA instead of a 401(k) plan for purchasing qualifying employer securities, the exemption under IRC Section 4975(d)(13) refers to ERISA, which does not govern IRAs since an IRA is an individual retirement account and not an employer plan," John said.

"OK, I got it. If I decided to do a ROBS solution to buy my water business, David and I would need to establish a C corporation and have it adopt a 401(k) plan. Using an LLC or IRA would not work, as it would not allow me to get around the prohibited-transaction rules under IRC Section 4975," Ken said.

"That is correct. Other than the Ellis case, which we talked about when discussing the self-directed IRA funding option, there is another case we previously discussed when looking at the prohibited transaction rules that really highlights the impact of failing to use a corporation and 401(k) plan when engaging in a business transaction."

PEEK V. COMMISSIONER, 140 T.C. NO. 12 (MAY 9, 2013)
In 2001, two taxpayers, Mr. Lawrence Peek and Mr. Darrel Fleck, sought to use self-directed IRAs to acquire a business. The taxpayers established self-directed IRAs using 401(k) rollovers, created a new company (FP

Company), and then directed the IRAs to purchase the common stock of FP Company with the cash in the IRAs. FP Company then sought to purchase the business. To consummate the purchase, in addition to the cash and other credit lines, FP Company provided a promissory note to the sellers. This promissory note was backed by the personal guarantee of the taxpayers, and the guarantees were then backed by the deeds to the taxpayers' homes. In 2003 and 2004, the taxpayers converted their traditional IRAs to Roth IRAs. In 2006 and 2007, the IRAs sold FP Company for a gain. Because a Roth IRA recognized the gain, there would be no tax on the gain from the sale of stock.

The IRS audited the income tax return for both Mr. Peek and Mr. Fleck for the tax years of 2006 and 2007. After reviewing the individuals' tax returns, the IRS adjusted their tax returns to include the capital gains income from the sale of the stock as well as imposed excise tax for excess IRA contributions. Both Mr. Peek and Fleck contested the IRS's adjustment and filed a petition with the tax court.

The IRS argued that Mr. Fleck's and Mr. Peek's personal guarantees of a $200,000 promissory note from FP Company to the sellers of the business in 2001 as part of FP Company's purchase of the business assets were prohibited transactions. The tax court agreed with the IRS and found that the taxpayers had committed prohibited transactions, that the IRAs had ceased to be IRAs as of the beginning of 2001, and that the capital gain from the sale of FP Company by the IRAs was immediately taxed to the taxpayers. The tax court agreed with the IRS and held that since IRC Section 4975 prohibits both "direct and indirect...lending of money or extensions of credit" between an IRA and its owner, it did not matter that the loan guarantee by the taxpayers was to FP Company and not the IRAs directly. IRC Section 4975 clears prohibits the lending of money or extension of credit between a retirement plan and a disqualified person.

Mr. Peek and Mr. Fleck argued that the IRS's notices issued in 2006 and 2007 were too late because the loan was made in 2001. The IRS contended, and the tax court agreed, that since the nonrecourse loan was ongoing, the prohibited transaction continued, and on January 1, 2006, it remained true that both Mr. Peek and Mr. Fleck personally guaranteed the company loan.

The Law

IRC Section 4975(c) prohibits specified transactions between (i) various plans including IRAs and (ii) "disqualified persons" (or "parties in interest" under the ERISA version of these rules), which in the case of an IRA includes the IRA owner. Subject to certain exemptions, pursuant to IRC Section 4975, a disqualified person cannot engage in transactions with the plan that, among other things, constitute direct or indirect

- sales, exchanges, or leasing of property;
- lending of money or other extension of credit;
- furnishing of goods, services, or facilities; or
- transfer to, or use by or for the benefit of, a disqualified person of the income or assets of a plan.

The Court's Opinion

The tax court ruled that a taxpayer's personal guarantee of a loan by a corporation owned by the individual's IRA is a prohibited transaction under IRC Section 4975(c)(1)(B). The court found that the taxpayers had provided an indirect extension of credit to the IRAs, a prohibited transaction under IRC Section 4975 that disqualified the IRAs. The tax court held that Peek and Fleck were liable for a 20 percent accuracy-related penalty because their underpayments of tax were a "substantial understatement of income tax" under IRC Section 6662.

While the penalty for an IRC Section 4975 violation is normally an excise tax, a prohibited transaction between an IRA and its owner results in the tax disqualification of the IRA under IRC Section 408(e)(2), in which case the IRA assets are treated for tax purposes as distributed to the IRA owner.

"That is really helpful," Ken said. "I assume that if Mr. Peek used a 401(k) plan instead of an IRA he would not have had a prohibited transaction issue."

"Correct; you are a quick learner. Like in Ellis, the problem in Peek is that a self-directed IRA was used to make the business investment. As a result, the exception to the IRC Section 4975(c) prohibited-transaction rules for the purchase of qualifying employer securities under IRC Section 4975(d) (13) was not satisfied, because 401(k) plan funds were not used. Even though Mr. Peek used a corporation, by using an IRA and not a 401(k) plan to make the purchase of corporate stock, he was not able to satisfy the definition of a qualifying employer security under ERISA Section 408," John said.

"I guess it makes sense to work with tax professionals when organizing these types of structures," Ken said.

"I couldn't agree with you more. The Peek case highlighted the importance of working with independent tax attorneys who can properly advise on a proposed investment. Mr. Peek and Mr. Fleck relied on the advice of Mr. Blees, a CPA, who was also the promoter of the transaction. As a result, Mr. Blees did not warn Mr. Peek and Mr. Fleck about triggering the prohibited-transaction rules when personally guaranteeing the business loan for their IRA investment. If Mr. Peek had been properly advised, he could have potentially used the ROBS solution to engage in the business transaction without violating the IRS prohibited-transaction rules," John said.

"Well, I am really glad I am speaking to you," Ken said.

"It is my pleasure. Now that we have touched upon the legal foundation of the ROBS solution, I think this is a great time to talk about the IRS's position on the ROBS solution."

"OK, this should be interesting," Ken said.

"As we now know, ERISA and the IRC clearly allows for the use of retirement funds to acquire or invest in a new or existing business as long as the transaction satisfies the exemption to the prohibited-transaction rules under IRC Section 4975(d)(13). I also mentioned that aspiring entrepreneurs have been using retirement funds to help acquire or invest in a business for a number of years. For over fifteen years, a number of promoters have promoted these types of transactions under the name "ROBS." Even though this type of transaction is permitted under IRS and ERISA rules, the IRS believed a significant number of the ROBS promoters were not taking the necessary steps to structure a transaction that is in full compliance with IRS and ERISA rules."

John gave Ken a handout from the Treasury Department titled "Guidelines Regarding Rollovers as Business Start-Ups" (See Exhibit F).

Ken took the document and started flipping through the fifteen or so pages.

"Don't worry. I will go through the main points of the document, which I will refer to as the ROBS memorandum. However, I do think it is a good idea for you to read it. In fact, I recommend that any client I talk with about the ROBS solution that shows some interest read it. The ROBS memorandum is written quite well, goes through the ROBS solution is some detail, and provides some important insight from the IRS on problem areas." John said.

"OK, I will definitely read it thoroughly when I get home." Ken said.

"Let me begin. On October 1, 2008, Michael Julianelle, director of employee plans, signed a memorandum approving IRS ROBS examination guidelines. The IRS stated that while this type of structure is legal and not considered an abusive tax-avoidance transaction, the execution of these types of transactions, in many cases, has not been found to be in full compliance with IRS and ERISA rules and procedures. In the ROBS memorandum, the IRS highlighted a number of compliance areas that they felt were not being adequately followed by the promoters implementing the structure during this time period."

"Can you explain?"

"As I previously mentioned, I did not work with the ROBS solution until after 2010, even though I had heard of people engaging in the transaction since the late 1990s. When I read the ROBS memorandum in October 2008, I felt good about my position. The IRS did not state that the ROBS solution was illegal or even prohibited, but the IRS did mention that they had audited a number of ROBS promoters and found a number of problem areas in its implementation, which concerned me. I did not want any of my clients to be audited or for their transaction to be deemed invalid because of noncompliance. I was also worried that the IRS could turn around at some point and treat the ROBS as illegal or prohibited so I wanted more guidance," John said.

"That makes sense, and I assume your clients understood your position," Ken said.

2008 IRS ROBS MEMORANDUM

"I think they did. But let's get back to discussing the ROBS memorandum," John said. "Prior to 2008, the IRS had not issued significant administrative guidance on business start-ups capitalized with retirement plan assets. That all changed in October 2008, when the Tax Exempt and Government Entities Division of the IRS issued the only real administrative guidance on rollovers of retirement plan assets to fund business start-ups—ROBS. The IRS issued the memorandum in light of a growing number of promoters marketing the ROBS solution. The memorandum mentioned that promoters nationwide were aggressively marketing the ROBS solution as a vehicle for prospective business owners to access accumulated tax-deferred retirement funds without paying applicable distribution taxes in order to cover new business start-up costs."

"Did the ROBS memorandum provide any info on the promoters they contacted?" Ken asked.

"Not specifically, but it mentioned that it had identified nine promoters of the ROBS transaction. The IRS did not mention names, but any search of the Internet would provide you a list of the more popular promoters of the ROBS solution, so coming up with a list is not too difficult. Most of these promoters (companies or individuals) are actively promoting the use of ROBS at seminars held to help individuals purchase business franchises. The ROBS memorandum mentioned that these promoters were referred to the Lead Development Center (LDC). The ROBS memorandum also mentioned that the IRS had been coordinating the review of the ROBS plans with the DOL. Additionally, the ROBS memorandum mentioned that the IRS had reviewed several returns of employers who engaged in ROBS transactions. Their examinations have largely started with a review of business tax returns and then moved on to a review of promoter activity.

"I guess this is what you wanted your clients to stay away from," Ken said.

"Exactly. After reading the ROBS memorandum, I was concerned that the IRS would start issuing summonses to all these ROBS promoters in order to try to get the names of all their clients. This type of summons is often referred to as a John Doe summons, and it is an IRS summons authorized by IRC Section 7609(f). Unlike other IRS summonses it does not list the name of the taxpayer under investigation, because the taxpayer is unknown to the IRS. The term "John Doe summons" achieved notoriety in July 2008 when the procedure was used to crack Swiss banking-secrecy laws, and ultimately ended up in Bank UBS turning over the names of about forty-five hundred holders of Swiss bank accounts to the IRS. I didn't want any of my clients to be in a situation where their retirement account would become subject to an IRS audit until I heard more from the IRS on the subject. I spent a lot of time talking with a number of tax attorneys and tax professionals about the ROBS solution prior to the issuance of the 2008 ROBS memorandum and sometime after, and most felt the same way—until the IRS issued more guidance it was best to stay away from the transaction," John said.

"As you will see when you start reading the ROBS memorandum, the IRS held that the ROBS solution would serve legitimate tax and business planning needs, but what is questionable is that the ROBS structure would serve solely to enable one individual's exchange of tax-deferred assets for currently available funds by using a qualified plan and its investment in employer stock as a medium. The IRS added that the ROBS solution allows for the avoidance of distribution taxes otherwise assessable on this exchange. The IRS then added that although a variety of business activity had been examined, the valuation of the newly established corporations might be questionable. The IRS then went into explaining how the ROBS solution works, which I will get into shortly, and then focused on the two main area of noncompliance that have been a common problem areas in the structures they reviewed."

"OK," Ken said.

"The first noncompliance area of concern the IRS highlighted in the ROBS memorandum was the lack of disclosure of the adopted 401(k) plan to the company's employees. The IRS believed that in too many instances the promoter was establishing a 401(k) plan that was not adequately disclosed to all eligible employees. IRC Section 401(a)(4) provides that under a qualified retirement plan, contributions or benefits provided under the plan must not discriminate in favor of highly compensated employees. In addition, the promoters were encouraging business owners who had used their retirement funds to purchase company stock not to provide the same benefit to their employees."

"Got it," Ken said.

"The second noncompliance area of concern the IRS highlighted in the ROBS memorandum was establishing an independent appraisal to determine the fair market value of the corporate stock being purchased (qualifying employer security). As we talked about, IRC Section 4975(d)(13) provides an exemption from prohibited transaction consideration for any transaction that is exempt from ERISA Section 406 (prohibited transactions), by reason of ERISA Section 408(e) (exemptions from prohibited transactions), which addresses certain transactions involving qualifying employer stock. ERISA Section 408(e), and ERISA Regulation Section 2550, 408e promulgated thereunder, provides an exemption from ERISA Section 406 (prohibited-transaction rules) for acquisitions or sales of qualifying employer securities, subject to a requirement that the acquisition or sale must be for adequate consideration. Except in the case of a marketable obligation, adequate consideration for this purpose means a price not less favorable than the price determined under ERISA Section 3(18). ERISA Section 3(18) provides in relevant part that, in the case of an asset other than a security for which there is no generally recognized market, adequate consideration means the fair market value of the asset as determined in good faith by the trustee or named fiduciary pursuant to the terms of the plan and in accordance with regulations."

"I see," said Ken.

"The ROBS memorandum outlines the IRS's concern that adequate consideration is not being paid for the qualifying employer security by the corporation in violation of the exemption under IRC Section 4975(d) (13), which requires that an exchange of company stock between the plan and its employer-sponsor would be a prohibited transaction, unless the requirements of ERISA Section 408(e) are met (the acquisition or sale of the qualifying employer securities must be for adequate consideration). Therefore, valuation of the qualifying employer security stock is a relevant issue to the IRS. Since, in some cases, the company may be newly established, there could be a question of whether the stock is indeed worth the purchase price exchanged. If the transaction has not been for adequate consideration, it would have to be corrected, for example, by the corporation redeeming stock from the plan and replacing it with cash equal to its fair market value, plus an additional interest factor for lost plan earnings. In addition, the IRS asserts that a valuation-related prohibited-transaction issue may arise when the start-up enterprise does not actually "start-up." Many promoters have been advising clients that they do not need to secure an appraisal, which would seemingly contradict the IRS's position outlined in the ROBS memorandum. In addition, the promoters who have provided clients with a valuation have been providing clients with a single line valuation statement generally approximating available retirement funds, which the IRS considers inadequate."

"I understand that the tax rules require that qualifying employer securities be for adequate consideration in order to take advantage of the exception under IRC Section 4975(d). My question is if the corporation is a start-up and essentially a shell company, as it is newly established, how do you value the stock?" Ken asked.

"You asked a really important question. This has been bothering many tax attorneys and CPAs for many years and has been one of the biggest unanswered questions and uncertainties involving the ROBS solution. The question then becomes how do you value a new company that has had no business activity and has no business assets? Since the majority of people who use the ROBS solution for start-ups are using a new corporation with no business activity, how do you put a value on the new company stock? Of course, getting a value on a publically traded company, such as Apple, is not a problem and is as simple as a click of the mouse. Even a private business that has been in business for a number of years and has assets, revenues, and has filed a tax return can be difficult to value. A small-business valuation may be subjective, but it can be done. For start-ups using the ROBS solution, I suggest that all my clients get an independent tax professional such as a CPA or a certified appraiser to value the new company stock. Typically what occurs is the appraiser will look at the assets the company will be purchasing as part of the ROBS transaction, either by reviewing the stock purchase agreement, asset purchase agreement, or franchise agreement. The appraiser will then look at all other relevant factors to come out with a fair market value of the company stock purchased (qualifying employer securities). In most cases, the valuation equals the amount of the 401(k) funds and other personal funds being used in the ROBS solution," John said.

"I guess that makes sense. How else would you value a company that was just formed?" Ken said.

"Agreed. It is quite subjective to put a value on a newly established company that has no customers, revenues, or even any equipment or inventory. The tax rules require that the qualifying employer security that is purchased be for adequate consideration, so we have to comply with the rules and make sure that the qualifying employer security that is purchased by the 401(k) plan is priced fairly. The issue is that putting a value on a newly established corporation with no assets or business activity is quite subjective. According to a number of CPAs and certified appraisers I have talked to, the most effective way of coming up with a fair market value for the new corporate stock being purchased is to take into account all the 401(k) and personal funds that will be invested in the company and then look at all the assets the new corporation will be buying with those funds. Of course, there may be other factors that can contribute to valuing the stock of the new corporation, such as the experience of the owners, goodwill, prior business relationships that can be leveraged, confirmed future orders or business arrangements, and the like. The bottom line is that valuing a start-up business is not an exact science and can be quite subjective. It is for this reason that in most cases, the corporate stock sold by the corporation to a 401(k) plan in the ROBS structure tends to equal the amount of 401(k) and personal funds being used in the transaction, which will ultimately be used to purchase business assets. For example, if you established a new corporation and rolled over $100,000 into the new corporation's 401(k) plan, invested $25,000 of personal funds into the corporation, and used the resulting $125,000 to buy business assets, most appraisals would value the company at $125,000 and would break down the purchase price to equal the assets that would be purchased by the business. The more details, analysis, and support the appraisal letter contains, the easier it will be to show that adequate consideration was paid for the qualifying employer securities purchased. A one-page appraisal letter that shows only the amount of funds invested, with no breakdown of the business assets to be purchased, and no review of the business, industry, or other relevant factors, will not convince the IRS that adequate consideration was paid for the stock. The IRS actually addressed this issue in the ROBS memorandum and commented that even if supportive analysis to back up the valuation or the stock purchase is presented it may not satisfy the exemption under IRC Section 4975(d)(13)."

"I'm following," Ken said.

"Of course, as I mentioned, there may be additional facts that can change the value of the company stock, but in most ROBS transactions, the appraisal letter tends to value the company stock at the amount of funds being used to purchase that stock. One issue is that no one really knows what kind of supportive analysis or information the IRS is looking for in order to satisfy the adequate consideration threshold. For a start-up with no business activity, other than the 401(k) plan or personal funds being used to purchase the company stock, without considering the business assets that will be ultimately purchased with such funds, there is really not much more supportive analysis that can be offered to back up the value of a start-up business. This is the issue many certified appraisers have with issuing valuation for a start-up corporation in a ROBS transaction. Clearly, the more evidence, analysis, support that can be provided by the independent appraiser when drafting the appraisal letter valuing the qualifying employer securities being purchased will be helpful. The IRS expanded on this in the memorandum by describing how in some cases, IRS examiners were provided with a single sheet of paper signed by a purported valuation specialist. This appraisal 'certifies' that the value of the enterprise stock is a sum certain, the amount of which approximates the amount of available proceeds from the individual's tax-deferred retirement account. The IRS stated that these types of appraisals are questionable. Because the valuation usually approximates available funds, consideration needs to be given to whether inherent value in the plan-acquired entity actually exists. The IRS went even further to state that the lack of a bona fide appraisal raises a question as to whether the entire exchange is a prohibited transaction," John said.

"Pretty scary stuff," Ken said.

"Yes. The IRS takes the valuation aspect of the ROBS transaction very seriously and so should all ROBS promoters. The problem is that it seems a lot of them do not and tend to look at the appraisal letter as an afterthought. As the ROBS memorandum states quite clearly, the IRS could hold that the lack of a bona fide appraisal could cause one to fail the requirements of IRC Section 4975(d)(13) and trigger a prohibited transaction," John said.

"I assume that if I bought into an existing C corporation or had established my C corporation some time ago and it had business activity, revenues, customers, and so forth, and was not a start-up, then valuing the company would be a bit more objective and precise?" Ken asked.

"Yes, that is for sure. The more business activity and business history the company has, the more accurate the business valuation can be. The valuation is important not so much so you know how much your company is worth from an owner's perspective, but it is required in order to satisfy the exemption to the prohibited-transaction rules under IRC Section 4975(d)(13), which is key to successfully using the ROBS solution. The rules under IRC Section 4975(d)(13) are clear that the qualifying employer securities purchased by the 401(k) plan be for adequate consideration," John said.

"Why does the IRS care so much about my 401(k) plan paying adequate consideration for the corporate stock?" Ken asked.

"It really comes down to the IRS being concerned about the value of your 401(k) plan. Remember the value of your pretax IRA or 401(k) plan is very important to the IRS because of the RMD regime. Making sure that you are valuing your retirement account accurately is important because it can have a significant impact on the tax revenues generated by the Treasury. It is for this reason that most tax practitioners believe that the IRS is so focused on the adequate consideration factor when evaluating the ROBS solution. Another reason for the valuation focus is that the IRS, upon reviewing a number of active ROBS structures, noticed that some businesses that used the ROBS transaction were actually not yet operational or even started, which opens up a slew of other potential problems, such as the plan being invalid because there is no business to adopt it. The ROBS memorandum expanded on this problem by stating that where the start-up has not actually started up and the appraisal letter shows 'cash' as its only asset, as no business assets or other assets necessary to start a bona fide business were purchased, the cash-only valuation may not be sufficient to satisfy the adequate consideration requirement," John said.

"I understand the position of the IRS on adequate consideration, but I still don't understand how a start-up business can provide an appraiser anything more than a breakdown of the cash and retirement funds to be used and anticipated business assets to be purchased for completing a valuation of the new corporate stock," Ken said.

"I know. This is one reason I don't love the ROBS solution. The compliance aspect is so difficult to satisfy, especially for start-ups, which are what make up most of the ROBS structures. For an established business with a business history, revenues, clients, and assets, providing a value for the corporate stock being purchased would be much more attainable. To this end, when someone is buying the business assets of an existing corporation, the IRS requires that the buyer and seller agree to a purchase price allocation of the purchased assets per IRC Section 1060. This tends to provide an appraiser with the necessary support on which to base an appraisal letter, whereas in the case of a start-up, where the corporation is newly established and has no cash or assets on hand, valuing the business tends to be based on invested cash and the projected value of assets to be purchased. This concerns the IRS since there is a likelihood that the business will not get started and the rollover funds could then be used by the business owner with no tax or early distribution penalty," John said.

"So is that what this really about?" Ken asked. "The IRS is worried that people are going to establish these ROBS solutions, never actually start a business, and just use the funds for personal purposes without paying tax or penalty?"

"I think you hit the nail on the head. That is undoubtedly something the IRS is concerned about when start-ups use the ROBS solution as a business-funding mechanism. The IRS makes reference to this in the ROBS memorandum when they state that in some cases the funds were used to purchase personal/nonbusiness assets. The concern on the part of the IRS is that the funds newly invested in the corporation will be used for personal reasons instead of business purposes, which will allow the individual to use the funds without paying a distribution tax or 10 percent early distribution penalty if the individual is under the age of fifty-nine and a half. The tax on retirement account distributions generates significant tax revenues for the Treasury and is an important set of rules that the IRS is steadfast in protecting. To allow someone to invest retirement funds through a ROBS solution and then use those funds for personal purposes will potentially create an abusive tax-avoidance scheme and will negatively impact the IRS at two points: once when the individual receives a tax deduction for the pretax retirement account contribution that was made, and again when the retirement funds are used for personal purposes without paying any tax. This is a nightmare scenario for the IRS and is a central reason they are so concerned about the ROBS structure and lack of compliance," John said.

"What about the high start-up business failure rate? Don't you think that is an important reason the IRS is not so in love with the ROBS structure?" Ken asked.

"I do. A big issue the IRS has with the ROBS solution is the high failure rate for new businesses and the potential negative impact the investment loss can be on tax revenues. I think the IRS has no issues with employees of larger corporations, such as Apple, using their 401(k) plan funds to buy Apple stock (qualifying employer securities) or even employees of established business who want to invest in the business they work for with their 401(k) funds, but when would-be entrepreneurs take all their hard-earned retirement funds and invest in a start-up, which has a fifty percent chance of failing, a red flag goes up."

"So does the IRS really care that much about me and my retirement funds?" Ken asked.

"Yes and no. They care about you and your retirement funds to the extent that you do not engage in any prohibited transactions, and they are certainly hopeful that your account grows in value, which usually means more tax revenue for the Treasury. As you now know, the IRS doesn't tell you what you can invest in with retirement funds, only what you are not able to invest in, so they are not looking to micromanage your retirement investments, but they do want to make sure you are staying within the rules. There are a number of reasons they have spent a considerable amount of time focusing on the ROBS solution. The first, which I have discussed in some detail, is lack of compliance, which, based on the ROBS memorandum, appears quite worrisome to the IRS. The second is the high failure rate of these new start-up businesses, which has a negative impact on the tax revenue generated by the Treasury from RMDs. The third is the failure of some of these businesses to launch, which has led to the use of retirement funds for personal purposes and the circumvention of the IRS distribution rules, which are crucial to the Treasury."

"I really appreciate your going through this fifteen-page IRS ROBS memorandum with me. To summarize, what are the main issues the IRS addressed with respect to the ROBS transaction?" Ken asked.

"Let me review them again as well as touch on a few extras I don't believe I mentioned," John said.

Plan Not Notified to Eligible Participants

"The first problem the IRS has with the ROBS structure is lack of compliance. Specifically, the fact that the 401(k) plan adopted by the new corporation is not being offered to all eligible participants. We spent some time discussing

401(k) plans earlier on, and I described how all eligible plan participants must be offered plan benefits per the plan documents, and the plan cannot be used exclusively by the owners or highly compensated employees. The IRS had some concerns on the amount of compensation paid to the business owner and whether that was kept below the dollar limit for highly compensated employees purposely in order to circumvent reporting. To that end, I mentioned the safe harbor 401(k) plan, which is commonly used by small businesses because its simpler administrative features usually require the employer to provide a minimum 3 percent matching contribution based on each eligible employee's salary. The ROBS memorandum addressed the fact that many 401(k) plans they examined as part of the overall ROBS structure audit were not being offered to all eligible participants. In fact, they mentioned that in some cases the employees were not even notified that a plan existed and were not offered any plan benefits or allowed to make any contributions. Furthermore, the ROBS memorandum mentioned that if the company issued additional shares, no other plan participant would ever be offered the ability to invest in employer stock, which violates ERISA rules. Furthermore, in some ROBS versions, the provision permitting the stock investment is eliminated immediately after the stock exchange by means of a second amendment that serves to prospectively redact that provision. The IRS is clearly concerned that the 401(k) plan is being used simply as a vehicle to fund the business and is not being used to benefit all eligible employees and provide retirement benefits as it is intended. The IRS revealed that because the ROBS transaction usually benefits only the principals involved with setting up the business, and does not enable rank-and-file employees to acquire employer stock, they believe that some of these plans could violate the antidiscrimination provisions of the IRC and regulations. This is a huge concern for the IRS and is something that can invalidate the ROBS structure."

Inadequate Valuations

"The second problem the IRS found with the ROBS solution, which they detailed in the 2008 ROBS memorandum, was the inadequate valuation given to the purchase of the qualifying employer security. As we spent lots of time discussing, in order to take advantage of the prohibited-transaction exemption under IRC Section 4975(d)(13), the purchase of qualifying employer security must be for adequate consideration. This is a major problem area for the IRS for a number of reasons. The first issue the IRS has is that the value of the stock is typically set to equal the value of the company's available assets, which tends to be the cash invested. In many situations, the appraisal that is drafted to show the value of the stock purchased (qualifying employer security) is often devoid of supportive analysis. Since in most cases the corporation used in the ROBS structure is newly established, the IRS feels that there could be a question of whether the stock purchased is indeed worth the value of the tax-deferred assets for which it was exchanged. Secondly, the IRS mentioned that a valuation-related prohibited transaction issue could arise when the start-up enterprise does not actually "start-up." In such a case, the start-up entity might record "cash" as its only asset without any real attempt to secure, for example, a franchise license, property, plant and equipment, or any other assets necessary to start a bona fide business. We have discussed at length why this troubles the IRS and how it can be used as an abusive tax-avoidance scheme, negatively impacting the levels of tax revenues generated for the Treasury. The IRS seems concerned that the valuations being presented lack substance. For example, many examiners have been provided with a single sheet of paper signed by a purported valuation specialist. This appraisal "certifies" that the value of the enterprise stock is a certain sum, the amount of which approximates the amount of available proceeds from the individual's tax-deferred retirement account. The IRS feels these appraisals are questionable. Because the valuation usually approximates available funds, consideration needs to be given to whether inherent value in the plan-acquired entity actually exists. The IRS feels that the lack of a bona fide appraisal raises a question as to whether the entire exchange is a prohibited transaction."

IRS Form 5500 Not Filed

"A 401(k) plan is a tax-exempt retirement plan, so it is not required to file a tax return; however, it still may be required to file an annual information return with the IRS, the Form 5500. In the case of a solo 401(k) plan, which is a plan adopted by a sole proprietorship or small-business owner with no full-time employees, an IRS Form 5500-EZ is required to be filed only if the plan's assets exceed $250,000. In the case of a 401(k) plan with full-time employees, the IRS Form 5500 or IRS Form 5500-SF must be filed, irrespective of plan asset value. With respect to the ROBS structure, an IRS Form 5500 must be filed even if there are no full-time employees other than the owners because of the purchase of qualifying employer securities. The ROBS memorandum outlined the IRS's concern that the IRS Form 5500 was not filed in a number of instances."

Promoter Fees

"The IRS outlined in the ROBS memorandum that if the promoter of the ROBS solution was considered a fiduciary as defined under IRC Section 4975(e)(2), fees paid to the promoter could trigger a prohibited transaction. A fiduciary is defined as any person who exercises any discretionary authority or control, who renders investment advice for a fee, or who has any discretionary authority or responsibility in the administration of the plan. The IRS details how the ERISA rules clarify the definition of a person deemed to render investment advice as someone who renders advice to the plan as to the value of securities or other property, or makes a recommendation as to the advisability of investing in, purchasing, or selling securities or other property, and such person either directly or indirectly has discretionary authority or control, whether or not pursuant to an agreement, arrangement, or understanding, with respect to purchasing or selling securities or other property for the plan. The advice would have to be rendered on a regular basis to the plan pursuant to a mutual agreement, arrangement, or understanding. In almost all cases, a ROBS promoter will not satisfy the definition of a fiduciary under the IRC or ERISA rules, thus, in my opinion, greatly reducing any prohibited transaction risk in this circumstance."

Permanency of Plan

"A 401(k) plan should not be intended to be temporary. The Treasury regulations under IRC Section 401 provide that a qualified plan must be created primarily for the purposes of providing systematic retirement benefits for employees. The Treasury regulations under Section 1.401-1(b)(2) require that the plan be permanent, as distinguished from temporary arrangement, and provide a general rule that if a plan is discontinued within a few years after its adoption, there is a presumption that it was not intended as a permanent program from its inception, unless business necessity required the discontinuance, termination, or partial termination. The IRS acknowledged that because ROBS benefits are designed to be used only once for the investment of retirement funds into the company, the permanency of the 401(k) plan is an issue that must be addressed, as a 401(k) plan must be permanent."

Personal Assets Being Purchased

"The IRS noted in the ROBS memorandum that they had reviewed several ROBS arrangements to determine whether the plan had been established for the exclusive benefit of employees or if it was being used for personal nonbusiness purposes. In a few cases, the IRS noted that the 401(k) funds used to purchase the company stock wound up purchasing personal assets like recreational vehicles, which is quite problematic as it would violate the exclusive benefit rules under IRC Section 401. IRC Section 401(a)(2) provides, in relevant part, that a plan is not qualified unless it is impossible—at any time prior to the satisfaction of all liabilities with respect to employees and their beneficiaries—for any part of the corpus or income to be used for or diverted to purposes other than for the exclusive benefit of employees or their beneficiaries. In addition, the Treasury regulations under Section 1.401-2 outline the specific provisions that a plan must follow to meet the exclusive benefit rule for purposes of Title II of ERISA."

Lack of Plan Activity

"The IRS noted that a large number of reviewed ROBS 401(k) plans contained election provisions in the adoption agreement to utilize a CODA (cash or deferred arrangement synonymous with a 401(k) plan). However, they found that often a low number of participants actually chose to make salary-reduction contributions to the plan. In some instances, the IRS found that the deferral option was 'inactive.' This is an area of concern to the IRS since a plan that did not allow employees to make elective deferrals would violate IRC Section 401(k)(2)(D). The IRS concluded the ROBS memorandum by acknowledging that the ROBS transaction may violate law in several regards. The IRS also called the ROBS structure a 'scheme,' which is not a very positive term from an IRS perspective."

"Now I understand why you still had some reservations about the ROBS solution after reading the IRS 2008 memorandum," Ken said.

"I did. The use of the word 'scheme' in the ROBS memorandum conclusion really worried me and told me that the IRS had some serious concerns about the ROBS structure. I also was troubled by the many problem areas and compliance issues the IRS raised. After reviewing the ROBS memorandum carefully, I was unsure what the IRS was going to do in the future with respect to the legality of the ROBS solution. On one hand, the IRS did not say flat out that the ROBS solution was illegal or prohibited, but it did call it a 'scheme' and stated that it 'may violate law in several regards.' This caused me apprehension, and I did not feel comfortable advising any of my clients to engage in a ROBS transaction. In addition, the IRS highlighted so many potential compliance violations and problem areas that I felt that the ROBS structure posed too much risk."

"So what changed?" Ken asked.

"Well, not much from 2008 through the summer of 2010. I still felt the same way about the ROBS structure and advised against doing the transaction to anyone who asked. I felt there was too much uncertainty as to how the IRS was going to treat these structures in the future, and I wanted to hear more from the IRS. From the release of the ROBS memorandum through the summer of 2010, neither the IRS nor the DOL said much about the ROBS transaction. That all changed in August 2010."

"What happened?"

August 2010 Public Forum

"On August 27, 2010, almost two years after publishing the 2008 ROBS memorandum, the IRS held a public phone forum that covered transactions involving using retirement funds to purchase a business."

John handed Ken a copy of the handout announcing the phone forum (See Exhibit I).

"I was on the call and was really excited to hear what the IRS had to say about the ROBS transaction in light of the 2008 memorandum. Monika Templeman, director of employee plans examinations and Colleen Patton, area manager of employee plans examinations for the Pacific Coast spent considerable time discussing the IRS's position on this subject. Templeman began the presentation by reaffirming the IRS's position that a transaction involving the use of 401(k) plan retirement funds to purchase a new business's qualifying employer stock is legal and not an abusive tax-avoidance transaction as long as the transaction complies with IRS and ERISA rules and procedures. This was a very important statement for me because it was the first time I heard the IRS state that the ROBS solution was not illegal, a prohibited transaction, or even a tax shelter. As I mentioned, after reading the ROBS memorandum I was not sure how the IRS was going to ultimately treat the ROBS transaction in the future, and when the IRS described the ROBS transaction as a 'scheme' in the 2008 memorandum, I was looking for more guidance from the IRS. In a perfect world I would have wished that the IRS's statement about the validity of the ROBS transaction was in writing, but the IRS repeatedly stated that the ROBS solution was legal and was not a prohibited transaction. I now had the validation from the IRS that I was looking for before I was willing to recommend the ROBS structure to a client who wanted to use retirement funds to invest in a business."

"Did the IRS also talk about the problem areas and compliance issues they referred to in the 2008 memorandum?" Ken asked.

"They sure did. The IRS spent a considerable amount of time on the call discussing those problem areas and compliance violations discussed in the ROBS memorandum. The IRS stressed that they were concerned that the ROBS promoters were not doing enough to ensure their clients were keeping the ROBS structure in full IRS and ERISA compliance. The IRS added that a large percentage of the transactions they reviewed were in noncompliance largely due to the following issues: (i) failure by the promoters to develop a structure that requires the new company to disclose the 401(k) plan to the company's employees and, (ii) the failure to require the client to secure an independent appraisal to determine the fair market value of the company stock being purchased by the 401(k) plan. The IRS was concerned about the 401(k) plan was not being offered to eligible employees and that the valuation drafted by an independent appraiser was inadequate because of a lack of support and substance. The IRS also noted that they were concerned that, in some cases, personal assets such as recreational vehicles, and not business assets, were being purchased by the company. Overall, the public phone forum was very helpful to me and many tax practitioners because it was important to hear directly from the IRS that the ROBS solution is not considered illegal or a prohibited transaction if done properly. Also, the IRS did not refer to the ROBS structure as a 'scheme,' which was comforting. On the other hand, the IRS still had real concerns about the way ROBS transactions had been implemented in many cases, and they continue to be focused on compliance," John said.

"So, if I did a ROBS transaction and made sure to keep the structure in full IRS and ERISA compliance in line with the 2008 ROBS memorandum, I would be OK?" Ken asked.

"Yes. I think that is correct, but it is easier said than done. Any individual who is looking to do a ROBS solution must really understand the compliance areas that must be satisfied, such as plan permanency, exclusive benefit, stock valuation, annual administration requirements, and of course business use of funds. The 2010 call did offer some validity to the ROBS transaction to me and to many tax practitioners, although the ROBS transaction still imposes a high degree of risk versus other retirement business-funding options, such as the 401(k) loan feature," John said.

"So what do you tell clients today who ask about your position on the ROBS transaction?" Ken asked.

"Well, I tell them that if done properly and in full IRS and ERISA compliance, is it legal and not a prohibited transaction. I also tell them to work with a tax attorney or firm that has experience in establishing these structures. Establishing a ROBS structure is a major commitment that should not be taken lightly. It can mean the difference between having a legal structure or engaging in a prohibited transaction. Besides completing due diligence on the business you will be investing in, the ROBS structure requires continuous attention, which for some of my clients could end up being too much of a burden. I have recommended the ROBS structure to a number of my clients I felt would be OK working in such a compliance-driven environment, but I have certainly advised more people against doing it. As I previously mentioned, the ROBS structure should be a last resort for anyone looking to fund a business because of the compliance requirements and restrictions imposes. In addition, there are costs and potential IRS scrutiny that must be considered. The ROBS solution can be a great way to fund the business of your dreams with your retirement funds, but it should be done only as a last resort after all other business-funding options have been exhausted. Reading the 2008 IRS ROBS memorandum in detail is a good start to get acquainted with some of the compliance areas that must be addressed. The next step is working with a tax professional or firm that has significant experience with the ROBS transaction is important to make sure the structure is set up correctly and provides a roadmap for keeping the structure in IRS and ERISA compliance," John said.

"I understand," Ken said. "I plan on going home and reading the 2008 ROBS memorandum in detail. To be honest, the compliance issues have really soured me on the ROBS structure and have given me some pause about using it. I have no doubt that if I used the ROBS transaction to fund my water business, the corporation would be using the 401(k) funds it receives in exchange for stock for business purposes, but I am anxious about the responsibilities of maintaining a 401(k) plan and the type of appraisal letter I would need in order to satisfy the IRS. I still can't get around the fact that the IRS expects me to receive an exhaustive appraisal letter from an independent appraiser when my corporation is newly established and has no cash or assets. I am worried that the IRS would not accept the appraisal letter even though it outlines the business assets that will ultimately be purchased by the corporation, which realistically seems like the only way to value a newly established start-up business that is essentially a shell company."

"I understand your apprehension and agree that the ROBS structure does come with a lot of compliance responsibility and risks and should be done only as a last resort," John said. "I think this is now a good time to get into some detail on how the ROBS structure actually works and some of the ins and outs. I know you are not particularly interested in establishing the structure, but I think it will be helpful to understand how it's done."

"OK," Ken agreed.

HOW DOES THE ROBS WORK?

Before beginning discussing the steps involved for establishing a ROBS, John handed Ken a flow chart.

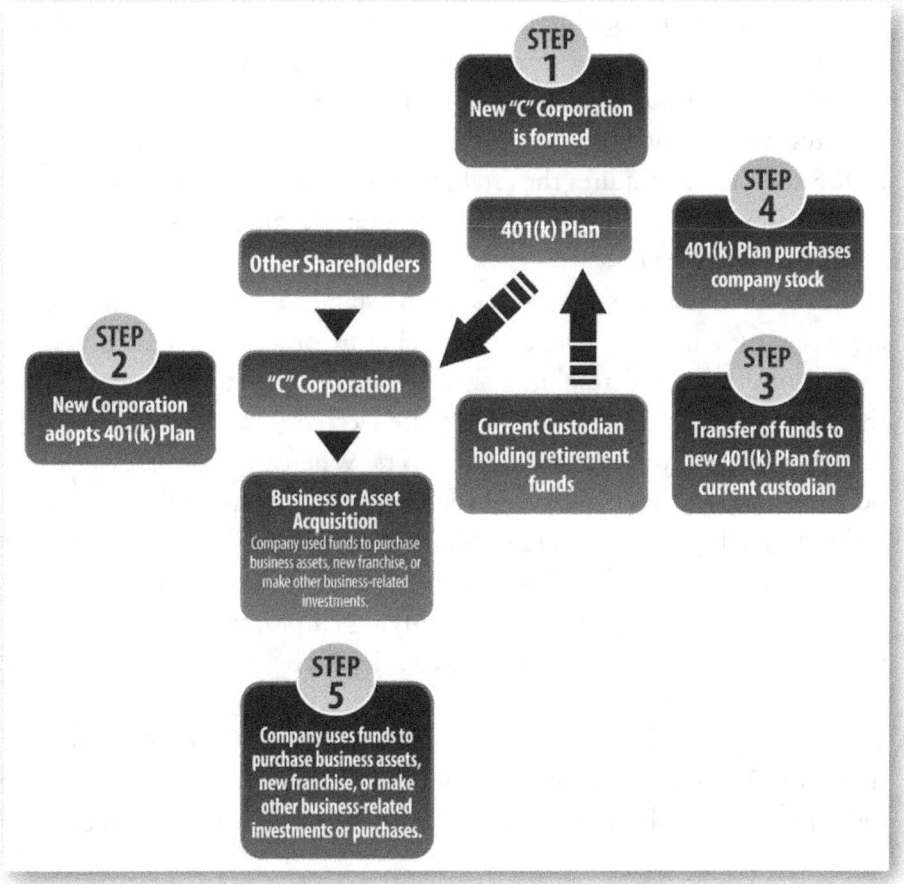

"Let's start with the first step, which is establishing the corporation or confirming that the entity you will be using or purchasing is a C corporation."

Step 1—Establish C Corporation

"In the typical ROBS transaction, an individual establishes a new C corporation that will operate the business. The corporation can be formed in any state. The entity must be a C corporation since taking advantage of the exception to the prohibited-transaction rules under IRC 4975(d)(13) requires the 401(k) plan to purchase qualifying employer securities, which is defined as corporate stock. Typically, the newly established corporation has no employees, assets, or business operations. In some cases, an individual will purchase an existing corporation in a stock purchase transaction, which will negate the need to establish a new corporation."

"Does the corporation need to be a US company?" Ken asked.

"Yes, because only a US company can adopt a 401(k) plan, and the ROBS transaction requires the establishment of a 401(k) plan," John said.

"I assume I have to take care of corporate formalities, such as annual minutes?" Ken asked.

"Yes, once the corporation has been established, there are additional corporate formalities associated with being incorporated, such as bylaws, annual meetings, and resolutions. The bylaws cover topics such as how the board of directors and/or officers are elected, how meetings are conducted, and the types and duties of officers. Whereas, the articles of incorporation state the basic outline of the company. A corporation is required to hold meetings of the shareholders and directors. Corporate meetings are to be recorded, and the important business actions, such as adopting a 401(k) plan and the purchase of qualifying employer securities are to be approved by the board and the shareholders. These actions are resolved in the form of corporate resolutions and meeting minutes are produced and then signed by the meeting attendees and finally by the corporate secretary. You may want to work with an attorney or CPA the first year just to make sure you have complied with all corporate requirements. In addition, you may want a tax professional to help you draft any important business resolutions."

"Will do," Ken said.

"Let's now move on to step two in the ROBS transaction, which is the adoption of a 401(k) plan."

Step 2—Corporation Adopts 401(k) Plan

"In addition to having a C corporation, we know the ROBS structure requires that the corporation adopt a 401(k) qualified retirement plan. The 401(k) plan documents must allow for the purchase of qualifying employer securities. Most qualified plans follow a standard form of plan (a master or prototype plan) approved by the IRS. Prototype plans are plans made available by plan providers for adoption by employers (including self-employed individuals)."

"So these 401(k) plans are preapproved by the IRS?" Ken asked.

"Yes. Most of the ROBS promoters out there are using prototype 401(k) plans that have been approved by the IRS under a preapproved opinion letter program. The plan is then customized to meet the needs of the client and is ultimately adopted by employers by the execution of the adoption agreement. The plan document from which client plans are administered is thus a preapproved prototype plan supplied by the provider, which was reviewed and approved by the IRS with a favorable opinion letter. In addition, the adopting employer is able to customize the prototype plan to offer all eligible plan participants the ability to make employee deferrals, in pretax or Roth, as well as take advantage of the loan feature. As I previously mentioned, most small-business plans tend to employ the safe harbor rules in order to minimize the plan-testing requirements and make administering the 401(k) plan less burdensome," John said.

"I got you. I know I need a C corporation and a 401(k) plan, so once those have been established, what's next?" Ken asked.

"OK. Step three involves the rollover of your pretax retirement funds to the newly adopted 401(k) plan," John said.

Step 3—Rollover/Transfer of Retirement Funds to 401(k) Plan

"Once the 401(k) plan has been established and the plan account has been opened, you are then able to roll over your existing pretax retirement funds into the 401(k) plan account. I am not sure if you remember our earlier conversation on rollovers, but the IRS essentially allows all pretax eligible retirement funds to be rolled into a 401(k) plan. That includes a traditional IRA, SEP-IRA, SIMPLE IRA (after two years), 401(k), 403(b), 457(b), defined benefit plan, and so forth."

John handed Ken the same IRS rollover chart he gave him a while back so he could get a full grasp of the IRS rollover rules (See Exhibit D).

"Can you explain how the rollover process happens?" Ken asked.

"The plan documents include a direct rollover form to assist you in transferring funds from your current retirement account to the new 401(k) plan. The purpose of the direct rollover request form is to notify the financial institution that is currently holding the retirement funds that the plan participant wishes to roll over your retirement funds to another retirement account. The direct rollover request form will inform the current retirement account custodian that the plan participant seeks to roll over his or her retirement funds to a 401(k) qualified retirement plan. This is important because a rollover to a 401(k) plan is treated as a tax-free rollover and not a taxable distribution—the funds are going from one retirement account to another. Therefore, the direct rollover request form alerts the custodian that the funds will be rolled over tax free and penalty free to a 401(k) qualified retirement plan and provides the name of the institution that will be receiving the funds. As soon as the rollover retirement funds have been deposited into the new 401(k) plan, either by check or wire, the trustee of the plan is now ready to make an investment."

"I assume there will be a rollover form provided?" Ken said.

"Yes. The plan documents you receive from the ROBS promoter should include a rollover request form. Otherwise, the institution that is currently holding your retirement funds will likely have a form you can use to indicate that the funds are going to a qualified retirement plan so that they are treated as a nontaxable rollover when reported to the IRS by the current custodian on the IRS Form 1099-R."

"What about doing a sixty-day indirect rollover?" Ken asked.

"Sure, that is an option, but the indirect rollover can be done only once every twelve months, and you have only sixty days to make sure the funds are rolled over into a retirement account, or they will be subject to tax and a 10 percent early distribution penalty if you are under the age of fifty-nine and a half. Also, doing an indirect rollover could cause IRS reporting issues down the road since an IRS Form 1009-R will be issued showing a taxable distribution. I would suggest doing a direct rollover over an indirect rollover whenever possible," John said.

"So at this point the 401(k) plan can invest the funds into the corporation?" Ken asked.

"Yes, essentially. Step four would be the 401(k) buying stock in the corporation in exchange for the cash investment."

Step 4—401(k) Plan Buys Stock of Corporation

"Once the funds have been deposited into the 401(k) plan account, the plan is now ready to buy corporate stock. It is important to make sure that all necessary corporate formalities, such as corporate meetings and resolutions, have been addressed, as this will allow the 401(k) plan to buy qualifying employer securities. Because in most ROBS transactions, the 401(k) plan will be purchasing greater than a 10 percent interest in the company, a resolution should be executed that allows for this," John said.

"What corporate documents are typically needed to execute the stock purchase?" Ken asked.

"That's a good question and is something the tax professional or firm you are working with will help you with. In general, in addition to corporate resolutions and bylaws, you will need a resolution adopted by the incorporator, a resolution appointing the officers and directors of the company, a document consenting to the issue of shares by the company, a document describing the company's plan to offer shares, stock purchase agreements for the 401(k) plan and any individual shareholders, stock certificates, and, of course, the appraisal letter that we discussed today. The stock purchase agreement will outline the terms of the stock purchase and identify the number and purchase price of shares purchased."

"So how do I decide how many shares my corporation should authorize and issue?" Ken asked.

"The term authorized shares means the maximum number of shares that a corporation is legally permitted to issue, as specified in its articles of incorporation. Authorized shares should not be confused with outstanding shares, which are the number of shares the corporation has actually issued that are held by its shareholders. Whereas, issued shares are the shares that have been authorized by the company that have been sold to and held by the shareholders of a company. In general, the number of shares to issue at incorporation is somewhat arbitrary. There is no wrong or right answer. I have some clients who wish to issue just a few hundred shares and some that want to issue millions of shares. A lot of my start-up companies will issue one million shares. Now that doesn't mean all one million shares will be issued or sold. All shares that are not issued are still authorized shares and can be issued in the future. For example, if your corporation authorized one million shares, you may want to keep an amount for reserve for future stock purchases, thus you would issue only up to nine hundred thousand shares initially," John said.

"OK, that makes sense. I would probably take your advice and authorize a million shares, issue just a few hundred thousand shares, and keep the rest for reserves. But what does 'par value' mean? I hear a lot about this but don't really understand the concept," Ken said.

"In general, par value—known as par, nominal, or face value—refers to the amount at which a security is issued or can be redeemed. For example, a bond with a par value of $1,000 can be redeemed at maturity for $1,000. Today most stocks are issued with either a very low par value (such as $0.01 per share) or no par value at all," John said.

"Why?" Ken asked.

"Usually corporations do this because it helps them avoid a liability to stockholders should the stock price take a turn for the worse. For example, if a stock was trading at $5 per share and the par value on the stock was $10, theoretically, the company would have a $5-per-share liability. Par value has no relation to the market value of a stock. A no-par-value stock can still trade for tens or hundreds of dollars—it all depends on what the market feels the company is worth. I recommend a par value of either zero of $0.01 per share," John said.

"OK, so how do I figure out the price per share?" Ken asked.

"The price per share is the cost in dollars that one would have to pay in order to purchase a single share of stock. In the context of start-up financing, the formula is generally 'per share price equals premoney valuation divided by total number of shares outstanding.' For example, if your water company start-up has a premoney valuation of $200,000 and one thousand shares of common stock outstanding, the price per share of would be $200 per share—$200,000 divided by one thousand shares outstanding," John said.

"Does 'shares outstanding' mean the amount of shares I want to issue or all the shares of the company?" Ken asked.

"Generally, shares outstanding are all the shares of a corporation or financial asset that have been, issued, and purchased by all investors and are held by them. They have rights and represent ownership in the corporation by the person that holds the shares. In other words, the maximum number of shares that a corporation is legally permitted to issue, as specified in its articles of incorporation. Authorized stock, also known as 'authorized shares' or 'authorized capital stock,' is also usually listed in the capital accounts section of the balance sheet. Authorized shares should not be confused with outstanding shares, which are the number of shares the corporation has actually issued that are held by the public."

"OK, I think I understand. The company will issue shares to the 401(k) plan, me, and any other investor. I would set the number of shares the company would issue for purchase, and the appraisal letter I receive from an independent appraiser or CPA would value the stock and set the value. We would execute all required corporate documents, such as the stock purchase agreements, to document the stock purchase. At that point, the 401(k) plan and all investors would receive company stock in exchange for the transfer of funds, which would be documented by the receipt of stock certificates," Ken said.

"That is pretty much how the ROBS transaction works," John responded. "Once the company receives the funds from the stock purchase transaction, it will use the funds to buy the business assets or acquiring company stock. As we learned from the IRS 2008 memorandum, the funds should be used only for business purposes and not personal use, including personal expenses or taking a salary."

"Can the 401(k) plan buy all the outstanding company stock?" Ken asked.

"I get this question all the time, and there is not much guidance from the IRS on this topic. If the 401(k) plan owns 100 percent of the outstanding company shares, the plan asset rules we discussed could kick in. The plan asset rules would apply if a retirement account owns 100 percent of an operating business. In that case, the plan asset rules could apply and treat the income earned by a disqualified person from the business as plan assets and trigger the prohibited-transaction rules. The IRS did not address this issue in the 2008 ROBS memorandum or the August 2010 public forum, probably because most ROBS transactions did not involve corporations wholly owned by a 401(k) plan. Nevertheless, a company owned 100 percent by a 401(k) plan could trigger the plan asset rules and place the ROBS transaction as risk. My advice is to not have the 401(k) plan own 100 percent of the company's outstanding stock. Company founders as well as third-party investors can purchase company stock."

"Wait, I assume I have to be an employee of the business in order to participate in the company 401(k) plan, but how do I get paid?" Ken asked.

"That is a great point, and I am happy you brought it up. In order to participate in a 401(k) plan you must meet the plan eligibility requirements. In general, you must be a full-time employee and work over one thousand hours during the year, although some plans lower the annual hours threshold to five hundred. That is why, even if you are a shareholder or owner of Apple or IBM stock, you cannot participate in their 401(k) plan because you are not an employee of the company. In other words, you may own the company shares, but if you are not a full-time employee of the company, you will likely not be able to participate in the company 401(k) plan. This is an important point because becoming an employee of a start-up business is sometimes a less than clear proposition. For example, how can you be an employee of a business that has no assets, revenues, clients, business activity, or revenues? In such cases, what is typically done is that the start-up company will enter into an employment agreement with the individual and have a deferred compensation arrangement or stock option mechanism to compensate an individual who is working for a business that is unable to pay that person."

"So is this an issue under the ROBS transaction? If being an employee of the corporation plan is necessary in order to participate in the company 401(k) plan, and since most start-ups don't have any business activity or revenues, showing the IRS you are an employee could prove difficult," Ken said.

"It is an issue and something the IRS addressed in the 2008 ROBS memorandum. The IRS mentioned that they were aware of some ROBS transactions where the individual transferring tax-deferred assets into the plan was not an employee, participant, or owner, such as when the arrangement was used to set up a business for a spouse. The IRS noted that these types of transactions could violate the exclusive benefit rules as the benefits derived by third-parties from the transaction are not merely an incidental side effect of an investment of trust assets, but are instead a major purpose of the investment. This is definitely something the IRS is looking at, and showing oneself as an employee of a start-up must be considered and well thought out," John said.

"How can I prove I am an employee of the business and thus eligible to participate in the company 401(k) plan?" Ken asked.

"According to the IRS, under common-law rules, anyone who performs services for you is your employee if you can control what will be done and how it will be done. This is the case even when you give the employee freedom of action. What matters is that you have the right to control the details of how the services are performed. The IRS goes on to state that in determining whether the person providing service is an employee or an independent contractor, all information that provides evidence of the degree of control and independence must be considered," John said.

"Does the IRS offer any guidance on the facts they look at when deciding whether one is an employee?" Ken asked.

"Yes, the IRS has provided several facts that they look at, such as

- **Behavioral**. Does the company control or have the right to control what the worker does and how the worker does his or her job?
- **Financial**. Are the business aspects of the worker's job controlled by the payer? These include how a worker is paid, whether expenses are reimbursed, who provides tools/supplies, and so forth.
- **Type of relationship**. Are there written contracts or employee-type benefits such as a pension plan, insurance, vacation pay, and the like? Will the relationship continue and is the work performed a key aspect of the business?

So even if you are not being paid by the business because it does not yet have any income or revenues, you can still be considered by the IRS as an employee of the business. To this end, I think having an employment agreement with the company documenting the relationship is also helpful, especially when it comes to identifying the terms of the deferred compensation," John said.

"Can the business just pay me out of the funds received from the 401(k) plan or other investors?" Ken asked.

"No. The reason is that the IRS could make the argument that receiving a salary out of the rollover funds transferred to the company in exchange for stock is a personal benefit. The IRS noted in the ROBS memorandum that they had reviewed several ROBS arrangements to determine whether they are truly for the exclusive benefit of employees or were being used for personal nonbusiness purposes. In a few cases, the IRS noted that the 401(k) funds used to purchase the company stock wound up purchasing personal assets like recreational vehicles, which is quite problematic as it would violate the exclusive benefit rules under IRC Section 401. By taking salary out of the 401(k) rollover funds, the IRS can make the argument that the transaction is for personal purposes and could violate the exclusive benefit rules under IRC Section 401. My recommendation is for my clients to not take salaries or derive any personal benefit from any of the 401(k) plan funds used to purchase corporate stock. One way to get some cash to use for personal purposes is to take a 401(k) plan loan, assuming your plan documents permit it. As we discussed, the 401(k) plan loan feature will allow you to borrow the lesser of $50,000 or 50 percent of your account value, and this is a lot safer from an IRS perspective than taking salary from the 401(k) plan funds used to buy the corporate stock," John said.

"OK, thanks. That makes sense. So I have to make contributions to the plan once I start getting paid?"

"No and yes. The 2008 IRS memorandum makes it clear that the IRS expects that the 401(k) plan be permanent. A 401(k) plan should not be intended to be temporary. The Treasury regulations under IRC Section 401 provide that a qualified plan must be created primarily for the purposes of providing systematic retirement benefits for employees. The Treasury regulations under Section 1.401-1(b)(2) requires that the plan be permanent. The IRS noted that a large number of reviewed plans contained election provisions in the adoption agreement to utilize a CODA. However, they found that often a low number of participants actually chose to make salary-reduction contributions to the plan. In some instances, the IRS found that the deferral option was 'inactive,' which is an area of concern for the IRS. That being said, a 401(k) plan is a defined contribution plan and it is up to the employee whether contributions are made to the plan. So to answer your question, the IRS cannot force you to make contributions to a 401(k) plan, but if no company employees are contributing to the plan, the IRS could argue that the plan is not active or permanent, thus, violating the tax rules and potentially invalidating the plan and the ROBS transaction," John said.

"I understand. If I decided to do the ROBS transaction, having a 401(k) plan would be a positive factor primarily because of the high employee deferral limits compared to an IRA," Ken said.

"Right."

"I'd like to briefly change the topic of conversation. If I did the ROBS transaction and then ultimately needed to borrow money from a bank, would that be an issue?" Ken asked.

"The IRS did not address this in the 2008 ROBS memorandum or even mention it in any public forum or document, so I assume it would not be an issue, much like being an employee of the business. I think the key would be to make sure the loan was for business purposes," John said.

"The only reason I am asking is because of the prohibited-transaction rules under IRC Section 4975. You spent a lot of time talking about the rules, but it always confuses me how the prohibited-transaction rules prohibit me from being an employee or personally guaranteeing a loan that my retirement account is involved in, but I am able to do it with the ROBS transaction. It seems a bit fishy to me," Ken said.

"Well, you are not alone. Prior to 2010, one of my biggest issues with the ROBS transaction was that it seemed like it was being used in a way that was not intended when the prohibited-transaction rule exception under IRC Section 4975(d)(13) was created. I still believed that the IRS intended the (d)(13) qualifying employer securities exemption to apply to large corporations such as public companies. The IRS clearly did acknowledge that a qualifying employer security need not have an ascertainable market value because the IRS provides guidance for instances where the stock cannot be readily valued. That being said, I am not sure they ever thought that the (d)(13) qualifying employer securities prohibited-transaction exemption would be used by so many start-ups, as is the case today. The fact of the matter is that the exemption does exist, and the IRS has repeatedly stated that using the ROBS structure to buy start-up corporate stock is legal and not a prohibited transaction. Thus, the exemption under (d)(13) allows the 401(k) plan to buy the corporate stock of the business, which employs a disqualified person (the 401(k) plan participant) and would seemingly allow the disqualified person to run the business like any other for-profit business. The IRS never addressed any prohibited transaction issue with a disqualified person being actively involved in the business or even personally guaranteeing a company loan. In reality, almost every ROBS transaction involving a start-up would have a situation where a disqualified person is employed by the start-up business and, in most cases, is running the business. How else would that person be eligible to do the rollover of retirement funds to the 401(k) plan if he or she were not an employee of the business? So, if a disqualified person can be an employee of a business in a ROBS transaction, why couldn't the disqualified person personally guarantee a company loan or operate the business like any other for-profit business in America? I would think if the IRS were concerned with these issues they would have addressed them in the 2008 ROBS memorandum or the 2010 public forum. The IRS is certainly not in love with the structure and would probably love to rewrite the exemption to where its application is more restricted, but that has not happened. The fact is that the IRC Section 4975(d)(13) prohibited-transaction exemption is valid and does allow one to use 401(k) plan funds to purchase qualifying employer securities so long as the transaction complies with all IRS and ERISA rules. You are not alone in feeling that the ROBS transaction seems a bit suspicious considering it allows you to do a prohibited transaction, and all you have to do is establish a corporation and use 401(k) plan funds. I had the same concerns and even today feel that if the ROBS transaction is not done in full satisfaction of all IRS and ERISA rules, and is not being used for any purpose other than funding a business, the IRS could argue that the transaction fails to meet the exclusive benefit rule for purposes of Title II of ERISA."

"And the Ellis and Peek cases you mentioned before, what is their impact on this?" Ken asked.

"I'm happy you brought that up because a lot of my clients get confused with this—they read Ellis and Peek and try to argue that they invalidate the ROBS transaction. Both the Ellis and Peek cases involved IRAs, which are not eligible to purchase qualifying employer securities under IRC Section 4975(d)(13). Therefore, because they used IRAs, not a 401(k), to invest in the business and thus did not purchase qualifying employer securities per IRC Section 4975(d)(13), they were not able to avail themselves of the prohibited-transaction rules exemption under (d)(13). If Ellis and Peek had both used 401(k) plans to purchase corporate stock (qualifying employer security) then their transactions would likely not have triggered a prohibited transaction," John said.

"OK, that clears that up for me. Thanks," Ken said. "So how many of these ROBS transactions are out there for start-ups?"

"It is hard to tell. There are millions of people who have used their 401(k) plan to buy company stock, but for start-ups, the best estimate I could come up with is anywhere from forty thousand to seventy thousand, but that includes only ROBS transactions promoted to start-up businesses or franchises," John said.

"Wow. There are a lot of these ROBS transactions out there. A lot more than I thought," Ken said.

"Just curious, but what are the fees involved in establishing a ROBS transaction?" Ken added.

"Another great question. Of course it depends on who you work with, but from what I understand the fees range from $2,500 to $5,500 to set up the structure, and the annual compliance and plan record-keeping fees can run from $750 to $2,500, depending on the number of employees," John said.

"Pretty pricey," Ken said.

"Yes, that is another reason I like the 401(k) plan loan option—you can usually get that done for half the cost. The annual compliance and record-keeping fees are pretty much standard for any type of 401(k) plan with employees because of the time and effort involved in satisfying plan testing and the completion and filing of IRS Form 5500. Whereas if your business adopted a solo 401(k) plan, since the IRS Form 5500-EZ is simple and easy to complete and is required only for plans valued in excess of $250,000, you are looking at annual fees anywhere from $125 to $350," John said.

"OK, that seems fair and about what I expected," Ken said. "If I did a ROBS transaction and was blessed to have a successful business, what is my exit strategy? How could I get out of the ROBS transaction and become more tax efficient?"

"Another really important question. Let's put aside the worst-case-scenario exit strategy where the business fails and the 401(k) investment is lost. On a more optimistic and positive note, the best-case-scenario exit strategy from the ROBS structure is the sale of the 401(k) plan stock to a third party. In this scenario the business has likely been a success and a third-party individual or business is interested in buying the company stock from its shareholders in order to acquire the business. All company selling shareholders would receive consideration in exchange for the stock and all proceed would go back to the 401(k) plan without tax," John said.

"That sounds really good. I hope I can be that lucky where I can have a successful business that someone would want to buy. What other options are there for moving away from the ROBS transaction?" Ken asked.

"Selling the 401(k) plan-owned stock to the company is probably the most common ROBS transaction exit strategy. The company share buyback will allow the 401(k) plan to sell its shares back to the company for fair market value. It is very important that the purchase be for fair market value as determined by an independent appraiser or third party. The stock buyback will remove the 401(k) plan as shareholder of the corporation, and the remaining corporate shareholders will have their ownership interest in the company increase proportionally. For example, if the 401(k) plan owned 95 percent of the outstanding corporate shares, and the other 5 percent of the shares was owned by an individual, and the company purchased all of the 401(k) plan shares back, then the individual's business ownership would increase from 5 percent to 100 percent since the 401(k) plan shares purchased by the company would technically be canceled. The company could also offer these shares for purchase to the other shareholders," John said.

"How exactly would the company buy back the 401(k) plan stock?" Ken asked.

"It is important to work with a local attorney on this so that you are properly advised. In general, a private company can purchase its own shares out of distributable profits, and out of capital.

"These steps should be taken to accomplish a stock buyback":

- The board of directors must formally resolve to proceed with a stock buyback.
- The directors should look at the company accounts, typically a four-month period before the share buy back and consider whether the company has sufficient distributable profits to go ahead with the share buyback.
- The shares in question should be canceled.
- The share buyback must be approved by way of a special resolution by the shareholders. Shareholders who are selling their shares are not entitled to vote.
- A share buyback agreement must be drawn up and made available to all shareholders.
- Any stamp duty tax or other transfer tax that applies may be payable by the company.
- Company board minutes must be prepared and refer to the relevant sections of company law.
- The directors must make a statement about the solvency of the company if purchased out of capital.
- An auditor's report is required if stock is to be purchased out of capital.

"Can a disqualified person purchase the company qualifying employer stock from the 401(k) plan?" Ken asked.

"That's a really tough question, and I wish there were some IRS guidance. The IRS did not address this question in either the 2008 ROBS memorandum or the 2010 public forum. My position is that a disqualified person should not purchase any of the qualifying employer securities from the 401(k) plan. That transaction would seem to violate the prohibited-transaction rules under IRC Section 4975(c), and I am not sure any exemption under IRC Section 4975(d) would apply," John said.

"I assume I can always just keep the 401(k) plan as a shareholder of the company?" Ken asked.

"Yes, which is also a really great scenario. One of the main comments I hear from clients wanting to do a ROBS transaction is that they would rather bet on themselves and their business than on some Wall Street stock. By having your 401(k) plan be a shareholder of your business, you would be able to issue tax-free dividends to the 401(k) plan. I am not sure if you remember the discussion we had on the UBTI tax rules, but in general, all capital gains, interest, royalties, rental income, and dividends are received tax free from a 401(k) plan. Therefore, if your company is doing well, you can issue dividends to all the company shareholders pro rata, and the 401(k) plan will be able to receive the dividends tax free," John said.

"That is really interesting. Does this get me around paying tax on the dividends?" Ken asked.

"Not really. Getting a tax-free dividend is great, but remember that a dividend is paid out of the company's net profits after taxes has been paid, so the amount you receive as a dividend has already been taxed. In addition, if you have used pretax 401(k) plan funds to buy the company stock, any time you take a distribution (or at age seventy and a half, when you will be required to take an RMD) you will have to pay tax on the amount of the distribution, including the amount of dividends you have received from the company. Therefore, receiving a tax-free dividend from the corporation is beneficial, but the funds can grow without tax (tax deferral). Ultimately when you take a distribution voluntarily or because you have reached the age of seventy and a half, you will have to pay tax on the dividend amount received," John said.

"I guess that is not so bad. I still have to pay tax on the dividend I receive from the company, but that can be many years down the road, and in the interim the funds can grow without tax. Also, the ROBS transaction allows me invest in my business and in myself without having to pay tax and penalty on the amount of funds used. I really see why the ROBS transaction is so popular among entrepreneurs, and if my business required more money to get started I would have to strongly consider it despite some of the concerns I have about potential IRS scrutiny. So what should I do?" Ken asked.

"Well, that's the million-dollar question," John said with a laugh.

"Let's do this. Why don't you go home and spend time reading the IRS 2008 ROBS memorandum and digest everything we discussed today and then let's meet for one final chat so we can try to put it all together," John said.

"That sounds great." Ken said.

6

Putting It All Together

As usual, Ken arrived at the coffee bar a few minutes early and picked up two cappuccinos and two scones. John arrived a few minutes later, but this time Pam joined them. John felt it would be helpful if Pam was part of this conversation, so that they could attempt to find the best business-funding option for Ken.

Ken started the conversation by thanking John for all his time and patience over the last several months trying to help him navigate all the different financing and retirement funding options available to entrepreneurs looking to start a business or franchise. Pam also thanked John for his time and his willingness to help Ken.

Ken told John that he and David had been spending the past week finalizing their business deal and had pretty much worked out how much would be needed initially to buy the franchise and operate the business for the first six months.

"David and I have each committed to invest $160,000 in the water franchise. I know this is $10,000 more than I initially mentioned, but after reworking all our numbers we think this number is more realistic. Especially after all we talked about I really want to make sure the business has enough cash flow to get us through the first six months—I am sure not everything will go as we planned or budgeted," Ken said.

"I think that is a good choice and probably makes a lot of sense. What I want to do today, since you and Pam are both present, is to go through all the financing and retirement funding options we talked about over the last several weeks and try to come up with a plan of action for you," John said.

"That would be awesome," Ken said.

"OK, let's start with the option of using cash to buy the business. I know this may not be a realistic option for you since coming up with $160,000 in cash just may not be possible. You are not alone—most entrepreneurs do not have six figures lying around to buy a business. Clearly, using cash to buy a business presents some exciting advantages, such as closing on a transaction quickly since all that is needed is a check or wire transfer. It would likely alleviate a lot of the stress of approaching family and friends about the business opportunity, and it would save time and energy from having to go through a tedious loan application. It may also prevent any friendship or family disruptions due to the performance of the business, and would likely free up cash for the business by not having to meet loan payment requirements. On the flip side, using all your personal cash or savings to buy a business instead of acquiring a loan to help finance a portion of the business may actually put added stress on your personal finances and end up being a major distraction. Like almost everything we discussed, a lot depends on the facts and circumstances. For Bill Gates, who is worth billions, investing a few hundred thousand dollars of personal funds on a business is a no-brainer. But if the purchase price of the business were $1 billion dollars, using leverage such as a loan would likely make more sense, even for Bill Gates, since interest rates are historically low and are tax deductible when paid by the business," John said.

"That makes sense. If Pam and I had $1 million in savings, then I think using personal funds to make the business acquisition would be right. However, based on our financial position and the level of savings we currently have, using personal cash to cover the full $160,000 will not work. I think we are ready to use $75,000 from our savings for the business, but we still need to come up with another $85,000," Ken said.

"I understand. Let's move on to the family and friends option. I know when we discussed this option you mentioned that you had spoken to certain family members and friends you thought could financially handle the business investment opportunity, yet they wouldn't bite. Have either of you spoken to anyone else regarding investing in the business since we last talked about this?" John asked.

"I did chat with my parents again and some colleagues at work," Ken said, "but no one seems willing to make the investment. The people I talked to were all supportive of me and showed interest in my business, but for whatever reason were not ready to make that investment. I also talked to them about a personal loan or loan to my business, and the feedback I got was mostly that they don't want a business transaction to impact our personal relationship. I guess I understand where they are coming from. I know there are a lot of negatives to having family and friends as investors, especially if the business does not succeed. However, I am very confident that the business will be successful, and I'm sure it would be neat to have my family and close friends who invested in the business share in my success. Unfortunately, it just has not happened, and I need to move on to the next option," Ken said.

"Well, everything happens for a reason, so I am sure one or more of the other funding options will work for you, and this way it won't impact your relationship with those family members and friends," John said.

"Pam and I have spent the last few weeks contemplating the bank and SBA loan options, and we have actually spoken with our bank as well as a number of other banks in our community. The feedback I got was that the loan could be an option but that a lot would come down to our credit scores. We checked them and were happy to know that they were in the 700s, so we are in good shape. I also reviewed the bank-loan applications and SBA-loan application and don't think I would have an issue meeting their requirements. The interest rates charged by the banks are quite fair. My main issue is the personal guarantee I would have to make in order to secure the loan. Based on my research, almost all bank and SBA loans are usually sanctioned against some collateral, often a house and property, which I could lose if the business fails. This is something that concerns me, and I would not want to put Pam and the kids in a position where we could lose our house if my business failed. The SBA-loan terms are a bit better, but I would still likely have to personally guarantee the business loan, which is not very attractive to me," Ken said.

"I understand. The loan option is quite common for many entrepreneurs, especially ones who can come up with 20 percent of the business purchase price. In your case, because you need only $85,000, the 401(k) plan loan may prove to be more attractive," John said.

"OK. Like the bank or SBA loan, using a personal or business credit card would seem to have the same drawbacks, although the application process is much easier. If I needed only $10,000 or $15,000 for the business I would probably just use my credit card, but because I need around $85,000 I think using a credit card would be tough, and if I ever missed a payment I would be in big trouble—the interest payments would be a blow to my cash flow," Ken said.

"That makes sense. Would you consider taking a taxable distribution for your 401(k) plan to cover the $85,000?" John asked.

"Pam and I talked about this. I have about $138,000 in my 401(k) plan, so I could technically take a taxable distribution from my account. But if I remember our chat on 401(k) plan distributions, I would need a triggering event from my plan to take a distribution. If I stayed at my job, that would not work. However, if I left my job I could roll the pretax 401(k) plan funds into a traditional IRA and take a taxable distribution from the IRA. I know I would be subject to ordinary income tax and a 10 percent early distribution penalty on the amount of the distribution since I am under the age of fifty-nine and a half. Since Pam and I file a joint return and are close to the highest tax bracket, adding the $85,000 of income from the taxable distribution would certainly push our income to the top bracket, which means that taking the $85,000 as a taxable distribution would probably cost me around 45 percent in taxes, and that's just too steep. If Pam and I had some losses we could use to offset the tax from the distribution that would be another story, but paying almost half of the distribution in taxes is just too expensive. For that reason, I just don't think taking a taxable distribution is a great option for me."

"I understand, and I actually agree with you. If you needed less money or were in a low tax bracket I would encourage you to reconsider, but based on everything you just said, I think you're right. That pretty much covers all the financing options for using nonretirement funds to buy a business. As of now, it appears that an SBA loan may be your best option compared to using all cash, securing funds from friends and family, using a credit card, or taking a taxable distribution from a retirement account. Let's now turn to the three main ways to use retirement funds to finance a business," John said.

"I thought there were only two options. Isn't the self-directed IRA not a business-funding option because of prohibited-transaction rules?" Ken asked.

"Yes, you are correct, but I still want to quickly go through the self-directed IRA so Pam can understand why it doesn't work as a business-funding option for you."

"Thanks," Pam said.

"In a lot of respects, using a self-directed IRA LLC or a 401(k) plan to purchase stock in a corporation would seem to work the same way as a ROBS transaction. But as we discussed last time we met, using IRA funds versus 401(k) funds prevents you from taking advantage of the prohibited-transaction exemption under IRC Section 4975(d)(13) for qualifying employer securities. Ask Mr. Peek and Mr. Ellis about using IRA funds to buy a business that involves a disqualified person. The IRS successfully argued that a prohibited transaction had occurred, which had painful repercussions," John said.

"I remember that discussion very well," Ken said.

"Using a self-directed IRA to make an investment in a business not involving a disqualified person is 100 percent legal and done all the time. However, it is important to remember that the business cannot be established through an S corporation, because of the shareholder ownership restrictions. In addition, if the business is being operated through a pass-through entity, such as an LLC, the UBTI rules could kick in and impose a tax on profits allocated to the self-directed IRA LLC in an amount greater than $1,000," John said.

"I also remember that conversation," Ken said.

"The bottom line is that a self-directed IRA cannot be used as a business-funding option for a business that is operated, owned, and controlled by a disqualified person—the retirement account holder—without triggering the prohibited-transaction rules. Of course, this would not apply to a public company such as Apple, which has millions of shareholders, where an Apple employee who runs a division could still use his or her self-directed IRA to buy Apple stock without triggering the prohibited-transaction rules. The self-directed IRA works best for passive forms of investments such as real estate, tax liens, IRS-approved precious metals and coins, and private business investments not involving a disqualified person. You must still be aware of the UBTI rules if the business is operated through a pass-through entity, such as an LLC, but the transaction would likely not be considered a prohibited transaction under IRC Section 4975," John said.

"OK, that makes sense to me. Do you get this, Pam?" Ken asked.

"Yes, I do. I didn't really understand the difference between the self-directed IRA and the ROBS, but thanks to John, I do now," Pam said.

401(K) PLAN LOAN OPTION

"Great. Now let's turn to the 401(k) plan loan option, which I think will be your best option."

"OK. I have spoken with Pam at length about this option, so I'm curious to hear your thoughts," Ken said.

"The 401(k) plan loan funding option is probably the easiest and cleanest way someone can use retirement funds to invest in their own business or do anything they want with it, including engaging in a prohibited transaction. The loan feature is truly helpful because it allows you to use retirement funds and do a prohibited transaction but not pay a tax or penalty. Plan loans from the 401(k) are legal because of a limited statutory exception to the prohibited-transaction rules as stated in IRC Section 4975(d)(1). Specifically, IRC Section 72(p) allows you to borrow money from your 401(k) plan tax free and without penalty. As long as the plan documents allow for it and the proper loan documents are prepared and executed, you can take such a loan for any reason. If the loan payments are made on time, there are no penalties or taxes due. The IRS doesn't care what you do with the loan proceeds; the only requirement is that the loan be paid back timely. The 401(k) plan loan must be paid back over a five-year period (fifteen years if you will be using the loan proceeds to purchase a primary residence), and the payments must be made at least quarterly—but can be made weekly, biweekly, or monthly—at an interest rate of at least prime per the Wall Street Journal. As of September 1, 2015, the prime interest rate was 3.25 percent. Loan payments not made in a timely manner will be considered delinquent and will become subject to tax and a 10 percent penalty if the borrower is under the age of fifty-nine and a half. A delinquent loan is not the same as a defaulted loan. A defaulted loan is an IRS-defined term, and a 401(k) plan loan is deemed to be in default when it no longer meets the requirements found in Treasury Regulation 1.72(p)-1. There is not usually a prepayment penalty for paying back a 401(k) loan early.

"Thanks for the summary," Pam said.

"I really think the 401(k) plan will work well for the both of you. What I was thinking is that because both of you have over $100,000 in your current 401(k) plans, you each have the option of borrowing $50,000 from your respective 401(k) plans. I know you only need $85,000, so maybe Ken borrows $50,000 from a 401(k) plan and Pam borrows $35,000. The $85,000 in funds plus the $75,000 in your savings could then be used to get Ken to the $160,000 he needs to fund the business," John said.

"Would I make the loan with my current employer?" Ken asked.

"You could because your current employer plan offers a 401(k) plan, but that likely won't be practical since you will be running your water business. What makes more sense is that the water company establishes a 401(k) plan. When you decide on the type of entity David and you want to use for the business—whether the LLC or S corporation you're currently considering—that entity would establish a 401(k) plan and you would be able to roll your employer 401(k) plan funds tax free into the new 401(k) plan now associated with the water business. At that point, we would make sure that the 401(k) plan documents your company adopts include a loan option. You would then be able to borrow up to $50,000 from the 401(k) plan and use that to fund your business. The good thing is that the $50,000 you will be borrowing will not be needed to buy the business and pay the franchisor, but will be used for working capital, which should make the whole loan process less time sensitive and stressful," John said.

"Would I just get a check from the plan for the $50,000?" Ken asked.

"Bingo. The 401(k) plan would send you a check made out to you personally that you would then be able to use for any purposes, including funding the business. You would be required to make timely loan payments back to the 401(k) plan by writing a check from your personal account to the plan. The plan administrator would be required to keep track of all loan payments to make sure they are being made in a timely manner," John said.

"What about me?" Pam said.

"For you, Pam, the process works pretty much the same way. I can put you in touch with the firm's 401(k) plan administrator and she can help you through the loan application process. You will receive a check made out to you from the plan in the amount of the loan you requested. Our plan allows you to pay back the loan from your salary via payroll deductions. This works out quite well and will guarantee that you don't miss a payment and put your loan in default," John said.

"I like this idea. Pam could borrow $35,000 at an interest rate of 3.25 percent, which would be approximately $632 a month in loan payments. My $50,000 loan at the same interest rate would be approximately $904 a month in loan payments. The monthly payments of around $1,500 for the both of us will be a bit tough, but I think we can make it work. The interest rate on the loan is quite low—much lower than a bank or SBA loan—and the great thing with the 401(k) plan loan option is that we are essentially paying ourselves back while at the same time getting tax-free and penalty-free use of the retirement funds. If my calculations are accurate, at the end of five years, Pam's and my 401(k) plans will have increased in value by around $2,968 and $4,200 respectively, the amount of interest paid back on the loans. That is a neat concept. The 401(k) plan gets you tax-free and penalty-free use of your retirement funds for any purposes, and it also increases the value of your plan," Ken smiled.

"Yes! The 401(k) plan loan allows you to serve as your own bank and fund a business by getting tax-free access of up to $50,000 of retirement funds. It's the only type of retirement plan that offers the loan feature, which makes it far more attractive than a SEP-IRA or SIMPLE IRA. Of course, the $50,000 limit doesn't work for everyone, but if you can make the 401(k) plan loan feature work, I think it is more flexible and safer from an IRS audit standpoint than the ROBS structure," John said.

"I agree. I just really like the fact that we are getting tax-free and penalty-free use of the retirement funds without having to take a taxable distribution, and we can use the funds for any purpose, including funding Ken's business. Best of all, all interest and principal payments go back to the 401(k) plan, so we are in fact growing the value of our retirement funds while being able to use the funds for Ken's business without tax or penalty. Seems like a win-win situation for us and our 401(k) plans," Pam said.

"I couldn't agree with you more. I always offer the 401(k) plan loan feature as a first option to my clients who are interested in using retirement funds to buy or finance a business. I just think it makes a lot of sense. Unfortunately, it doesn't work for everyone, because in many cases the funds needed for the business are significantly more than the $50,000 maximum 401(k) loan amount. In fact, I prepared a chart that summarizes some of the pros and cons of the 401(k) plan loan option," John said.

John handed Ken and Pam a copy of the chart.

401(K) PLAN LOAN FEATURE—PROS AND CONS

401(k) Plan Loan Option—Pros	401(k) Plan Loan Option—Cons
Can use loan funds for any purpose	Limited to the lesser of 50 percent of 401(k) account value or $50,000
Tax-free and penalty-free use of funds	Loan must be paid over five years, at least quarterly
Pay back 401(k) plan instead of a third party	Straight line loan of interest and principal—no balloon payments allowed
Get tax-free access to funds while growing 401(k) plan value	Tax and 10 percent early distribution penalty if payments on outstanding balance not made on time

"Before you get set on the 401(k) plan loan option for borrowing the $85,000 needed for Ken's water business, let's spend some time discussing the pros and cons of the ROBS transaction. I think it only makes sense to let Pam hear more about the ROBS transaction so you can both make a more qualified decision on the best retirement financing option for the water business," John said.

"Great. I was actually curious to hear more about some of the pros and cons of the ROBS transaction," Pam said.

"OK, I am an eternal optimist, so let's start with the positives of the ROBS transaction," John said. "To recap, when it comes to using retirement funds to buy or finance a business that you or another disqualified person will be involved in personally, other than the 401(k) plan loan option, there is only one legal way to do it, and that is through the ROBS solution. As we discussed, it takes advantage of an exception in the tax code under IRC Section 4975(d)(13) that allows a person to use 401(k) plan funds to buy stock in a C corporation, which is known as 'qualifying employer securities,' defined as stock of a C corporation. There's a reason you should not use a self-directed IRA LLC to invest in a business that the IRA holder or a disqualified person will be personally involved in—it would trigger a prohibited transaction as in the Ellis and Peek cases," John said.

OK, thanks for the summary," Pam said.

ADVANTAGES OF USING A ROBS TO BUY A BUSINESS
"Let's start discussing some of the main advantages of the ROBS solution."

Save Money
"The primary advantage of establishing a ROBS solution is the ability to use your retirement funds to invest in a business you will be personally involved in without having to pay tax or penalty on the retirement funds you wish to use as a distribution. By being able to invest retirement funds into the business without having to take a taxable distribution and a 10 percent early distribution penalty if under the age of fifty-nine and a half, a ROBS solution could save someone close to 45 percent of the distribution

amount. For example, if someone under the age of fifty-nine and a half was looking to use $100,000 of retirement funds to fund a business and ended up taking a taxable distribution of that amount, that individual would likely have to pay approximately 45 percent of the $100,000, or $45,000, in tax to the IRS when declaring the distribution on his or her tax return. The tax rate could be lower if the individual was in a lower income tax bracket or the retirement funds needed were insignificant, but using a ROBS solution would save having to pay tax and potentially a 10 percent penalty on that amount of retirement funds needed for a business investment."

Invest in Yourself

"The ROBS solution allows you to invest your retirement funds in a business that will be actively run by you, the retirement account holder. As a result, you are essentially investing your retirement funds in yourself rather than Wall Street. Of course, not all businesses are successful. According to the SBA, close to 50 percent of new businesses fail in the first five years, so investing your hard-earned retirement funds in a new business is certainly a risk. However, it is a risk that you are legally entitled to take per the IRC. Using retirement funds to invest in your business is not for everyone, but for those entrepreneurs who would rather invest in themselves than Wall Street, the ROBS solution is an option."

Diversification

"There is a growing sentiment among financial advisors, especially after the 2008 financial crisis, that in order to protect your retirement funds from a market downturn, your retirement funds should be well diversified. You cannot eliminate investment risk, but you can manage the level of risk. Every investment has some amount of risk; however, having your retirement funds invested in different types of investments, such as stocks, real estate, and even private businesses, can be a way of diversifying your retirement portfolio and better protecting your retirement funds. Of course, investing all your retirement funds in your start-up business does not offer much diversification, but using just a percentage of your retirement funds to invest in a start-up business can offer some investment diversification. Diversification can enable a retirement portfolio to grow both when markets grows and and when they correct. You should certainly work with a financial planner and tax professional when looking at investment options, especially when it comes to using retirement funds to buy a business."

Earn a Salary
"In order for you to participate in a 401(k) plan, you need to be an employee of the business that adopted the plan. This is why if you own Apple or IBM stock but don't work at those companies, you cannot participate in their company 401(k) plans. Hence, to be eligible to participate in the corporation 401(k) plan you must become a W-2 employee of the C corporation. For many entrepreneurs the ability to earn a salary and be actively involved in the business is the reason they are using a ROBS solution versus using a self-directed IRA."

Benefit from Having a 401(k) Retirement Plan
"One of the best ways for you to save toward your own retirement and ensure your future security is through an employer-sponsored 401(k) plan. Below are some of the advantages of offering and participating in a 401(k) plan."

- **Matching contributions**. Many employers will match a portion of your savings; it's like passing up free money if you don't participate. A safe harbor 401(k) plan, which is a popular type of 401(k) plan for small businesses, offers participants a minimum 3 percent matching contribution by the employer. For example, if the employee earns $40,000 in salary during the year and contributes 3 percent of the salary ($1,200) to the 401(k) plan, the employer would contribute an additional $1,200 (3 percent of the salary) to the individual 401(k) plan account, providing the employee with a total or $2,400 of plan contributions for the year.
- **Employee retention**. With most successful businesses offering their employees retirement benefits, it is worthwhile for small businesses to compete for talented workers by implementing 401(k)

benefits. Offering 401(k) plan benefits is a great way to retain key employees. In general, when potential hires are considering multiple job offers, they'll compare those offers based on corporate culture, growth opportunities, and benefits packages.

- **Easy administration**. 401(k) plan administration is now easier and more cost effective than ever thanks to the safe harbor rules. If a plan elects to be governed by the safe harbor rules, the level of plan testing and administration will significantly decrease. In addition, plan investment and administration costs have become much less expensive.

- **Owner participation**. You are eligible to participate in the company 401(k) plan if you are an owner or an employee of the company that sponsors the plan. Current regulations allow plan participants to contribute up to $18,000 ($24,000 if over the age of fifty) of their income on a pretax basis each year. That means that, in addition to employee-retention advantages for offering a 401(k) plan, you will receive tax savings for participating in and contributing to a 401(k) plan. These savings can be substantial—an owner in the 35 percent tax bracket who made the maximum contribution would have saved approximately $6,500 in taxes in 2014.

"OK, that is really helpful," Ken said. "The ROBS transaction clearly has a lot of benefits. I guess that is why it is so popular with entrepreneurs and start-ups."

"It does, but it does have some drawbacks, which we have discussed in detail. Let me review some of them for Pam so she gets a better handle of why the ROBS transaction is something that the IRS is concerned with," John said.

The C Corporation Requirement
"Although there are advantages to establishing a C corporation, such as owner's liability protection from the actions of the company, there are several disadvantages as well."

Double Taxation
"Corporations, unlike other companies that are considered sole proprietorships or partnerships (i.e., LLC), file their own taxes separately from their owners at their own tax rates. After the company's profits are taxed at the corporate level, they are then distributed to the shareholders, who have to report the amount received on their individual tax returns (double taxation). The corporate tax rate is usually 15 percent for corporate profits under $50,000 and 35 percent for profits above $50,000. This isn't the case for S corporations or LLCs, where the profits bypass being taxed at the corporate level and are distributed and taxed at the shareholder's level. That is called pass-through taxation. For example, if we assume a 20 percent income tax rate for both corporation and individuals, and a C corporation earned $100 of profits, the C corporation would be required to pay tax of $20 (20 percent of $100) and then the shareholder would be required to pay tax of $16 (20 percent of $80) on any dividend issued by the C corporation to the shareholder. In contrast, in the case of an LLC or S corporation, there is no entity-level tax, so the $100 would flow directly to the shareholder or LLC member, and a tax of only 20 percent would be imposed at the shareholder level. In comparison, when using a pass-through entity such as an S corporation or LLC, the individual would save $16 in our example (total tax of $36 with a C corporation versus $20 with an LLC or S corporation).

"It is important to note that it can be argued that the disadvantage of the double taxation bite does not impact retirement accounts (i.e., 401(k) plans) as much as individuals, since the dividend from the C corporation to the 401(k) plan shareholder would be exempt from tax because a 401(k) plan is a tax-exempt retirement account. However, double taxation is not eliminated but simply deferred until the 401(k) plan participant elects to take a 401(k) plan distribution, which would be subject to a second tax (the first tax would be applied at the C corporation level). In contrast, if a 401(k) plan invested in an LLC, a pass-through entity for taxation, the income or gains from the LLC would flow back to the 401(k) plan without tax and the 401(k) plan participant would be required to pay only one tax when a distribution is taken.

"Unfortunately, the IRS rules under IRC Section 4975(d)(13) require a C corporation be used when a retirement account holder wishes to use retirement funds to invest in a business the holder or another disqualified person will be involved in. The issue of double taxation is certainly one disadvantage of the ROBS solution, but it is generally perceived as better than paying tax and potentially a 10 percent early distribution penalty on a distribution from your retirement account.

Regulations and Formalities
"Subchapter C corporations usually involve more corporate formalities than LLCs. C corporations have to report annually to the states in which they're incorporated and to the states in which they do a lot of business. They must observe certain formalities to be considered corporations, including holding regular board and shareholder meetings and issuing stock. Also, the names of corporate officers are made public, which is not required by businesses formed under different organizational structures."

401(k) Plan Administration
"Even though 401(k) plan administration costs have come down significantly over the years, there is still a cost in offering a 401(k) plan to employees. In addition to making a 3 percent safe harbor contribution, 401(k) plans cost money to administer because there are many compliance issues to be monitored, numerous ongoing administration functions to be provided, and a host of education and communication services required to be offered to plan participants. It is not uncommon for a small business to pay anywhere from $750 to $1,500 annually for a third-party administration company to administer the plan and file the annual IRS Form 5500."

Matching Contributions
"A safe harbor 401(k) plan, a popular type of 401(k) plan for small businesses, offers employees who participate in the plan a 3 percent matching contribution by the employer. For example, if the employee earns $40,000 in salary during the year and contributes 3 percent of the salary, or $1,200, to the 401(k) plan,

the employer would contribute an additional $1,200 (3 percent of the salary) to the individual's 401(k) plan account. Taking this a step further, if the business has five employees each making $40,000 a year, the employer now has to make $6,000 in matching contributions. Although the contributions are tax deductible to the employer, it is still additional funds that are removed from the company and could impact the cash flow of a new small business."

Potential IRS Audit

"Dating back to 2005 or so, the IRS started focusing some attention on the ROBS structure for funding start-up businesses because of the high level of abuse they perceived was occurring. This resulted in the publication of the 2008 ROBS memorandum. The IRS highlighted numerous problem areas and compliance issues they found in many of the ROBS transactions they reviewed, and concluded that in many cases the transactions failed to comply with all required IRS and ERISA rules and procedures. As we discussed in detail, in the ROBS memorandum, the IRS highlighted several problem areas and a number of compliance issues that they felt were not being adequately satisfied, such as plan permanency, exclusive benefit, stock valuation, annual administration requirements, and, of course, business use of funds."

"So does the ROBS solution trigger an audit?" Ken asked.

"No one knows what factors trigger an IRS audit, but while legal, the ROBS solution is something the IRS and DOL are looking at with extra scrutiny. Again, if your ROBS structure is set up properly in full compliance with IRS and ERISA rules as set forth in the 2008 ROBS memorandum, the establishment of a ROBS transaction should pose very little risk from an IRS audit standpoint. Specifically, the retirement funds must be used for business purposes; the 401(k) plan must be established for the exclusive benefit of employees, must be offered to all eligible employees, and must be intended to be permanent; a detailed and accurate valuation of the stock purchased must be performed, and the plan must be compliant with all annual testing and IRS filing requirement," John said.

"OK, that is really useful," Pam said. "Ken and I discussed the ROBS transaction at length over the last few days, as we have been considering the 401(k) plan loan option versus the ROBS structure. I think if Ken needed more funds for the business, we would have had to seriously entertain doing the ROBS transaction because it seems like the only way he would be able to use his retirement funds to invest in a business he will personally be involved in without tax or penalty. Because we are in a very high tax bracket and Ken is under the age of fifty-nine and a half, a taxable distribution would be just too painful. My calculations suggest that we would pay close to 45 percent tax on a taxable distribution from his 401(k) plan. However, because the loan option allows us to get tax-free and penalty-free use of the funds without having to establish a C corporation or deal with a lot of compliance issues, I think it makes a lot of sense for us."

"I agree with Pam," Ken said. "I do think the ROBS transaction has many positives, and I feel that if I worked with you, John, the structure would be set up properly and in full IRS compliance. I like the idea of having a 401(k) plan and would make sure to offer benefits to all my full-time employees. I also have no interest in using the funds for any personal purposes and could live with using a C corporation, but my main concern is attaining an appraisal of the new start-up C corporation that would satisfy the IRS requirements. The IRS, in the 2008 ROBS memorandum, stressed the lack of an adequate valuation as one of their major compliance issues with the ROBS transaction. I am just not sure how you can accurately value a start-up with no business activities, clients, revenues, equipment, or inventory, only cash that will be used to buy assets. The IRS has not seemed to offer any guidance as to what would satisfy their annual valuation concerns, and I would not want my transaction invalidated because the IRS did not feel that the price paid for the qualifying employer security was adequate and at fair market value. If I were buying an existing business, I would not have the concern since the purchase agreement would set forth the price of the assets or shares being purchased."

"I understand your concerns, and many tax attorneys and tax practitioners have the same worries with the ROBS transaction. The fact of the matter is that the ROBS transaction is legal and is not a prohibited transaction if done in full IRS and ERISA compliance, but as we read in the 2008 ROBS memorandum and heard in the 2010 public forum, there are many problem areas and points of concern for the IRS. That being said, if the ROBS transaction is established correctly and the structure satisfies all the IRS and

ERISA requirements, I think you would not have any IRS issues regarding it. That is not to say that you won't be targeted for an audit, but if you satisfied all IRS and ERISA rules and areas of compliance, there would be nothing to worry about. I would still recommend that my clients first explore the 401(k) plan loan feature as a way to fund the business before considering the ROBS transaction. I like the fact that with the 401(k) plan loan option you are getting tax-free and penalty-free use of your retirement funds and can use the funds for any purpose, including funding a business, while simultaneously growing your 401(k) plan account. Of course, you are limited to using the lesser of $50,000 or 50 percent of your account value, but that is not really an issue for your business transaction. Based on the circumstances surrounding your water business transaction, I agree that using the 401(k) plan loan option is your best course of action. I think if you needed more funds and were not ready to take a taxable distribution, then the ROBS transaction is something that you would need to consider, but since both you and Pam can take 401(k) loans and handle the repayment terms, I think the 401(k) plan loan feature makes a whole lot of sense for the both of you and is probably the best way for you to fund your water business."

"Thanks so much for all of your time and effort in helping me over the last month or so. I don't know how I can ever repay you. Pam and I would love to take you and your wife for dinner as a small token of gratitude for helping us come up with the best way to fund the new water business. I would never have been able to navigate all the financing and retirement funding options without your help," Ken said.

"It was my pleasure. My wife and I would love to take you up on your dinner invitation. Also, I have really enjoyed talking with you and am glad I was able to help. I wish you and David all the luck in the world on your new water business venture. Of course, if you need an attorney to help you get your business off the ground, I would love to help you out," John said.

"Yes, of course we will be hiring you and your firm to help us get the business going. I will just let David know which funding route I will be using and will get back to you in a few days about going forward," Ken said.

"Great. Can't wait to get started," John said.

"Same here and thanks again," Ken said.

CONCLUSION

I t's almost always harder to raise capital than you thought it would be, and it always takes longer. So plan for that.—Richard Harroch, venture capitalist and author

I think almost every entrepreneur who is looked into starting a business has felt frustrated and overwhelmed by the difficulty of raising sufficient capital to start or fund a business. Just ask Mark Zuckerberg of Facebook, who needed $30,000 or so from Eduardo Saverin to start the company, or take the story of twenty-five-year-old dropout John Mackey and twenty-one-year-old Renee Lawson Hardy.

In 1978, Mackey and Hardy saved and borrowed money from family and friends to open the doors of a small natural foods store in Austin, Texas. Within a year of opening the store, the couple was evicted from their home for using their apartment as storage for the store. Homeless and with no place to go they decided to save costs by moving and living at their store full time. Eventually Mackey and Hardy moved out of the store and into their own place, and within two years merged with another natural foods store to open the first Whole Foods Market in Austin, Texas, on September 20, 1980. Starting with just 10,500 square feet of floor space and nineteen employees, Whole Foods Market has become the largest market of its kind and had revenues of $12.3 billion in 2013.

Facebook and Whole Foods illustrate the many different ways to build a successful business. Whether from personal savings, family and friends, third-party loans, credit cards, or taxable distributions, businesses can get funding from a wide variety of sources. What many entrepreneurs and small-business owners still don't know is that using retirement funds to start or fund a business is a viable option that, if done correctly, is perfectly legal.

The primary objective of this book is to reveal the many different ways one can buy or finance a business, including the less common approach of using retirement funds. I used the characters of Ken and John to illustrate the kind of dialogue I have experienced in talking with many thousands of entrepreneurs and small-business owners looking to buy or finance a business. The questions and answers they exchanged were designed to give you a sense of the types of issues and matters to consider when (1) deciding to buy or start a business, (2) examining the different funding and financing options for buying or funding a business, (3) thinking about using retirement funds to buy or fund a business, and (4) deciding what funding or financing option works best for you.

Ken represented the typical entrepreneur with retirement funds who is contemplating buying or funding a business. Most of the individuals I speak to are looking to buy a business or franchise and have heard about the option of using retirement funds but are looking for additional information and guidance. The questions Ken posed to John are typical of the questions someone looking to buy or fund a business with personal or retirement funds would ask a tax professional. It was my hope that using this type of dialogue format would allow the book to address the subject of start-up business funding options in detail while still being engaging and interesting.

I hope I've helped you understand the different types of business financing and funding options, including the use of retirement funds, that are available to you, along with some of their advantages and disadvantages. Most importantly, I hope the book has been able to show you how important it is to carefully consider all factors before starting or buying a business, considering the high failure risk and the challenging financing environment. The good news is that if you have retirement funds, the available business-funding options increase materially and potentially offer tax-efficient ways to buy or start a business. I'm not telling you that you should consider starting a business or use your retirement funds as a funding vehicle. That's not the purpose of this book, and that's a conversation best left for you to have with your tax professional, investment adviser, or financial planner.

First, I want to make sure you understand that aside from the traditional start-up business funding options, such as savings, friends and family, crowdfunding, credit cards, or third-party or SBA loans, the 401(k) plan loan and the ROBS structure do offer legal ways to use retirement funds to buy or finance a business acquisition.

Second, I also want to impress upon you that there are advantages and disadvantages to using retirement funds to buy or finance a business and that working with a tax professional is crucial.

Finally, I know many of you are probably wondering why this is the first book you've read on the ability to use retirement funds to buy or finance a start-up business or franchise. People ask me, "How can that be?" They think that it sounds almost too good to be true.

Don't blame yourself for not knowing. You are not alone. I have talked to tens of thousands of retirement account holders and am always amazed at how few people realize you can buy, finance, or invest in your own business without triggering an IRS prohibited transaction. I understand how they feel. I have a law degree and a masters in taxation from a top law school and have worked at some of the largest law firms in the world. While I am not the most sophisticated investor, I have a diverse tax and investment background. But I learned about using retirement funds as a business-funding option only through research I did for a client.

Since then, I've helped many entrepreneurs use their retirement funds to fund their business dreams, including a number of attorneys and CPAs—one who even went to Harvard Law School—who were unaware that retirement assets can be used to buy or finance a business or franchise.

I hope this book has been able to provide you with details on the many popular ways an entrepreneur or small-business owner can buy or fund a business. Whether you wish to use your personal savings, approach friends and family, look into crowdfunding, think a bank or SBA loan fits your bill, or feel a personal or business credit card will get you the quick cash you need, there are options available to you. Now, if you have retirement funds, your business-funding options increase significantly. From taking a taxable distribution, to considering the self-directed IRA, to contemplating the 401(k) plan loan option, to pondering the ROBS transaction, buying or funding a business gets a little easier. No matter what type of business-funding or financing options you choose, it is important that you consider the pros and cons of all options and work with a tax professional to help you make the right decision.

If you have gotten this far, you are obviously interested in becoming a business owner or seeking alternative ways to finance a business. The good part is that you probably have done all your due diligence and examined all the risks of becoming a business owner and are still committed to moving forward. You should know that the deck is stacked against you since half of new businesses fail within the first five years according to the SBA, but you should also know that America has always been a land of opportunity, where the idea of "pulling yourself up by your bootstraps" is widely believed. Entrepreneurial spirit is what makes America great. Consider the example of Howard Schultz. A trip to Milan gave a young marketer working for a Seattle coffee roaster an idea for upscale espresso cafes like they have all over Italy. His employer had no interest in owning coffee shops but agreed to finance Schultz's endeavor. They even sold him their brand name, Starbucks. Or the case of Joe Coulombe. After operating a small chain of convenience stores in Southern California, Joe Coulombe had an idea that upwardly mobile college grads might want something better than 7-11. So he opened a tropical-themed market in Pasadena, stocked it with good wine and other products, hired good people, and paid them well. He added more locations near universities, then healthy foods, and that's how Trader Joe's got started. The history books are filled with rags-to-riches stories of entrepreneurs who overcame enormous odds to strike it rich with an idea and a dream. If you stay with your dream, build on your ideas, and acquire the necessary funding to get started, with a little luck and hard work you could become the next great American entrepreneur. Nothing is guaranteed, and no business idea is a sure thing, but what makes America great is that with hard work and some luck, anything is possible. With a multitude of personal and retirement business-funding options now available, your dream of becoming your own boss and a successful entrepreneur is a lot closer than you think.

EXHIBIT A

STATE	FILING FEES
Alabama - Tel: 334-242-1170 Press 8	$100 ($75 plus county fee) Business Privilege Tax Return $10 No Annual Report filing
Alaska - Tel: 907-465-2530	$250 (online) $25 fee for reserving an LLC name
Arizona - Tel: 602-542-6187	LLCS are formed through the Arizona Corporations Commission $85 ($50 +35 Expedited fee) Application to Reserve Limited Liability Company Name $10 Regular $45 Expedited $150 publishing fee (within 3 months of formation) Need original signature of registered agent
Arkansas - Tel: 888-233-0325	Form LL-01 $45 Online $50 Paper $150-franchise tax report must be filed by May 1st of each year.
California - Tel: 916-653-6814	$85 ($70 + $15 walk in fee) Within 90 days of your formation, you will need to send in your statement of information along with a $20 filing fee. LLCs also pay an $800 annual tax, due within 3 1/2 months of your LLC's formation and every April 15 thereafter.
Colorado - Tel: 303-894-2200	File $60 Amend $25 Amend and Restate $ 25 Dissolve $25
Connecticut - Tel: 860-509-6002 Department of Revenue - Tel: 860-297-5962	$120 Filing Fee $100 Expedited Service
Delaware - Tel: 302-739-3073	$140 ($90 + $50 for certified copy) If necessary the expedite fee for Delaware LLC $100 Same Day $ 50 24-Hour Fee
D.C. - Tel: 202-442-4411	$220
Florida - Tel: 850-245-6500	$155 ($125 +30 for certified copy)
Georgia - Tel: 404-656-2817	$25 for Name reservation $100 for filing articles online (articles immediate online if name reservation has been done first) = $125 $50 annual filing fee due within 90 days of filing – client obligation
Hawaii - Tel: 808-586-2744 Alt: 808-586-2727	$75 ($50 + $25 expedited fee)
Idaho - Tel: 208-334-2301	$120 ($100 filing fee +$20 expedited fee)
Illinois - Tel: 217-782-6961	$500 by hand (receive in 7 days) or $600 online (receive in 24hrs)
Indiana - Tel: 317-232-6576	$90 Mail $85 Online
Iowa - Tel: 515-281-5204	$50
Kansas - Tel: 785-296-4564	$160 Online $165 Paper
Kentucky - Tel: 502-564-2848	$40
Louisiana - Tel: 225-925-4704	$130 ($100 +30 expedited fee)
Maine - Tel: 207-626-8400	$225 ($175 +$50 expedited fee)

STATE	FILING FEES
Maryland - Tel: 410-767-1340	$150 ($100 +$50 expedited fee) $300 annual fee for personal property return filing fee due each year
Massachusetts - Tel: 617-727-9640	$500 $20 Expedite Fee
Michigan - Tel: 888-767-6424	$50
Minnesota - Tel: 651-296-2803	$135 Mail $155 In Person or Online
Mississippi - Tel: 601-359-1633	$50 Online only
Missouri - Tel: 573-751-4153	$50 Online $105 In Person
Montana - Tel: 406-444-3665	$70 $ 20 Expedited Fee within 24 hours
Nebraska - Tel: 402-471-4079	$100 plus $10 for a certificate and $5 a page ($125)
Nevada - Tel: 775-684-5708	$75 (plus $125 expedited fee is client wants = $200) – Need signature of registered agent IF FILE ONLINE - $75
New Hampshire - Tel: 603-271-3244	$100 $50 for certification
New Jersey - Tel: 609-292-9292	$125 Online or In Person
New Mexico - Tel: 505-827-4508	$50
New York - Tel: 518-473-2492	$200 +$25 (expedited fee) = $225 Publication requirement within 120 days of forming LLC. Onetime fee – amount varies by county. Cost can vary from $400 to $1800 for Manhattan.
North Carolina - Tel: 919-807-2225	$125 (plus $100 if client wants expedited)
North Dakota - Tel: 701-328-2900	$135
Ohio - Tel: 614-466-3910	$125 $100 Expedite
Oklahoma - Tel: 405-521-3912	$104 e-filing $100 by mail
Oregon - Tel: 503-986-2200	$100 Online
Pennsylvania - Tel: 717-787-1057	$125
Rhode Island - Tel: 401-222-3040	$150
South Carolina - Tel: 803-734-2158	$110 (need signature of registered agent)
South Dakota - Tel: 605-773-4845	$150
Tennessee - Tel: 615-741-2286 Department of Revenue – Tel: 615-253-0700	$300
Texas - Tel: 512-463-5555	$300 ($20 expedited fee if client is in a big hurry)
Utah - Tel: 801-530-4849	$70 Online $5 extra for Expedite
Vermont - Tel: 802-828-2386	$125
Virginia - Tel: 804-371-9733	$100
Washington - Tel: 360-725-0377	$200 Online $180 Mail
West Virginia - Tel: 304-558-8000	$100 Online
Wisconsin - Tel: 608-261-7577	$130 Online $170 Mail

EXHIBIT B

ENTITY COMPARISON CHART

A business can take a number of forms, such as a limited liability company or partnership, a "C" corporation, or an "S" corporation. When one starts a business, they must choose the form in which they will operate. Both non-tax and tax considerations should guide the choice. Until recently, the choice was essentially between the corporate form of doing business, and the partnership form (either general or limited partnership). In recent years a third alternative has become available in all states, the LLC.

	LLC	Sole Proprietorship	"C" Corporation	"S" Corporation	General Partnership
Formation	File Articles of Organization with State agency	Automatically formed upon start of business. No filings necessary	File Certificate of Formation with State agency	File Certificate of Formation with State agency	Two or more persons intend to operate a business. No filings necessary
Management	Can be manager or member managed	Owner managed. May be manager managed	Corporate management structure is fixed. Shareholders can be officers and directors	Corporate management structure is fixed. Shareholders can be officers and directors	Must be partner managed. Cannot be manager managed
Liability	Limited liability for all members. Members not liable for LLC debts. Piercing the LLC veil possible	Owner personally liable. Owner liable for all debts.	Limited liability for all shareholders. Shareholders not liable for corporate debts. Piercing the corporate veil allowed	Limited liability for all shareholders. Shareholders not liable for corporate debts. Piercing the corporate veil allowed	All partners are personally liable. All partners are jointly and severally liable for all partnership debts. No veil piercing theories
Tax Treatment	Generally treated as a partnership or sole proprietorship. Subject to one level of tax. May be taxed as a "C" or "S" corporation. Distributions may be subject to self-employment income tax.	Always taxed as a sole proprietorship	Generally taxed as a "C" corporation. Shareholders subject to double taxation. No self-employment income tax on distributions	Always taxed as a "S" corporation - one level of tax - but can lose "S" status. Shareholders not subject to double taxation. No self-employment income tax on distributions in most cases	Always taxed as a partnership - one level of tax.

	LLC	Sole Proprietorship	"C" Corporation	"S" Corporation	General Partnership
Owners	One or more members. Can have single member LLC. No limit on maximum number of members	Single owner only. Cannot have two or more owners	One or more shareholders. Can have single owner corporation. No limit on maximum number of shareholders	One or more shareholders. Can have single owner corporation. Limit to hundred shareholders. Limit in type of shareholders	Two or more partners required. Cannot have single partner partnership. No limit on maximum number of members
Ownership Interests	May share in profits and losses. May participate in management. Interest may be treated differently. Restrictions can prevent interest from being assigned or transferred	Entire business owned by owner. All property is personal property of owner. All profits and losses belong to owner. All management controlled by owner	May receive dividends. May participate in management. Free transferability of stock. Each stock class must be treated identically but can have different classes of stock	May receive dividends. May participate in management. Free transferability of stock. Limited to one class of stock but can have different voting rights	Right to share in profits and losses. Right to participate in management. Interest may be assignable.

271

EXHIBIT C

OMB Control No. 3245-0348
Expiration Date: 04/17/2017

BORROWER INFORMATION FORM
For use with all 7(a) Programs

The purpose of this form is to collect identifying information about the applicant, loan request, indebtedness, information about the principals, information about current or previous government financing, and certain other disclosures. The information also facilitates background checks as authorized by Section 7(a)(1)(B) of the Small Business Act, 15 U.S.C. 636(a)(1)(B). This form is to be completed by the Small Business Applicant and submitted to an SBA Participating Lender.

To be completed by the following:

(With the exception of guarantors, all parties listed below are considered "Associates" of the small business applicant.)

- For a sole proprietorship, the sole proprietor;
- For a partnership, all general partners and all limited partners owning 20% or more of the equity of the firm;
- For a corporation, all owners of 20% or more of the corporation and each officer and director;
- For limited liability companies (LLCs), all members owning 20% or more of the company, each officer, director, and managing member;
- Any person hired by the business to manage day-to-day operations; and
- Any other person who is guaranteeing the loan, if required by SBA.

For clarification regarding any of the questions, you should contact the SBA Participating Lender that will be processing the loan request.

NAME OF BUSINESS APPLYING FOR LOAN ("APPLICANT"): _____

YOUR NAME: _____ TITLE: _____

SOCIAL SECURITY NUMBER: _____ DATE OF BIRTH: _____

PLACE OF BIRTH (City & State or Foreign Country): _____

Veteran**	1=Non-Veteran; 2=Veteran-Other; 3=Service-Disabled Veteran; 4=Not Disclosed.					
Gender**	M=Male; F=Female; N=Not Disclosed					
Race**	1=American Indian or Alaska Native; 2=Asian; 3=Black or African-American; 4=Native Hawaiian or Pacific Islander; 5=White; X=Not Disclosed					
Ethnicity**	H=Hispanic or Latino; N=Not Hispanic or Latino; Y=Not Disclosed					
Owner	% Owned	Veteran	Gender	Race	Ethnicity	List proprietors, partners, officers, directors, all holders of outstanding stock. 100% of ownership must be shown. Use separate sheet if necessary. Please reference the above codes to complete this table for each owner of the applicant business. More than one race may be selected.

** The gender/race/ethnicity/veteran data is collected for program reporting purposes only. Disclosure is voluntary and has no bearing on the credit decision.

ALL QUESTIONS MUST BE ANSWERED AND ARE SUBJECT TO VERIFICATION BY SBA

(1) Are you presently subject to an indictment, criminal information, arraignment, or other means by which formal criminal charges are brought in any jurisdiction? ....Yes ☐...No ☐

(2) Have you been arrested in the past six months for any criminal offense? ....Yes ☐...No ☐

(3) For any criminal offense – other than a minor vehicle violation – have you ever: 1) been convicted; 2) plead guilty; 3) plead nolo contendere; 4) been placed on pretrial diversion; or 5) been placed on any form of parole or probation (including probation before judgment)? ....Yes ☐...No ☐

(4) Has an application for the loan you are applying for now ever been submitted to SBA or to a Certified Development Company or lender in connection with any SBA program? ....Yes ☐.....No ☐

SBA Form 1919 (Revised 4/14)   1

(5) Are you presently debarred, suspended, proposed for debarment, declared ineligible, or
   voluntarily excluded from participation in this transaction by any Federal department or agency?Yes ☐ ...No ☐

(6) If you are at least a 50% or more owner of the applicant business, are you more than 60 days
   delinquent on any obligation to pay child support arising under an administrative order, court
   order, repayment agreement between the holder and a custodial parent, or repayment agreement
   between the holder and a state agency providing child support enforcement services? ....Yes ☐...No ☐

If "YES" to Question 1, the loan request is ineligible for SBA assistance. If there is a "YES" response to
Question 2 or 3, you must complete SBA Form 912 and furnish details on a separate sheet, including dates,
location, fines, sentences, whether misdemeanor or felony, dates of parole/probation, unpaid fines or penalties,
name(s) under which charged, and any other pertinent information. If "YES" to Questions 2 or 3, the lender
will be required to conduct a background check and make a character determination in accordance with the
procedures described in SOP 50 10 5. If "YES" to Question 3 and you are currently on parole or probation
(including probation before judgment), the loan request is ineligible for SBA assistance. If the charge resulting
in a "YES" was a single misdemeanor that was subsequently dropped without prosecution, you must provide
documentation from the appropriate court or prosecutor's office along with the completed Form 912.

If "YES" to Questions 4, 5 or 6, this application may not be submitted to SBA under any delegated or
expedited processing method, but must be submitted to the Standard 7(a) Loan Guaranty Processing Center
(LGPC) for non-delegated processing. The only exception is an application that was declined under a 7(a)
Small Loan due to the applicant's credit score may be submitted under SBA Express procedures. Note: This
does not mean that your loan will be denied, only that your lender will need to use different SBA procedures
to process the loan.

(7) Are you a U.S. Citizen?...Yes ☐...No ☐
   If "No," are you a Lawful Permanent resident alien?...Yes ☐...No ☐
   Provide Alien Registration Number _____

(8) Are any of your business' products or services exported or do you plan to begin exporting as a
   result of this loan?..Yes ☐...No ☐
   If ""Yes," provide the estimated total export sales this loan will support: $_____

(9) Is your business a franchise?..Yes ☐...No ☐

(10) Does the Applicant business have any Affiliates? ....Yes ☐...No ☐

   Affiliation exists when one individual or entity controls or has the power to control another or when a third
   party or parties control or have the power to control both. SBA considers factors such as ownership,
   management previous relationships with or ties to another entity, and contractual relationships when
   determining whether affiliation exists. The complete definition of affiliation is found at 13 CFR 121.103. (See
   also, 13 CFR 121.107 and 121.301.) An "Affiliate" includes, for example: (1) a parent company; (2)
   subsidiaries and other companies that are owned or controlled by the Applicant; (3) companies in which an
   officer, director, general partner, managing member or party owning 20% or more is also an officer, director,
   general partner, managing member or 20% or greater owner of the Applicant; (4) companies or individuals with
   unexercised options to own 50% or more of the Applicant's stock; and (5) companies that have entered into
   agreements to merge with the Applicant.
      If answered "yes," attach a listing of all Affiliates to this form.

(11) Have you, the Applicant, its Affiliates, or any business owned or controlled by you or any
   Associate ever obtained a direct or guaranteed loan from SBA or any other Federal agency or
   been a guarantor on such a loan? (This includes student loans and disaster loans.) ....Yes ☐...No ☐
   (a) If you answered "Yes" to Question 11, is any of the financing currently delinquent?...........Yes ☐...No ☐
   (b) If you answered "Yes" to Question 11, did any of this financing ever default and cause a
   loss to the Government? ....Yes ☐...No ☐

(12) What is the existing number of employees currently employed by the business? _____

(13) Number of jobs to be created as a result of the loan? _____ Number of jobs that will be retained as a
   result of the loan that would have been lost otherwise?_____

(14) Have you or the Applicant used (or intend to use) a packager, broker, accountant, lawyer, etc.to assist
   in (a) preparing the loan application or any related materials and/or (b) referring the loan to the
   lender?..Yes ☐...No ☐
   If answer is "Yes," a SBA Form 159 7(a) will need to be completed by the Applicant and the lender.

(15) Will more than $10,000 of the loan proceeds be used for construction? .... Yes ☐ ... No ☐
 If answer is "Yes," a SBA Form 601 will need to be completed.

(16) Are any of the Applicant's revenues derived from gambling or from the sale of products or services, or the presentation of any depiction, displays or live performances, of a prurient sexual nature? .... Yes ☐ ... No ☐

(17) Is the loan request for a Community Advantage Pilot Program loan?   Yes ☐ ...No ☐
 If answer is "Yes," a SBA Form 2449, Community Advantage Addendum will need to be completed.

SBA may not provide financial assistance to an applicant where there is any appearance of a conflict of interest with an SBA or other governmental employee. If any of the questions below are answered "False", this application may not be submitted under any delegated or expedited processing method, but must be submitted to the LGPC for non-delegated processing. Note: This does not mean that your loan will be denied, only that your lender will need to use different SBA procedures to process the loan.

(18) No SBA employee, or the household member (see definition at * below) of an SBA employee, is a sole proprietor, partner, officer, director, or stockholder with a 10 percent or more interest, of the Applicant. [13 CFR 105.204]   True____ False____

(19) No former SBA employee, who has been separated from SBA for less than one year prior to the request for financial assistance, is an employee, owner, partner, attorney, agent, owner of stock, officer, director, creditor or debtor of the Applicant. [13 CFR 105.203]   True____ False____

(20) No member of Congress, or an appointed official or employee of the legislative or judicial branch of the Federal Government, is a sole proprietor, general partner, officer, director, or stockholder with a 10 percent or more interest, or household member of such individual, of the Applicant.
 [13 CFR 105.301(c)]   True____ False____

(21) No Government employee having a grade of at least GS-13 or higher is a sole proprietor, general partner, officer, director, or stockholder with a 10 percent or more interest, or a household member of such individual, of the Applicant. [13 CFR 105.301(a)]   True____ False____

(22) No member or employee of a Small Business Advisory Council or a SCORE volunteer is a sole proprietor, general partner, officer, director, or stockholder with a 10 percent or more interest, or a household member of such individual, of the Applicant. [13 CFR 105.302(a)]   True____ False____

* A "household member" of an SBA employee includes: a) the spouse of the SBA employee; b) the minor children of said individual; and c) the blood relatives of the employee, and the blood relatives of the employee's spouse who reside in the same place of abode as the employee.[13 CFR 105.201(d)]

Turning Retirement Funds into Start-Up Dreams

Please read the following restrictions regarding use of federal financial assistance programs. If you understand them fully and agree to them, sign your name at the end of this document.

SBA is required to withhold or limit financial assistance, to impose special conditions on approved loans, to provide special notices to applicants or borrowers and to require special reports and data from borrowers in order to comply with legislation passed by the Congress and Executive Orders issued by the President and by the provisions of various inter-agency agreements. SBA has issued regulations and procedures that implement these laws and executive orders. These are contained in Parts 112, 113, and 117 of Title 13 of the Code of Federal Regulations and in Standard Operating Procedures.

Privacy Act (5 U.S.C. 552a) -- Any person can request to see or get copies of any personal information that SBA has in his or her file when that file is retrieved by individual identifiers such as name or social security numbers. Requests for information about another party may be denied unless SBA has the written permission of the individual to release the information to the requestor or unless the information is subject to disclosure under the Freedom of Information Act.

Under the provisions of the Privacy Act, you are not required to provide your social security number. Failure to provide your social security number may not affect any right, benefit or privilege to which you are entitled. Disclosures of name and other personal identifiers are, however, required for a benefit, as SBA requires an individual seeking assistance from SBA to provide it with sufficient information for it to make a character determination. In determining whether an individual is of good character, SBA considers the person's integrity, candor, and disposition toward criminal actions. Additionally, SBA is specifically authorized to verify your criminal history, or lack thereof, pursuant to section 7(a)(1)(B), 15 USC Section 636(a)(1)(B) of the Small Business Act (the Act). Further, for all forms of assistance, SBA is authorized to make all investigations necessary to ensure that a person has not engaged in acts that violate or will violate the Act or the Small Business Investment Act, 15 USC Sections 634(b)(11) and 687(b)(a), respectively. For these purposes, you are asked to voluntarily provide your social security number to assist SBA in making a character determination and to distinguish you from other individuals with the same or similar name or other personal identifier.

The Privacy Act authorizes SBA to make certain "routine uses" of information protected by that Act. One such routine use is the disclosure of information maintained in SBA's investigative files system of records when this information indicates a violation or potential violation of law, whether civil, criminal, or administrative in nature. Specifically, SBA may refer the information to the appropriate agency, whether Federal, State, local or foreign, charged with responsibility for, or otherwise involved in investigation, prosecution, enforcement or prevention of such violations. Another routine use is disclosure to other Federal agencies conducting background checks; only to the extent the information is relevant to the requesting agencies' function. See, 74 F.R. 14890 (2009), and as amended from time to time for additional background and other routine uses.

Right to Financial Privacy Act of 1978 (12 U.S.C. 3401) -- This is notice to you as required by the Right to Financial Privacy Act of 1978, of SBA's access rights to financial records held by financial institutions that are or have been doing business with you or your business, including any financial institutions participating in a loan or loan guaranty. The law provides that SBA shall have a right of access to your financial records in connection with its consideration or administration of assistance to you in the form of a Government guaranteed loan. SBA is required to provide a certificate of its compliance with the Act to a financial institution in connection with its first request for access to your financial records, after which no further certification is required for subsequent accesses. The law also provides that SBA's access rights continue for the term of any approved loan guaranty agreement. No further notice to you of SBA's access rights is required during the term of any such agreement. The law also authorizes SBA to transfer to another Government authority any financial records included in an application for a loan, or concerning an approved loan or loan guarantee, as necessary to process, service or foreclose on a loan guaranty or collect on a defaulted loan guaranty.

Freedom of Information Act (5 U.S.C. 552) -- This law provides, with some exceptions, that SBA must supply information reflected in agency files and records to a person requesting it. Information about approved loans that will be automatically released includes, among other things, statistics on our loan programs (individual borrowers are not identified in the statistics) and other information such as the names of the borrowers (and their officers, directors, stockholders or partners), the collateral pledged to secure the loan, the amount of the loan, its purpose in general terms and the maturity. Proprietary data on a borrower would not routinely be made available to third parties. All requests under this Act are to be addressed to the nearest SBA office and be identified as a Freedom of Information request.

Flood Disaster Protection Act (42 U.S.C. 4011) -- Regulations have been issued by the Federal Insurance Administration (FIA) and by SBA implementing this Act and its amendments. These regulations prohibit SBA from making certain loans in an FIA designated floodplain unless Federal Flood insurance is purchased as a condition of the loan. Failure to maintain the required level of flood insurance makes the applicant ineligible for any financial assistance from SBA, including disaster assistance.

Executive Orders -- Floodplain Management and Wetland Protection (42 F.R. 26951 and 42 F.R. 26961) -- SBA discourages settlement in or development of a floodplain or a wetland. This statement is to notify all SBA loan applicants that such actions are hazardous to both life and property and should be avoided. The additional cost of flood preventive construction must be considered in addition to the possible loss of all assets and investments due to a future flood.

Occupational Safety and Health Act (15 U.S.C. 651 et seq.) -- This legislation authorizes the Occupational Safety and Health Administration in the Department of Labor to require businesses to modify facilities and procedures to protect employees or pay penalty fees. Businesses can be forced to cease operations or be prevented from starting operations in a new facility. Therefore, SBA may require additional information from an applicant to determine whether the business will be in compliance with OSHA regulations and allowed to operate its facility after the loan is approved and disbursed. Signing this form as an applicant is certification that the OSHA requirements that apply to the applicant business have been determined and that the applicant, to the best of its knowledge, is in compliance. Furthermore, applicant certifies that it will remain in compliance during the life of the loan.

Civil Rights Legislation (13 C.F.R. 112, 113, 117) -- All businesses receiving SBA financial assistance must agree not to discriminate in any business practice, including employment practices and services to the public on the basis of categories cited in 13 C.F.R., Parts 112, 113, and 117 of SBA Regulations. This includes making their goods and services available to handicapped clients or customers. All business borrowers will be required to display the "Equal Employment Opportunity Poster" prescribed by SBA.

Equal Credit Opportunity Act (15 U.S.C. 1691) -- The Federal Equal Credit Opportunity Act prohibits creditors from discriminating against credit applicants on the basis of race, color, religion, national origin, sex, marital status or age (provided the applicant has the capacity to enter into a binding contract); because all or part of the applicant's income derives from any public assistance program, or because the applicant has in good faith exercised any right under the Consumer Credit Protection Act.

Executive Order 11738 -- Environmental Protection (38 F.R. 251621) -- The Executive Order charges SBA with administering its loan programs in a manner that will result in effective enforcement of the Clean Air Act, the Federal Water Pollution Act and other environment protection legislation.

Debt Collection Act of 1982, Deficit Reduction Act of 1984 (31 U.S.C. 3701 et seq. and other titles) -- These laws require SBA to collect aggressively any loan payments which become delinquent. SBA must obtain your taxpayer identification number when you apply for a loan. If you receive a loan, and do not make payments as they come due, SBA may take one or more of the following actions: (1) report the status of your loan(s) to credit bureaus, (2) hire a collection agency to collect your loan, (3) offset your income tax refund or other amounts due to you from the Federal Government, (4) suspend or debar you or your company from doing business with the Federal Government, (5) refer your loan to the Department of Justice or other attorneys for litigation, or (6) foreclose on collateral or take other action permitted in the loan instruments.

Immigration Reform and Control Act of 1986 (Pub. L. 99-603) -- If you are an alien who was in this country illegally since before January 1, 1982, you may have been granted lawful temporary resident status by the United States Immigration and Naturalization Service pursuant to the Immigration Reform and Control Act of 1986. For five years from the date you are granted such status, you are not eligible for financial assistance from the SBA in the form of a loan guaranty under Section 7(a) of the Small Business Act unless you are disabled or a Cuban or Haitian entrant. When you sign this document, you are making the certification that the Immigration Reform and Control Act of 1986 does not apply to you, or if it does apply, more than five years have elapsed since you have been granted lawful temporary resident status pursuant to such 1986 legislation.

Lead-Based Paint Poisoning Prevention Act (42 U.S.C. 4821 et seq.)
Borrowers using SBA funds for the construction or rehabilitation of a residential structure are prohibited from using lead-based paint (as defined in SBA regulations) on all interior surfaces, whether accessible or not, and exterior surfaces, such as stairs, decks, porches, railings, windows and doors, which are readily accessible to children under 7 years of age. A "residential structure" is any home, apartment, hotel, motel, orphanage, boarding school, dormitory, day care center, extended care facility, college or other school housing, hospital, group practice or community facility and all other residential or institutional structures where persons reside.

Executive Order 12549, Debarment and Suspension (13 C.F.R. 145) -- The prospective lower tier participant certifies, by submission of this loan application, that neither it nor its principals are presently debarred, suspended, proposed for debarment, declared ineligible, or voluntarily excluded from participation in this transaction by any Federal department or agency. Where the prospective lower tier participant is unable to certify to any of the statements in this certification, such prospective participants shall attach an explanation to the loan application.

Turning Retirement Funds into Start-Up Dreams

_____   _____
Signature   Date

_____
Print Name

NOTE: According to the Paperwork Reduction Act, you are not required to respond to this collection of information unless it displays a currently valid OMB Control Number. The estimated burden for completing this form, including time for reviewing instructions, gathering data needed, and completing and reviewing the form is 9 minutes per response. Comments or questions on the burden estimates should be sent to U.S. Small Business Administration, Chief, AIB, 409 3rd St., SW, Washington DC 20416, and/or SBA Desk Officer, Office of Management and Budget, New Executive Office Building, Rm 10202, Washington DC 20503. **PLEASE DO NOT SEND FORMS TO THESE ADDRESSES.**

SBA Form 1919 (Revised 4/14)   6

Adam Bergman, Esq.

EXHIBIT D

ROLLOVER CHART

5/7/2011

	Roll To							
Roll From	Roth IRA	IRA (traditional)	SIMPLE IRA	SEP-IRA	457(b) (government)	Qualified Plan[1] (pre-tax)	403(b) (pre-tax)	Designated Roth Account (401(k), 403(b) or 457(b)[5])
Roth IRA	YES	NO	NO	NO	NO	NO	NO	NO
IRA (traditional)	YES[3]	YES	NO	YES	YES[4]	YES	YES	NO
SIMPLE IRA	YES,[3] after two years	YES, after two years	YES	YES, after two years	YES,[2] after two years	YES, after two years	YES, after two years	NO
SEP-IRA	YES[3]	YES	NO	YES	YES[4]	YES	YES	NO
457(b) (government)	YES[3]	YES	NO	YES	YES	YES	YES	YES,[3,5] after 12/31/10
Qualified Plan[1] (pre-tax)	YES[3]	YES	NO	YES	YES[2]	YES	YES	YES,[3,5] after 9/27/10
403(b) (pre-tax)	YES[3]	YES	NO	YES	YES[4]	YES	YES	YES,[3,5] after 9/27/10
Designated Roth Account (401(k), 403(b) or 457(b)[5])	YES	NO	NO	NO	NO	NO	NO	Yes, if a direct trustee to trustee transfer

[1]Qualified plans include, for example, profit-sharing, 401(k), money purchase, and defined benefit plans
[2]Governmental 457(b) plans, after December 31, 2010
[3]Must include in income
[4]Must have separate accounts
[5]Must be an in-plan rollover
For more information regarding retirement plans and rollovers, visit Tax Information for Retirement Plans Community.

EXHIBIT E

26 U.S. Code § 4975 - Tax on prohibited transactions

...

(c) Prohibited transaction

(1) General rule

For purposes of this section, the term "prohibited transaction" means any direct or indirect—

(A) sale or exchange, or leasing, of any property between a plan and a disqualified person;

(B) lending of money or other extension of credit between a plan and a disqualified person;

(C) furnishing of goods, services, or facilities between a plan and a disqualified person;

(D) transfer to, or use by or for the benefit of, a disqualified person of the income or assets of a plan;

(E) act by a disqualified person who is a fiduciary whereby he deals with the income or assets of a plan in his own interests or for his own account; or

(F) receipt of any consideration for his own personal account by any disqualified person who is a fiduciary from any party dealing with the plan in connection with a transaction involving the income or assets of the plan.

(2) Special exemption

The Secretary shall establish an exemption procedure for purposes of this subsection. Pursuant to such procedure, he may grant a conditional or unconditional exemption of any disqualified person or transaction, orders of disqualified persons or transactions, from all or part of the restrictions imposed by paragraph (1) of this subsection. Action under this subparagraph may be taken only after consultation and coordination with the Secretary of Labor. The Secretary may not grant an exemption under this paragraph unless he finds that such exemption is—

(A) administratively feasible,

(B) in the interests of the plan and of its participants and beneficiaries, and

(C) protective of the rights of participants and beneficiaries of the plan.

Before granting an exemption under this paragraph, the Secretary shall require adequate notice to be given to interested persons and shall publish notice in the Federal Register of the pendency of such exemption and shall afford interested persons an opportunity to present views. No exemption may be granted under this paragraph with respect to a transaction described in subparagraph (E) or (F) of paragraph (1) unless the Secretary affords an opportunity for a hearing and makes a determination on the record with respect to the findings required under subparagraphs (A), (B), and (C) of this paragraph, except that in lieu of such hearing the Secretary may accept any record made by the Secretary of Labor with respect to an application for exemption under section 408(a) of title I of the Employee Retirement Income Security Act of 1974.

(3) Special rule for individual retirement accounts

An individual for whose benefit an individual retirement account is established and his beneficiaries shall be exempt from the tax imposed by this section with respect to any transaction concerning such account (which would otherwise be taxable under this section) if, with respect to such transaction, the account ceases to be an individual retirement account by reason of the application of section 408 (e) (2) (A) or if section 408 (e) (4) applies to such account.

(4) Special rule for Archer MSAs

An individual for whose benefit an Archer MSA (within the meaning of section 220 (d)) is established shall be exempt from the tax imposed by this section with respect to any transaction concerning such account (which would otherwise be taxable under this section) if section 220 (e) (2) applies to such transaction.

(5) Special rule for Coverdell education savings accounts

An individual for whose benefit a Coverdell education savings account is established and any contributor to such account shall be exempt from the tax imposed by this section with respect to any transaction concerning such account (which would otherwise be taxable under this section) if section 530 (d) applies with respect to such transaction.

(6) Special rule for health savings accounts

An individual for whose benefit a health savings account (within the meaning of section 223 (d)) is established shall be exempt from the tax imposed by this section with respect to any transaction concerning such account (which would otherwise be taxable under this section) if, with respect to such transaction, the account ceases to be a health savings account by reason of the application of section 223 (e)(2) to such account.

(d) Exemptions

Except as provided in subsection (f)(6), the prohibitions provided in subsection (c) shall not apply to—

   (1) any loan made by the plan to a disqualified person who is a participant or beneficiary of the plan if such loan—

      (A) is available to all such participants or beneficiaries on a reasonably equivalent basis,

      (B) is not made available to highly compensated employees (within the meaning of section 414 (q)) in an amount greater than the amount made available to other employees,

      (C) is made in accordance with specific provisions regarding such loans set forth in the plan,

      (D) bears a reasonable rate of interest, and

      (E) is adequately secured;

   (2) any contract, or reasonable arrangement, made with a disqualified person for office space, or legal, accounting, or other services necessary for the establishment or operation of the plan, if no more than reasonable compensation is paid therefor;

   (3) any loan to an [1] leveraged employee stock ownership plan (as defined in subsection (e)(7)), if—

      (A) such loan is primarily for the benefit of participants and beneficiaries of the plan, and

      (B) such loan is at a reasonable rate of interest, and any collateral which is given to a disqualified person by the plan consists only of qualifying employer securities (as defined in subsection (e)(8));

   (4) the investment of all or part of a plan's assets in deposits which bear a reasonable interest rate in a bank or similar financial institution supervised by the United States or a State, if such bank or other institution is a fiduciary of such plan and if—

      (A) the plan covers only employees of such bank or other institution and employees of affiliates of such bank or other institution, or

      (B) such investment is expressly authorized by a provision of the plan or by a fiduciary (other than such bank or institution or affiliates thereof) who is expressly empowered by the plan to so instruct the trustee with respect to such investment;

   (5) any contract for life insurance, health insurance, or annuities with one or more insurers which are qualified to do business in a State if the plan pays no more than adequate consideration, and if each such insurer or insurers is—

      (A) the employer maintaining the plan, or

      (B) a disqualified person which is wholly owned (directly or indirectly) by the employer establishing the plan, or by any person which is a disqualified person with respect to the plan, but only if the total premiums and annuity considerations written by such insurers for life insurance, health insurance, or annuities for all plans (and their employers) with respect to which such insurers are disqualified persons (not including premiums or annuity considerations written by the employer maintaining the plan) do not exceed 5 percent of the total premiums and annuity considerations written for all lines of insurance in that year by such insurers (not including premiums or annuity considerations written by the employer maintaining the plan);

   (6) the provision of any ancillary service by a bank or similar financial institution supervised by the United States or a State, if such service is provided at not more than reasonable compensation, if such bank or other institution is a fiduciary of such plan, and if—

      (A) such bank or similar financial institution has adopted adequate internal safeguards which assure that the provision of such ancillary service is consistent with sound banking and financial practice, as determined by Federal or State supervisory authority, and

      (B) the extent to which such ancillary service is provided is subject to specific guidelines issued by such bank or similar financial institution (as determined by the Secretary after consultation with Federal and State supervisory authority), and under such guidelines the bank or similar financial institution does not provide such ancillary service—

      (C) in an excessive or unreasonable manner, and

      (D) in a manner that would be inconsistent with the best interests of participants and beneficiaries of employee benefit plans;

   (7) the exercise of a privilege to convert securities, to the extent provided in regulations of the Secretary but only if the plan receives no less than adequate consideration pursuant to such conversion;

(8) any transaction between a plan and a common or collective trust fund or pooled investment fund maintained by a disqualified person which is a bank or trust company supervised by a State or Federal agency or between a plan and a pooled investment fund of an insurance company qualified to do business in a State if—

(A) the transaction is a sale or purchase of an interest in the fund,

(B) the bank, trust company, or insurance company receives not more than a reasonable compensation, and

(C) such transaction is expressly permitted by the instrument under which the plan is maintained, or by a fiduciary (other than the bank, trust company, or insurance company, or an affiliate thereof) who has authority to manage and control the assets of the plan;

(9) receipt by a disqualified person of any benefit to which he may be entitled as a participant or beneficiary in the plan, so long as the benefit is computed and paid on a basis which is consistent with the terms of the plan as applied to all other participants and beneficiaries;

(10) receipt by a disqualified person of any reasonable compensation for services rendered, or for the reimbursement of expenses properly and actually incurred, in the performance of his duties with the plan, but no person so serving who already receives full-time pay from an employer or an association of employers, whose employees are participants in the plan or from an employee organization whose members are participants in such plan shall receive compensation from such fund, except for reimbursement of expenses properly and actually incurred;

(11) service by a disqualified person as a fiduciary in addition to being an officer, employee, agent, or other representative of a disqualified person;

(12) the making by a fiduciary of a distribution of the assets of the trust in accordance with the terms of the plan if such assets are distributed in the same manner as provided under section 4044 of title IV of the Employee Retirement Income Security Act of 1974 (relating to allocation of assets);

(13) any transaction which is exempt from section 406 of such Act by reason of section 408(e) of such Act (or which would be so exempt if such section 406 applied to such transaction) or which is exempt from section 406 of such Act by reason of section 408(b)(12) of such Act;

(14) any transaction required or permitted under part 1 of subtitle E of title IV or section 4223 of the Employee Retirement Income Security Act of 1974, but this paragraph shall not apply with respect to the application of subsection (c)(1) (E) or (F);

(15) a merger of multiemployer plans, or the transfer of assets or liabilities between multiemployer plans, determined by the Pension Benefit Guaranty Corporation to meet the requirements of section 4231 of such Act, but this paragraph shall not apply with respect to the application of subsection (c) (1)(E) or (F);

(16) a sale of stock held by a trust which constitutes an individual retirement account under section 408 (a) to the individual for whose benefit such account is established if—

(A) such stock is in a bank (as defined in section 581) or a depository institution holding company (as defined in section 3(w)(1) of the Federal Deposit Insurance Act (12 U.S.C. 1813 (w)(1)), [2]

(B) such stock is held by such trust as of the date of the enactment of this paragraph,

(C) such sale is pursuant to an election under section 1362 (a) by such bank or company,

(D) such sale is for fair market value at the time of sale (as established by an independent appraiser) and the terms of the sale are otherwise at least as favorable to such trust as the terms that would apply on a sale to an unrelated party,

(E) such trust does not pay any commissions, costs, or other expenses in connection with the sale, and

(F) the stock is sold in a single transaction for cash not later than 120 days after the S corporation election is made;

(17) Any [3]transaction in connection with the provision of investment advice described in subsection (e)(3)(B) to a participant or beneficiary in a plan that permits such participant or beneficiary to direct the investment of plan assets in an individual account, if—

(A) the transaction is—

(B) the provision of the investment advice to the participant or beneficiary of the plan with respect to a security or other property available as an investment under the plan,

(C) the acquisition, holding, or sale of a security or other property available as an investment under the plan pursuant to the investment advice, or

(D) the direct or indirect receipt of fees or other compensation by the fiduciary adviser or an affiliate thereof (or any employee, agent, or registered representative of the fiduciary adviser or affiliate) in connection with the provision of the advice or in connection with an acquisition, holding, or sale of a security or other property available as an investment under the plan pursuant to the investment advice; and

(B) the requirements of subsection (h)(8) are met,   [4]

(18) any transaction involving the purchase or sale of securities, or other property (as determined by the Secretary of Labor), between a plan and a disqualified person (other than a fiduciary described in subsection (e)(3)) with respect to a plan if—

  (A) the transaction involves a block trade,

  (B) at the time of the transaction, the interest of the plan (together with the interests of any other plans maintained by the same plan sponsor), does not exceed 10 percent of the aggregate size of the block trade,

  (C) the terms of the transaction, including the price, are at least as favorable to the plan as an arm's length [5] transaction, and

  (D) the compensation associated with the purchase and sale is not greater than the compensation associated with an arm's length [5] transaction with an unrelated party,   [4]

(19) any transaction involving the purchase or sale of securities, or other property (as determined by the Secretary of Labor), between a plan and a disqualified person if—

  (A) the transaction is executed through an electronic communication network, alternative trading system, or similar execution system or trading venue subject to regulation and oversight by—

    (i) the applicable Federal regulating entity, or

    (ii) such foreign regulatory entity as the Secretary of Labor may determine by regulation,

  (B) either—

    (i) the transaction is effected pursuant to rules designed to match purchases and sales at the best price available through the execution system in accordance with applicable rules of the Securities and Exchange Commission or other relevant governmental authority, or

    (ii) neither the execution system nor the parties to the transaction take into account the identity of the parties in the execution of trades,

  (C) the price and compensation associated with the purchase and sale are not greater than the price and compensation associated with an arm's length [5] transaction with an unrelated party,

  (D) if [6] the disqualified person has an ownership interest in the system or venue described in subparagraph (A), the system or venue has been authorized by the plan sponsor or other independent fiduciary for transactions described in this paragraph, and

  (E) not less than 30 days prior to the initial transaction described in this paragraph executed through any system or venue described in subparagraph (A), a plan fiduciary is provided written or electronic notice of the execution of such transaction through such system or venue,

(20) transactions described in subparagraphs (A), (B), and (D) of subsection (c)(1) between a plan and a person that is a disqualified person other than a fiduciary (or an affiliate) who has or exercises any discretionary authority or control with respect to the investment of the plan assets involved in the transaction or renders investment advice (within the meaning of subsection (e)(3)(B)) with respect to those assets, solely by reason of providing services to the plan or solely by reason of a relationship to such a service provider described in subparagraph (F), (G), (H), or (I) of subsection (e)(2), or both, but only if in connection with such transaction the plan receives no less, nor pays no more, than adequate consideration, [4]

(21) any foreign exchange transactions, between a bank or broker-dealer (or any affiliate of either) and a plan (as defined in this section) with respect to which such bank or broker-dealer (or affiliate) is a trustee, custodian, fiduciary, or other disqualified person person, [7] if—

  (A) the transaction is in connection with the purchase, holding, or sale of securities or other investment assets (other than a foreign exchange transaction unrelated to any other investment in securities or other investment assets),

  (B) at the time the foreign exchange transaction is entered into, the terms of the transaction are not less favorable to the plan than the terms generally available in comparable arm's length [5] foreign exchange transactions between unrelated parties, or the terms afforded by the bank or broker-dealer (or any affiliate of either) in comparable arm's-length foreign exchange transactions involving unrelated parties,

  (C) the exchange rate used by such bank or broker-dealer (or affiliate) for a particular foreign exchange transaction does not deviate by more than 3 percent from the interbank bid and asked rates for transactions of comparable size and maturity at the time of the transaction as displayed on an independent service that reports rates of exchange in the foreign currency market for such currency, and

  (D) the bank or broker-dealer (or any affiliate of either) does not have investment discretion, or provide investment advice, with respect to the transaction, [4]

(22) any transaction described in subsection (c)(1)(A) involving the purchase and sale of a security between a plan and any other account managed by the same investment manager, if—

(A) the transaction is a purchase or sale, for no consideration other than cash payment against prompt delivery of a security for which market quotations are readily available,

(B) the transaction is effected at the independent current market price of the security (within the meaning of section 270.17a–7(b) of title 17 (/uscode/text/17), Code of Federal Regulations),

(C) no brokerage commission, fee (except for customary transfer fees, the fact of which is disclosed pursuant to subparagraph (D)), or other remuneration is paid in connection with the transaction,

(D) a fiduciary (other than the investment manager engaging in the cross-trades or any affiliate) for each plan participating in the transaction authorizes in advance of any cross-trades (in a document that is separate from any other written agreement of the parties) the investment manager to engage in cross trades at the investment manager's discretion, after such fiduciary has received disclosure regarding the conditions under which cross trades may take place (but only if such disclosure is separate from any other agreement or disclosure involving the asset management relationship), including the written policies and procedures of the investment manager described in subparagraph (H),

(E) each plan participating in the transaction has assets of at least $100,000,000, except that if the assets of a plan are invested in a master trust containing the assets of plans maintained by employers in the same controlled group (as defined in section 407(d)(7) of the Employee Retirement Income Security Act of 1974), the master trust has assets of at least $100,000,000,

(F) the investment manager provides to the plan fiduciary who authorized cross trading under subparagraph (D) a quarterly report detailing all cross trades executed by the investment manager in which the plan participated during such quarter, including the following information, as applicable;

    (i) the identity of each security bought or sold;
    (ii) the number of shares or units traded;
    (iii) the parties involved in the cross-trade; and
    (iv) trade price and the method used to establish the trade price.

(G) the investment manager does not base its fee schedule on the plan's consent to cross trading, and no other service (other than the investment opportunities and cost savings available through a cross trade) is conditioned on the plan's consent to cross trading,

(H) the investment manager has adopted, and cross-trades are effected in accordance with, written cross-trading policies and procedures that are fair and equitable to all accounts participating in the cross-trading program, and that include a description of the manager's pricing policies and procedures, and the manager's policies and procedures for allocating cross trades in an objective manner among accounts participating in the cross-trading program, and

    (I) the investment manager has designated an individual responsible for periodically reviewing such purchases and sales to ensure compliance with the written policies and procedures described in subparagraph (H), and following such review, the individual shall issue an annual written report no later than 90 days following the period to which it relates signed under penalty of perjury to the plan fiduciary who authorized cross trading under subparagraph (D) describing the steps performed during the course of the review, the level of compliance, and any specific instances of non-compliance.

The written report shall also notify the plan fiduciary of the plan's right to terminate participation in the investment manager's cross-trading program at any time, [4] or

(23) except as provided in subsection (f)(11), a transaction described in subparagraph (A), (B), (C), or (D) of subsection (c)(1) in connection with the acquisition, holding, or disposition of any security or commodity, if the transaction is corrected before the end of the correction period.

[1] So in original. Probably should be "a".

[2] So in original. Another closing parenthesis probably should precede the comma.

[3] So in original. Probably should not be capitalized.

[4] So in original. The comma probably should be a semicolon.

[5] So in original. Probably should be "arm's-length".

[6] So in original. The word "if" probably should not appear.

[7] So in original.

[8] So in original. Probably should be "subsection (d)(17)(A)(ii)".

[9] So in original. The comma probably should not appear.

[10]   So in original. Probably should be "of the".

EXHIBIT F

DEPARTMENT OF THE TREASURY
INTERNAL REVENUE SERVICE
WASHINGTON, D.C. 20224

TAX EXEMPT AND
GOVERNMENT ENTITIES
DIVISION

OCT 1 2008

MEMORANDUM FOR DIRECTOR, EMPLOYEE PLANS EXAMINATIONS
DIRECTOR, EMPLOYEE PLANS RULINGS & AGREEMENTS

FROM: Michael D. Julianelle, Director, Employee Plans, SE:T:EP

SUBJECT: Guidelines regarding rollovers as business start-ups

Recently, personnel in our examination and determination letter functions have
identified a retirement plan design that appears to operate primarily to transact in
employer stock, resulting in the avoidance of taxes otherwise applicable to distributions
from tax-deferred accumulation accounts.

Although we do not believe that the form of all of these transactions may be challenged
as non-compliant *per se*, issues such as those described within this memorandum
should be developed on a case-by-case basis. Those cases currently in process or
held in suspense should be worked within the context of these guidelines. Please
cascade this memorandum to your managers and technical employee staff as
appropriate.

EXECUTIVE SUMMARY

A version of a qualified plan is being marketed as a means for prospective business
owners to access accumulated tax-deferred retirement funds, without paying applicable
distribution taxes, in order to cover new business start-up costs. For purposes of this
memorandum, these arrangements are known as Rollovers as Business Startups, or
ROBS. While ROBS would otherwise serve legitimate tax and business planning
needs, they are questionable in that they may serve solely to enable one individual's
exchange of tax-deferred assets for currently available funds, by using a qualified plan
and its investment in employer stock as a medium. This may avoid distribution taxes
otherwise assessable on this exchange. Although a variety of business activity has
been examined, an attribute common to this design is the assignment of newly created
enterprise stock into a qualified plan as consideration for these transferred funds, the
valuation of which may be questionable.

BACKGROUND

Employee Plans first identified ROBS provisions giving rise to these transactions through our regular compliance processes, including determination letter submissions and later project examination activity. They are proprietary defined contribution plans, generally established in the form of profit sharing plans coupled with a cash or deferred arrangement (CODA). Several different promoters have crafted variations on this design, but the elements of each are sufficiently similar that they can be addressed generally.

Although ROBS arrangements may operate as profit sharing plans, their primary purpose appears to be to provide funding for the establishment of a business or franchise. They are designed to allow a newly created business entity to retrieve available tax-exempt accumulation funds from its principal in exchange for its capital stock, simultaneously avoiding all otherwise imposable distribution income and excise taxes that would ordinarily apply to the transaction.

The typical ROBS customer is an individual seeking to start up a personal business, and having accumulated tax-deferred investment funds, usually in the form of a defined contribution account created under a prior employer's plan.[1] From our review of open cases, franchises are often the business form of choice, and this design is marketed as a funding method on various internet sites.

After client engagement, the practitioner-promoter apparently advises the individual to create a C-corporation. A number of corporate shares may be created, but they are not issued. After incorporation is complete, the practitioner installs a qualified profit sharing plan, sponsored by the shell corporate entity. The plan document used is generally a "pre-approved" specimen, but is usually supplemented with a single amendment. This amendment generally exists as either a stand-alone amendment or a tack-on addition to a qualified plan adoption agreement, and consists of a one paragraph provision to permit the plan to invest plan assets attributable to rollover accounts up to 100% in employer securities.

The individual then executes either a rollover or direct trustee-to-trustee transfer of the proceeds from the available tax-deferred investment account into this newly created plan. At this point, the prior account is usually liquidated; all proceeds are parked in a rollover account held in trust under the shell corporation's plan.

The amendment provision is then acted on immediately, and the individual directs the corporation to issue and then exchange all of its capital stock into its qualified plan in exchange for the proceeds held in the rollover account. The corporate shares, now held as plan assets, are valued and booked equal to the value of available account proceeds.

---

[1] At the time the ROBS transaction is executed, some of these amounts may remain as deferred separated accounts held under a prior plan trust, and some appear to have been rolled over into a "conduit IRA", which was a common utility for individual retirement arrangements prior to the expanded portability provisions enacted by the Economic Growth Tax Relief and Reconciliation Act of 2001.

2

Usually, after the exchange of stock is complete, no other plan participant will ever receive any ability to invest in employer stock. In some ROBS versions, the provision permitting the stock investment is eliminated immediately after exchange, by means of a second amendment that serves to prospectively redact that provision. In all versions, the exchange fully allocates all of the stock to the rollover sub-account created for the benefit of the individual, and no further allocations of stock to future participants are permitted.

A ROBS transaction therefore takes the form of the following sequential steps:

> ➢ An individual establishes a shell corporation sponsoring an associated and purportedly qualified retirement plan. At this point, the corporation has no employees, assets or business operations, and may not even have a contribution to capital to create shareholder equity.

> ➢ The plan document provides that all participants may invest the entirety of their account balances in employer stock.

> ➢ The individual becomes the only employee of the shell corporation and the only participant in the plan. Note that at this point, there is still no ownership or shareholder equity interest.

> ➢ The individual then executes a rollover or direct trustee-to-trustee transfer of available funds from a prior qualified plan or personal IRA into the newly created qualified plan. These available funds might be any assets previously accumulated under the individual's prior employer's qualified plan, or under a conduit IRA which itself was created from these amounts. Note that at this point, because assets have been moved from one tax-exempt accumulation vehicle to another, all assessable income or excise taxes otherwise applicable to the distribution have been avoided[2].

> ➢ The sole participant in the plan then directs investment of his or her account balance into a purchase of employer stock. The employer stock is valued to reflect the amount of plan assets that the taxpayer wishes to access.

> ➢ The individual then uses the transferred funds to purchase a franchise or begin some other form of business enterprise. Note that all otherwise assessable taxes on a distribution from the prior tax-deferred accumulation account are avoided.

---

[2] Distributions from tax-deferred accumulation accounts would generally be taxed under IRC § 72, which specifies treatment for various forms of annuity or non-annuity payments. In general, a single sum distribution would be taxed as ordinary income, at the individual's effective tax rate. Of particular concern here, the distribution would generally also be subject to the 10% "premature distribution" penalty provided by IRC § 72(t), unless the individual was at least 59½ years old on the transaction date, or met one of the other limited statutory exceptions. ROBS transactions effectively avoid all § 72 concerns.

➤ After the business is established, the plan may be amended to prohibit further investments in employer stock. This amendment may be unnecessary, because all stock is fully allocated. As a result, only the original individual benefits from this investment option. Future employees and plan participants will not be entitled to invest in employer stock.

➤ A portion of the proceeds of the stock transaction may be remitted back to the promoter, in the form of a professional fee. This may be either a direct payment from plan to promoter, or an indirect payment, where gross proceeds are then transferred to the individual and some amount of his gross wealth is then returned to promoter.

PROCEDURAL DEVELOPMENT OF CASES

Employee Plans has received numerous alerts from practitioners regarding the promotion of this scheme in the marketplace. Questions regarding the legitimacy of ROBS-type transactions have been posed to the Service at various employee benefits and practitioner conferences.[3]

We have currently identified 9 promoters of this transaction. Most are actively promoting the use of ROBS at seminars that are held to assist individuals purchase business franchises. A referral to the Lead Development Center (LDC) has already been made and an LDC Investigator has been assigned.

We have also coordinated our consideration of ROBS plans with the Department of Labor (DOL). As will be noted later, the transfer of enterprise stock within a ROBS arrangement could raise ERISA Title I prohibited transaction issues. Although our coordination efforts are not yet finalized, they remain ongoing.

Additionally, SB/SE has reviewed several returns of employers who have engaged in ROBS transactions. Their examinations have largely started with a review of business tax returns, and then moved on to a review of promoter activity.

Determination Letter Contacts

EP Determinations identified numerous determination letter submissions for taxpayer adoptions of these plans. Most are filed by a named representative who is also a pre-approved document platform provider. Since the type of plan used for this promotion is a prototype plan with a minor amendment that permits the investment in employer securities, we have issued some favorable determination letters for these plans. We are also likely to receive many more submissions within the two-year EGTRRA pre-approved adoption window created by Announcement 2008-23, 2008-14 I.R.B. 731.

---

[3] For example, a fact pattern describing a ROBS arrangement was presented at the American Bar Association's 2003 Joint Committee on Employee Benefits "Q&A". See *http://www.abanet.org/jceb/2003/qa03irs.pdf.* question 9 therein.

4

A major promoter was first identified through our determination letter program as the sponsor of a pre-approved prototype, or "M&P", which has been approved by the Service under our pre-approved opinion letter program. This document is then marketed to clients, and is ultimately adopted by employers by the execution of adoption agreements. The base document from which client plans are administered is thus a pre-approved M&P specimen supplied by the provider which was reviewed and approved by the Service with a favorable opinion letter.

Because of the unique rules regarding scope of reliance applicable to M&P adopters, a modification of an M&P generally requires submission for a determination letter application as an individually designed plan. Thus, we are confident that the determination letter database will eventually hold a registry of most, if not all, of this promoter's clients, once the two-year window closes on April 30, 2010.

Current Examination Contacts

We have examined a number of these plans – having opened a specific examination project on them based off referrals from our determination letter program – and found significant disqualifying operational defects in most. For example, employees in some arrangements have not been notified of the existence of the plan, do not enter the plan or receive contributions or allocable shares of employer stock. Additionally, we have identified that plan assets are either not valued or are valued with threadbare appraisals. Required annual reports for some plans have not been filed. In several situations, we have also found that the business entity created from the ROBS exchange has either not survived, or used the resultant assets on personal, non-business purchases.

Again, considering business activity that occurs, it is likely that many ROBS plans did in fact file returns that are currently in place on RICS. The amount of the asset transfer is likely to exceed the minimum $100,000 that would otherwise eliminate filing of Form 5500EZ, *Annual Return/Report of Employee Benefit Plan.*[4]

In those cases, however, where the appropriate Form 5500 or 5500EZ was not filed, issues may arise as to the proper way to correct a failure to file. For example, issues may arise due to DOL's mandate for electronic filing beginning with the 2009 plan year and the resulting limitations on filing paper returns. It is anticipated that additional guidelines will be issued to address these situations.

---

[4] Form 5500 filing is triggered by when the value of trust assets reaches a specified level. See Treas. Reg.§ 301.6058-1(a)(1), et seq. Note that Section 1103(a) of the Pension Protection Act of 2006, Pub. L. 109-280, increased the amount of assets required for filing by one-participant plans from $100,000 to $250,000 effective for plan years beginning after December 31, 2006. Note also that Form 5500EZ will be replaced with Form 5500-SF, beginning with year 2009 filings.

PRIMARY ISSUES RAISED:

The two primary issues raised by ROBS arrangements are (1) violations of nondiscrimination requirements, in that benefits may not satisfy the benefits, rights and features test of Treas. Reg. § 1.401(a)(4)-4, and (2) prohibited transactions, due to deficient valuations of stock.

Benefits, Rights & Features Discrimination

Because ROBS transactions generally benefit only the principal involved with setting up a business, and do not enable rank-and-file employees to acquire employer stock, we believe that some of these plans violate the anti-discrimination provisions of the Code and Regulations, on a case-by-case basis.

IRC § 401(a)(4) provides that, under a qualified retirement plan, contributions or benefits provided under the plan must not discriminate in favor of highly compensated employees (HCEs).

IRC § 414(q)(1)(A) provides that an HCE is defined as either (1) a 5% owner, defined under the attribution rules of § 318, or (2) receives compensation over $80,000 (indexed, and subject to a "top-paid group" election by the employer.)

IRC § 318(a)(2)(B)(i) precludes attribution of stock owned by a plan described in § 401(a) to any participant in the plan for whom the stock is held for the benefit of, in trust.

Treas. Reg. § 1.401(a)(4)-1(b)(2) provides that in order to satisfy § 401(a)(4), either the contributions or the benefits under a plan must be nondiscriminatory in amount.

Treas. Reg. § 1.401(a)(4)-4(e)(3) provides that the plan's benefits, rights and features (BRFs) are tested to see if they are nondiscriminatory in effect. BRF testing considerations can arise in many forms, including as here, the right to make investments in employer securities.

Treas. Reg. § 1.401(a)(4)-4(b)(1) indicates that whether any given BRF is "currently available" (i.e. nondiscriminatory in result) should be tested under the nondiscriminatory classification test used for coverage testing. Further, Reg. § 1.401(a)(4)-4(c) provides that a BRF must also be "effectively available" to non-highly compensated employees (NHCEs), on the basis of all facts and circumstances.

Treas. Reg. § 1.401(a)(4)-5 provides that whether the timing of a plan amendment or series of plan amendments has the effect of discriminating specifically in favor of HCEs involves a facts and circumstances determination.

In a typical ROBS arrangement, there may not be any individual who meets the statutory HCE definition. At the time when rollover funds are used to purchase

6

employer stock, the stock acquires identity as a trust asset and is not attributed to the individual participant. Compensation paid then becomes the determining factor in resolving HCE status questions.[5]

In most of our cases, the amount of compensation being paid to the individual who starts-up the business is ostensibly below the IRC § 414(q)(1)(B) dollar limit, at least for initial years. While this may leave open the question as to whether true compensation being paid to the individual is actually higher than reported compensation, absent a personal tax review of the individual no one may receive compensation at or above the HCE indexed dollar limit.

Even if the ROBS initiator is an HCE, in many of our cases, there are no other employees in the initial year of the transaction or for some number of future years thereafter. Therefore, as no finding regarding discrimination can be made in absence of NHCEs in the transaction year, the current availability testing standard for plan BRFs is satisfied. This does not, however, signify that the effective availability standard is similarly resolved.

Effective availability testing requires a facts and circumstances determination regarding whether a plan feature benefits NHCEs. This determination requires consideration of factors or conditions precedent that must be satisfied in order to accrue a benefit, including timing elements and whether the transaction was structured to intentionally avoid BRF testing issues. Furthermore, Treas. Reg. § 1.401(a)(4)-5 requires consideration as to whether the timing of plan amendments serves to preclude other NHCEs from receiving stock allocations.

Given that ROBS arrangements are designed to take advantage of a one-time only stock offering, the investment feature generally would not satisfy the effectively available benefit requirement. The issue of discrimination arises because the plan is designed in a manner that the BRF will never be available to any NHCEs. For this reason, ROBS cases should be developed for discrimination issues whenever a given plan covers both HCEs and NHCEs, and no extension of the stock investment option is afforded to NHCEs.

Prohibited Transactions – Valuation of Stock

In all ROBS arrangements, an aspiring entrepreneur creates capital stock for the purpose of exchanging it for tax-deferred accumulation assets. The value of the stock is set as the value of the available assets. An appraisal may be created to substantiate this value, but it is often devoid of supportive analysis. We find this may create a prohibited transaction, depending on true enterprise value.

---

[5] In several of our examined cases, the transaction did not exactly follow the sequential series of steps outlined earlier. Instead, the principal received shares of the shell corporation prior to the sale back to the plan. This timing made the principal a 100% owner for a short period of time. In such a case, HCE status is conferred on start-up, perhaps creating an imminent BRF testing issue. This might also raise related prohibited transaction concerns.

7

IRC § 4975(a) imposes a tax on a prohibited transaction equal to 15% of the amount involved in the transaction. IRC § 4975(b) imposes a tax equal to 100% of the amount involved in any case where a prohibited transaction is not corrected within the taxable period, as defined at § 4975(f).

IRC § 4975(c)(1)(A) defines a prohibited transaction as a sale, exchange or lease of any property between a plan and a disqualified person.

IRC § 4975(e)(1)(F) defines a plan as any trust, plan, account or annuity that is exempt from tax under § 501(a), or was ever determined by the Secretary to be so exempt.

IRC § 4975(e)(2)(C) defines a disqualified person as an employer, any of whose employees are covered by the plan.

IRC § 4975(e)(2)(E)(i) defines a disqualified person as an owner, direct or indirect, of 50% or more of the combined voting power of all classes of stock entitled to vote or the total value of shares of all classes of stock of a corporation which is an employer described in § 4975(e)(2)(C).

IRC § 4975(d)(13) provides an exemption from prohibited transaction consideration for any transaction which is exempt from ERISA § 406, by reason of ERISA § 408(e), which addresses certain transactions involving employer stock.

IRC § 4975(f)(2) defines the taxable period as the period beginning with the date on which the prohibited transaction occurs and ending on the earlier of the dates on which a) a notice of deficiency with respect to the tax imposed by § 6212(a) is mailed, b) the date on which the tax imposed by § 4975(a) is assessed, or c) the date on which correction of the prohibited transaction is completed.

IRC § 4975(f)(5) defines correction as the undoing of the transaction, to the extent possible, such that the plan is restored to a financial position not worse than it would have been absent the transaction.

ERISA § 408(e), and ERISA Reg. § 2550.408e promulgated thereunder, provides an exemption from ERISA § 406 for acquisitions or sales of qualifying employer securities, subject to a requirement that the acquisition or sale must be for "adequate consideration." Except in the case of a "marketable obligation", adequate consideration for this purpose means a price not less favorable than the price determined under ERISA § 3(18).

ERISA § 3(18) provides in relevant part that, in the case of an asset other than a security for which there is no generally recognized market, adequate consideration means the fair market value of the asset as determined in good faith by the trustee or named fiduciary pursuant to the terms of the plan and in accordance with regulations.

An exchange of company stock between the plan and its employer-sponsor would be a prohibited transaction, unless the requirements of ERISA § 408(e) are met. Therefore, valuation of the capitalization of the new company is a relevant issue. Since the company is new, there could be a question of whether it is indeed worth the value of the

8

tax-deferred assets for which it was exchanged. If the transaction has not been for adequate consideration, it would have to be corrected, for example, by the corporation's redemption of the stock from the plan and replacing it with cash equal to its fair market value, plus an additional interest factor for lost plan earnings.

A valuation-related prohibited transaction issue may arise where the start-up enterprise does not actually "start-up." Here, the start-up entity might record "cash" as its only asset, without any real attempt to secure, for example, a franchise license, property, plant and equipment or other assets necessary to start a bona fide business. The valuation ostensibly legitimizing the exchange is unsupported.

Many examiners have been provided with a single sheet of paper, signed by a purported valuation specialist. This appraisal "certifies" that the value of the enterprise stock is a sum certain, the amount of which approximates the amount of available proceeds from the individual's tax deferred retirement account.

These appraisals are questionable. Because the valuation usually approximates available funds, consideration needs to be given to whether inherent value in the plan-acquired entity actually exists. The lack of a bona fide appraisal raises a question as to whether the entire exchange is a prohibited transaction.[6]

Prohibited Transactions – Promoter Fees

In the case where the plan purchases the stock of the employer, and the employer immediately pays professional fees to the promoter out of the proceeds, prohibited transactions may occur.

IRC § 4975(c)(1)(E) prohibits a fiduciary from dealing with the assets of the plan in his own interest or his own account.

IRC § 4975(e)(3) defines a fiduciary as any person who exercises any discretionary authority or control, renders investment advice for a fee, or has any discretionary authority or responsibility in the administration of the plan.

Treas. Reg. § 54.4975-9(c) defines when a person would be providing investment advice as defined in § 4975(e)(3)(B).

ERISA Reg. § 2510-3.21(c) further clarifies the meaning of the term "investment advice." Under that regulation, a person is deemed to render investment advice if such person renders advice to the plan as to the value of securities or other property, or makes a recommendation as to the advisability of investing in, purchasing, or selling securities or other property and such person either directly or indirectly has discretionary authority or control, whether or not pursuant to an agreement, arrangement or understanding, with respect to purchasing or selling securities or other property for the plan. The advice would have to be rendered on a regular basis to the plan pursuant to a mutual agreement, arrangement or understanding, written or

---

[6] We note that deficient valuations can also raise qualification issues. See e.g. Rev. Rul. 80-155, 1980-1 CB 84.

otherwise, between such person and the plan or a fiduciary with respect to the plan, that such services will serve as a primary basis for investment decisions with respect to plan assets, and that such person will render individualized investment advice to the plan based on the particular needs of the plan regarding such matters as, among other things, investment policies or strategy, overall portfolio composition, or diversification of plan investments.[7]

If the promoter meets these requirements, his status may rise to that of plan fiduciary. Where a fiduciary directly receives a remit-back from the plan of a portion of tax-deferred accumulation assets, this payment may be a violation of IRC § 4975(c)(1)(E). Essentially, plan assets are being transferred in exchange for services and investment advice. Specialists will need to ascertain whether this is discernable from the facts presented on their examination, and whether the requirements of Treas. Reg. § 54.4975-9(c) have been met.

Note that IRC § 4975(f)(1) provides that where more than one person is liable for prohibited transaction excise taxes, all persons are jointly and severally liable for any deficiency. Therefore, assessments against promoters for direct receipt of plan assets may be made even where assessments are proposed against the corporation or individual for invalid appraisal of the underlying stock.[8]

OTHER ISSUES:

Permanency

Because ROBS benefits are designed to be used only once, we have considered whether they are truly a "permanent" retirement program. Permanency is a qualification requirement for all retirement plans.

IRC § 401(a)(1) provides that a trust is established for the purpose of distributing to such employees or their beneficiaries the corpus and income of the fund accumulated by the trust in accordance with such plan.

Treas. Reg. § 1.401-1(b)(1)(ii) provides that a profit sharing plan is established to enable employees or their beneficiaries to participate in the profits of the employer's trade or business, or in the profits of an affiliated employer who is entitled to deduct his contributions to the plan under IRC § 404(a)(3)(B), pursuant to a definite formula for allocating the contributions and for distributing the funds accumulated under the plan.

---

[7] DOL has taken the position that this definition of fiduciary also applies to investment advice provided to a participant or beneficiary in an individual account plan that allows participants or beneficiaries to direct the investment of their accounts. See ERISA Reg. § 2509.96-1(c).

[8] In an attempt to "insulate" client adopters against prohibited transaction issues, one promoter has apparently created a multiple employer plan within the meaning of IRC § 413(c), with each client adopting-in as a participating employer. Notwithstanding this attempt, the analysis supplied by this memorandum should be applied to these cases.

Treas. Reg. § 1.401-1(b) provides that a qualified plan must be created primarily for the purposes of providing systematic retirement benefits for employees. Treas. Reg. § 1.401-1(b)(2) requires that the plan be a permanent, as distinguished from temporary, arrangement, and provides a general rule that if a plan is discontinued within a few years after its adoption, there is a presumption that it was not intended as a permanent program from its inception, unless business necessity required the discontinuance, termination or partial termination.

Rev. Rul. 69-25, 1969-1 C.B. 113, provides that for purposes of invoking this "business necessity" exception, the necessity must have been unforeseeable when the plan was adopted, and cannot be within the control of the employer.

Consider that business reasons – tax motivated or otherwise – are generally the only reasons why a retirement arrangement is installed. Similarly, they are likely to be the only reason why they are terminated as well. For this reason, permanency is not an area where the Service has aggressively challenged plan terminations or design considerations. Additionally, Regulations address permanency within the context of an entire plan arrangement, not necessarily to a feature within a plan.

Therefore, a plan containing a ROBS arrangement would have to be shown to be non-permanent in its entirety. Many of the ROBS arrangements we have examined also contain a CODA feature. Plans which suffer from permanency failures are generally deficient in that they do not receive substantial and recurring contributions. Because CODA features receive contributions only if participants make contributions, the issue of permanence is resolvable in favor of the employer.

Under the specific facts presented by the cases we have examined, we are unable to find that all ROBS arrangements violate the permanency rule. However, facts of particular cases should be considered on a case-by-case basis.[9]

Exclusive Benefit

As noted earlier, ROBS arrangements typically involve direction of some amount of plan assets to the promoter in payment of professional fees for setting up the transaction. In some cases, the newly created business purchased assets that were essentially personal assets for the benefit of the individual. We considered whether this violates the "exclusive benefit" requirements of the Code.

IRC § 401(a)(2) provides, in relevant part, that a plan is not qualified unless it is impossible, at any time prior to the satisfaction of all liabilities with respect to employees and their beneficiaries, for any part of the corpus or income to be used for or diverted to purposes other than for the exclusive benefit of employees or their beneficiaries.

---

[9] In fact, as will be noted later, some plans appear to have been established with CODAs that do not receive contributions and may not have been adequately communicated to employees. These plans would not be insulated against permanency issues.

Treas. Reg. § 1.401-1(a)(3)(iv) provides that it must be impossible "under the trust instrument at any time before the satisfaction of all liabilities with respect to employees and their beneficiaries under the trust, for any part of the corpus or income to be used for, or diverted to, purposes other than for the exclusive benefit of the employees or their beneficiaries.

Treas. Reg. § 1.401-2 outlines the specific provisions that a plan must follow to meet the exclusive benefit rule for purposes of Title II of ERISA. Other applicable exclusive benefit issues are contained in corresponding Title I provisions.

We have reviewed ROBS arrangements to determine whether they are truly for the exclusive benefit of employees. The facts unique to each of our ROBS cases are disparate as to the eventual disposition of tax deferred accumulation assets. In a few cases, these assets wound up purchasing personal assets, like recreational vehicles. But in many, if not most of the transactions, the assets were in fact used to purchase legitimate business or franchises, plus attendant start-up costs. Courts have generally held that whether a Title II exclusive benefit violation has occurred largely depends on whether benefits to third parties are not merely an incidental side effect of an investment of trust assets, but are instead a major purpose of the investment.

Therefore, we believe that the typical ROBS design does not violate the exclusive benefit requirement in form.[10] Examiners will need to develop specific operational issues, such as where trust assets were used to pay purely non-business expenses prior to pursuing exclusive benefit violations.[11]

Plan not communicated to employees

In some cases, we have found that the existence of the plan is not communicated to people hired after the newly created business is up and running. "Participants", as identified on employee census information provided to our examiners, are not even aware that they merit this classification. If this can be established, the plan may be in violation of Treas. Reg. § 1.401-1(a)(2), requiring that it be a definite, written program communicated to employees. In some cases, employees may not reach participation status into the plan on their required entry dates, causing the plan to fail IRC § 410(a) requirements.

Inactivity in cash or deferred arrangement

A large number of reviewed plans contain election provisions in the adoption agreement to utilize a CODA. Often, low number of participants actually chose to make salary reduction contributions. However, many of our examiners found this issue and raised it, and usually received a response that the CODA was "inactive." In fact, many of these

---

[10] However, we are aware of arrangements in which the individual transferring tax-deferred assets into the plan is not an employee, participant or owner, such as where the arrangement is used to set up a business for a spouse. Such a transfer might be one where the exclusive benefit issue is properly raised.

[11] As a reminder, exclusive benefit revocation cases must be submitted for technical advice consideration under established procedures within each business unit.

plans have provisions describing a CODA feature, including applicable elections in the employer's signed adoption agreement. There being no such thing as an "inactive" CODA, examiners should consider whether all the procedures for allowing employees to participate in the CODA were followed, whether new employees just chose not to defer, or whether employees were not even offered salary reduction elections. If it is established that employees were not permitted to make elective deferrals, the plan would violate IRC § 401(k)(2)(D) in that it did not permit eligible employees to elect salary deferral contributions.[12]

COMPLETION AND MOVEMENT OF CASES

Determination Letter Contacts

We have specifically considered whether the form of the plan, as presented, is entitled to a favorable determination letter ruling. There is no inherent violation in the form of a plan containing a ROBS arrangement that would otherwise prevent a favorable ruling. The issues described herein are inherently operational, and beyond the scope of a determination letter ruling. Accordingly, determination letter applications for plans with ROBS features can be reviewed and approved as appropriate. However, we will monitor the volume of approval letters issued to these plans in a manner similar to those issued to IRC § 412(i) arrangements. Current procedures for these notifications, including review by EP Determinations Quality Assurance, are to be followed for ROBS determination letter submissions.

Open Examination Cases

Open examination cases should be worked within the context of these guidelines. Cases presenting prohibited transaction issues should be worked under existing procedures for processing delinquent returns in agreed cases, and under unagreed procedures for all other circumstances, including appropriate referral to and coordination with DOL. Cases in which BRF discrimination is an issue should be processed first under the appropriate Employee Plans Compliance Resolution System (EPCRS) correction program. If EPCRS is not appropriate or available, then unagreed qualification procedures should be followed.

Statute of Limitation Concerns

For BRF discrimination and other disqualification cases, normal control procedures for protection of applicable statutes of limitation on trust and related taxable returns should be followed. This may involve converting non-calendar year plans, and annualizing income in accordance with IRC § 645(a). Related returns should be protected, generally for the individual and employer sponsor only.

---

[12] Also, to the extent that a CODA supports the permanency of a plan, that support expires if in fact the CODA is not in fact communicated to employees.

13

Similar procedures are also applicable for prohibited transaction cases, however, specialists are cautioned that one other consideration may block pursuing deficiency determinations for these cases.

IRC § 6501(a) provides that the amount of any tax, including those imposed by Chapter 43 (such as IRC § 4975) may be assessed within three years after the "return" was filed.

IRC § 6501(l) further provides that, for this purpose, the term "return" means the annual Form 5500 series return required to be filed by plan/trust for the year in which the act occurred. Therefore, in most instances, the statute of limitation to make a prohibited transaction assessment on a ROBS transaction begins with the filing of Form 5500 for the year in which the stock transaction is executed.

IRC § 6501(e)(3) provides, however, that if this information return does not adequately disclose the existence of this transaction, the ordinary limitation period on assessment is extended to six years. Adequacy of disclosure is largely a facts and circumstances determination, developed through judicial interpretation.[13]

Prohibited transactions are classifiable into either "discrete" one-time transactions, or "continuous" recurring transactions.[14] ROBS arrangements fall into the former. In a discrete transaction, a taxable event occurs in the initial or "source" year when the prohibited exchange of stock occurs, and is deemed to be carried forward into later taxable periods until corrected.[15]

The Service's position with respect to administering the limitation period on assessment applicable to discrete transactions is that the source year must be open in order to make any assessment in the source or any later year. If this source year is barred by elapse of the relevant limitation statute, no excise tax deficiency may be assessed. Given the length of time that has elapsed since many of these transactions first were created and the time involved moving these cases through our determination letter and audit cycle processes, it is likely that the three-year limitation period has either elapsed or is imminent for most of these transactions.

Therefore, ROBS prohibited transaction cases are likely to require a determination as to whether a six-year statute is open, under a failure to make adequate disclosure of the existence of the transaction in the source year. For this purpose, coordination with Area Counsel will be required.[16] Specialists are reminded that statutes are to be protected, and assessments perfected, against the correct parties. Where the 3-year limitation period is open, it should be protected in lieu of relying on a 6-year period.

---

[13] See e.g. *Janpol v. Commissioner*, 102 T.C. 499 (1994)

[14] Note that these terms are not derived from statute or regulation, but are administrative creations.

[15] Unlike a continuous transaction, in which the taxable amount involved accumulates with a future interest factor in the manner known as "pyramiding", a discrete transaction's taxable amount is simply replicated forward in later years.

[16] Peter Gavagan, of Northeast Area Counsel, will coordinate application of 6-year statutes of limitation to open ROBS examination cases.

14

CONCLUSION

ROBS transactions may violate law in several regards. First, this scheme might create a prohibited transaction between the plan and its sponsor. At the time of the exchange between plan assets and newly-minted employer stock, the value of the capitalization of the entity is equivalent to the value of all plan assets, when in reality, the entity may be valueless and asset-less for an indefinite period of time. Additionally, this scheme may not satisfy the benefits, rights and features requirement of the Regulations. The primary utility of the arrangement may only be available the business's principal individual.

Specific facts will need to be evaluated on a case by case basis in order to make a proper determination as to whether these plans operationally comply with established law and guidance. Technical advice requests may be submitted after consultation with group managers. For this reason, employee plans specialists are directed to resolve open ROBS cases as described herein.[17]

---

[17] As additional reference material, see IRM § 4.72.8, *Valuation of Assets*, and § 4.72. ., *Prohibited Transactions*.

www.ingramcontent.com/pod-product-compliance
Lightning Source LLC
Chambersburg PA
CBHW072301200526
45168CB00014B/90